Practical Simulations for Machine Learning
Using Synthetic Data for AI

Paris and Mars Buttfield-Addison,
Tim Nugent, and Jon Manning

Beijing · Boston · Farnham · Sebastopol · Tokyo

Practical Simulations for Machine Learning

by Paris Buttfield-Addison, Mars Buttfield-Addison, Tim Nugent, and Jon Manning

Published by O'Reilly Media, Inc., 1005 Gravenstein Highway North, Sebastopol, CA 95472.

O'Reilly books may be purchased for educational, business, or sales promotional use. Online editions are also available for most titles (*http://oreilly.com*). For more information, contact our corporate/institutional sales department: 800-998-9938 or *corporate@oreilly.com*.

Acquisitions Editor: Rebecca Novack	**Indexer:** nSight, Inc.
Development Editor: Michele Cronin	**Interior Designer:** David Futato
Production Editor: Christopher Faucher	**Cover Designer:** Karen Montgomery
Copyeditor: Piper Editorial Consulting, LLC	**Illustrator:** Kate Dullea
Proofreader: Audrey Doyle	

June 2022:   First Edition

Revision History for the First Edition

2022-06-07:   First Release

See *http://oreilly.com/catalog/errata.csp?isbn=9781492089926* for release details.

The O'Reilly logo is a registered trademark of O'Reilly Media, Inc. *Practical Simulations for Machine Learning*, the cover image, and related trade dress are trademarks of O'Reilly Media, Inc.

978-1-492-08992-6

[LSI]

Table of Contents

Preface

Welcome to *Practical Simulations for Machine Learning*! This book combines two of our favorite things: *video game engines* and *artificial intelligence*. We hope you enjoy reading it as much as we enjoyed writing it.

Specifically, this book explores the use of Unity, a product that used to be called a *game engine* but now likes to be called a *platform for creating and operating interactive, real-time 3D content*. That's a lot of words, but they basically boil down to this: Unity is a platform for building things in 3D, and though it has traditionally been used for video game development, it can be used to build anything that can be represented in 3D, by using a combination of 3D graphics, physics simulations, and inputs of some kind.

By combining a *platform for creating and operating interactive, real-time 3D content* with machine learning tools, you can use the 3D world you create to train a machine learning model, kind of like it's the real world. It's not actually like the real world, but it's fun to imagine, and there are some legitimately useful connections to the real world (such as being able to generate both data for use in real-world machine learning applications, as well as models that can be transposed to physical, real-world objects, like robots).

 When we say real-world, we actually mean physical.

Combining Unity with machine learning is a great way to create both *simulations* and *synthetic data*, which are the two different topics we cover in this book.

Resources Used in This Book

We recommend following along with the book by writing code yourself as you progress through each chapter.

If you become stuck, or just want to archive a copy of our version of the code, you can find what you need via our website (*http://www.secretlab.com.au/books/practical-simulations*).

For some activities we work through in the book, you'll need a copy of the resources to get certain assets, so we do recommend you download it.

Audience and Approach

We wrote this book for programmers and software engineers who are interested in machine learning, but are not necessarily machine learning engineers. If you have a passing interest in machine learning, or are starting to work more in the machine learning space, then this book is for you. If you're a game developer, who kind of already knows Unity, or another game engine, and wants to learn machine learning (for either games or some other application) then this book is for you too.

If you're already a machine learning expert, this book is for you as well, but in a different way: we don't go *too* deep on the *whys* and *hows* of machine learning. So, if you already know what's going on deep within PyTorch, and similar frameworks, you'll do just fine here. And if you don't already know what's deep within the world of machine learning, you'll be fine too because everything is *very* accessible. The point of simulations and synthesis with Unity is that you don't need to know the ins and outs of what's going on. It all kind of just *works* (famous last words, we know).

Anyway, this book is for you if you're coming from software, machine learning, or games. There's something for everyone here. We teach you just enough Unity and just enough machine learning to be dangerous and we'll provide you with jumping-off points to learn more about the paths that you're interested in.

Organization of This Book

This book is divided into three parts.

Part I, "The Basics of Simulation and Synthesis", introduces the topics of simulation and synthesis, and eases you in gently with a simple activity based on each.

Part II, "Simulating Worlds for Fun and Profit", is dedicated to simulation. This is the biggest part of the book, because simulations are a much, much bigger topic than synthesis. In this part, we go almost step-by-step through a collection of simulation activities, building additional concepts and approaches as we go. By the end of this part, you'll have been exposed to many of the different paths through simulation that you can take.

Part III, "Synthetic Data, Real Results", is dedicated to synthesis. This is a much smaller part than simulation, but is still crucial. You'll learn the fundamentals of creating synthetic data with Unity, and by the end you'll be equipped to make basically any kind of synthesis you might need.

Using This Book

We've structured this book around activities. We hope you'll work through the activities with us, and add your own spin where you're so inclined (but don't feel like you have to).

We took an activity-based approach because we feel it's the best way to learn the bits you need from both the Unity game engine, and the machine learning side of things. We didn't want to have to teach you everything about Unity, and there's no room in the book to unpack all the details of machine learning.

By going from activity to activity, we can introduce or exclude things as needed. We really hope you enjoy our choice of activities!

Our Tasks

For simulation, we'll be building:

- A ball that can roll itself to a target, in Chapter 2 (we know, it sounds too amazing to be true, but it is!)
- A cube that can push a block into a goal area, in Chapter 4
- A simple self-driving car, navigating a track, in Chapter 5
- A ball that seeks a coin, trained by imitating human demonstrations, in Chapter 6
- A ballistic launcher agent that can launch a ball at a target, using curriculum learning, in Chapter 8
- A group of cubes that work together to push blocks to goals, in Chapter 9
- An agent that can balance a ball on top of itself, using visual inputs (i.e. cameras) instead of precise measurements, in Chapter 10
- A way to connect to, and manipulate simulations from Python, in Chapter 11

And for synthesis, we will:

- Generate images of randomly thrown and placed dice, in Chapter 3
- Improve the dice image generator, changing the floor and colors of the dice, in Chapter 13
- Generate images of supermarket products, to allow for out-of-Unity training on images with complex backdrops, and haphazard positioning, in Chapter 14

Conventions Used in This Book

The following typographical conventions are used in this book:

Italic

Indicates new terms, URLs, email addresses, filenames, and file extensions.

`Constant width`

Used for program listings, as well as within paragraphs to refer to program elements such as variable or function names, databases, data types, environment variables, statements, and keywords. Also used for commands and command-line output.

`Constant width bold`

Shows commands or other text that should be typed literally by the user.

`Constant width italic`

Shows text that should be replaced with user-supplied values or by values determined by context.

 This element signifies a tip or suggestion.

 This element signifies a general note.

 This element indicates a warning or caution.

Using Code Examples

Supplemental material (code examples, exercises, errata, etc.) is available for download at *http://secretlab.com.au/books/practical-simulations*.

This book is here to help you get your job done. In general, if example code is offered with this book, you may use it in your programs and documentation. You do not need to contact us for permission unless you're reproducing a significant portion of the code. For example, writing a program that uses several chunks of code from this book does not require permission. Selling or distributing examples from O'Reilly books does require permission. Answering a question by citing this book and quoting example code does not require permission. Incorporating a significant amount of example code from this book into your product's documentation does require permission.

We appreciate, but do not require, attribution. An attribution usually includes the title, author, publisher, and ISBN. For example: "*Practical Simulations for Machine Learning*, by Paris and Mars Buttfield-Addison, Tim Nugent, and Jon Manning. Copyright 2022 Secret Lab, 978-1-492-08992-6."

If you feel your use of code examples falls outside fair use or the permission given above, feel free to contact us at *permissions@oreilly.com*.

O'Reilly Online Learning

 For over 40 years, *O'Reilly Media* has provided technology and business training, knowledge, and insight to help companies succeed.

Our unique network of experts and innovators share their knowledge and expertise through books, articles, conferences, and our online learning platform. O'Reilly's online learning platform gives you on-demand access to live training courses, in-depth learning paths, interactive coding environments, and a vast collection of text and video from O'Reilly and 200+ other publishers. For more information, please visit *http://oreilly.com*.

How to Contact Us

Please address comments and questions concerning this book to the publisher:

O'Reilly Media, Inc.
1005 Gravenstein Highway North
Sebastopol, CA 95472
800-998-9938 (in the United States or Canada)
707-829-0515 (international or local)
707-829-0104 (fax)

We have a web page for this book, where we list errata, examples, and any additional information. You can access this page at *https://oreil.ly/practical-sims-for-ML*.

Send an email to *bookquestions@oreilly.com* to comment or ask technical questions about this book.

For more information about our books, courses, conferences, and news, see our website at *http://www.oreilly.com*.

Find us on Facebook: *http://facebook.com/oreilly*

Follow us on Twitter: *http://twitter.com/oreillymedia*

Watch us on YouTube: *http://youtube.com/oreillymedia*

Acknowledgments

Mars would like to thank her family and coauthors for their support, as well as the people of the University of Tasmania's School of ICT and the broader tech community in Australia for all the opportunities they have afforded her.

Jon thanks his mother, father, and the rest of his crazily extended family for their tremendous support.

Paris thanks his mother, without whom he wouldn't be doing anything nearly as interesting, let alone writing books, and his wife (and co-author) Mars, as well as all his friends (several of whom he is lucky enough to have written this book with!).

Tim thanks his parents and family for putting up with his rather lackluster approach to life.

We'd all like to thank Michele Cronin, who is absolutely amazing, and whose skills and advice were invaluable to completing the book. Paris is sorry for the regular diversions in our meetings, but it's too much fun to have a good conversation! We're really excited to work on more projects with you in the future!

Special thanks to our friend and former editor at O'Reilly Media, Rachel Roumeliotis. We miss our conference coffee breaks together.

Really, thanks must go to all the O'Reilly Media staff we've interacted with over the course of writing this book. A particular thanks must go to Chris Faucher for both being wildly good at their job, and fantastically patient with us. Thanks also to our fantastic copyeditor, Elizabeth Oliver. You're all so professional, so interesting, and so talented. It's truly terrifying.

A huge thank you to Tony Gray and the Apple University Consortium (*http://www.auc.edu.au*) for the monumental boost they gave us and others listed on this page. We wouldn't be writing this book if it weren't for them. And now you're writing books too, Tony—sorry about that!

Thanks also to Neal Goldstein, who deserves full credit and/or blame for getting us into the whole book-writing racket.

We're thankful for the support of the goons at MacLab (who know who they are and continue to stand watch for Admiral Dolphin's inevitable apotheosis), as well as professor Christopher Lueg, Dr. Leonie Ellis, and the rest of the current and former staff at the University of Tasmania for putting up with us.

Additional thanks to Dave J., Jason I., Adam B., Josh D., Andrew B., Jess L., and everyone else who inspires us and helps us. And very special thanks to the team of hard-working engineers, writers, artists, and other workers at Apple, without whom this book (and many others like it) would not have reason to exist.

Thanks also to our tech reviewers! We couldn't write a book without their thoroughness and professionalism, and general enthusiasm for our work. Also extreme levels of nitpicking. We appreciate it. Truly!

Finally, thank *you* very much for buying our book—we appreciate it! And if you have any feedback, please let us know.

PART I

The Basics of Simulation and Synthesis

CHAPTER 1

Introducing Synthesis and Simulation

The world is hungry for data. Machine learning and artificial intelligence are some of the most data-hungry domains around. Algorithms and models are growing ever bigger, and the real world is insufficient. Manual creation of data and real-world systems are not scalable, and we need new approaches. That's where Unity, and software traditionally used for video game development, steps in.

This book is all about synthesis and simulation, and leveraging the power of modern video game engines for machine learning. Combining machine learning with simulations and synthetic data sounds relatively straightforward on the surface, but the reality is the idea of including *video game* technology in the serious business world of machine learning scares an unreasonable number of companies and businesses away from the idea.

We hope this book will steer you into this world and alleviate your concerns. Three of the authors of this book are video game developers with a significant background in computer science, and one is a serious machine learning and data scientist. Our combined perspectives and knowledge, built over many years in a variety of industries and approaches, are presented here for you.

This book will take you on a journey through the approaches and techniques that can be used to build and train machine learning systems using, and using data generated by, the Unity video game engine. There are two distinct domains in this book: *simulation* and *synthesis*. Simulation refers to, for all intents and purposes, building virtual robots (known as *agents*) that learn to do something inside a virtual world of your own creation. Synthesis refers to building virtual objects or worlds, outputting data about those objects and worlds, and using it to train machine learning systems outside of a game engine.

Both simulation and synthesis are powerful techniques that enable new and exciting approaches to data-centric machine learning and AI.

A Whole New World of ML

We'll get to the structure of the book shortly, but first, here's a synopsis of the remainder of this chapter, which is split into four sections:

- In "The Domains", we'll introduce the domains of machine learning that the book explores: simulation and synthesis.
- In "The Tools" on page 6, we'll meet the tools we'll be using—the *Unity engine*, the *Unity ML-Agents Toolkit*, *PyTorch*, and *Unity Perception*—and how they fit together.
- In "The Techniques" on page 9, we'll look at the techniques we'll be using for machine learning: *proximal policy optimization* (PPO), *soft actor-critic* (SAC), *behavioral cloning* (BC), and *generative adversarial imitation learning* (GAIL).
- And finally, in "Projects" on page 13, we'll summarize the projects that we'll be building throughout this book, and how they relate to the domains and the tools.

By the end of this chapter, you'll be ready to dive into the world of simulations and synthesis, you'll know at a high level how a game engine works, and you'll see why it's a nearly perfect tool for machine learning. By the end of the book, you'll be ready to tackle any problem you can think of that might benefit from game engine-driven simulation or synthesis.

The Domains

The twin pillars of this book are *simulation* and *synthesis*. In this section, we'll unpack exactly what we mean by each of these terms and how this book will explore the concepts.

Simulation and synthesis are core parts of the future of artificial intelligence and machine learning.

Many applications immediately jump out at you: combine simulation with deep reinforcement learning to validate how a new robot will function before building a physical product; create the brain of your self-driving car without the car; build your warehouse and train your pick-and-place robots without the warehouse (or the robots).

Other uses are more subtle: synthesize data to create artificial data using simulations, instead of information recorded from the real world, and then train traditional machine learning models; take real user activity and, with behavioral cloning combined with simulations, use it to add a biological- or human-seeming element to an otherwise perfect, machine-learned task.

A video game engine, such as Unity, can simulate enough of the real world, with enough fidelity, to be useful for simulation-based machine learning and artificial intelligence. Not only can a game engine allow you to simulate enough of a city and a car to test, train, and validate a self-driving car deep learning model, but it can also simulate the hardware down to the level of engine temperatures, power remaining, LIDAR, sonar, x-ray, and beyond. Want to incorporate a fancy, expensive new sensor in your robot? Try it out and see if it might improve performance before you invest a single cent in new equipment. Save money, time, compute power, and engineering resources, and get a better view of your problem space.

Is it literally impossible, or potentially unsafe, to acquire enough of your data? Create a simulation and test your theories. Cheap, unlimited training data is only a simulation away.

Simulation

There's not one specific thing that we refer to when we say *simulation*. Simulation, in this context, can mean practically any use of a game engine to develop a scene or environment where machine learning is then applied. In this book, we use simulation as a term to broadly refer to the following:

- Using a game engine to create an environment with certain components that are the agent or agents
- Giving the agent(s) the ability to move, or otherwise interact or work with, the environment and/or other agents
- Connecting the environment to a machine learning framework to train a model that can operate the agent(s) within the environment
- Using that trained model to operate with the environment in the future, or connecting the model to a similarly equipped agent elsewhere (e.g., in the real world, with an actual robot)

Synthesis

Synthesis is a significantly easier thing to pin down: *synthesis*, in the context of this book, is the creation of ostensibly fake training data using a game engine. For example, if you were building some kind of image identification machine learning model for a supermarket, you might need to take photos of a box of a specific cereal brand from many different angles and with many different backgrounds and contexts.

Using a game engine, you could create and load a 3D model of a box of cereal and then generate thousands of images of it—synthesizing them—in different angles, backgrounds, and skews, and save them out to a standard image format (JPG or PNG, for example). Then, with your enormous trove of training data, you could use a perfectly standard machine learning framework and toolkit (e.g., TensorFlow, PyTorch, Create ML, Turi Create, or one of the many web services-based training systems) and train a model that can recognize your cereal box.

This mode could then be deployed to, for example, some sort of on-trolley AI system that helps people shop, guides them to the items on their shopping list, or helps store staff fill the shelves correctly and conduct inventory forecasting.

The synthesis is the creation of the training data by using the game engine, and the game engine often has nothing, or very little, to do with the training process itself.

The Tools

This chapter provides you with an introduction to the tools that we'll be using on our journey. If you're not a game developer, the primary new tool you'll encounter is Unity. Unity was traditionally a game engine but is now billed as a real-time 3D engine.

Let's go one by one through the tools you'll encounter in this book.

Unity

First and foremost, Unity is a game and visual effects engine. Unity Technologies describes Unity as a *real-time 3D development platform*. We're not going to repeat the marketing material from the Unity website for you, but if you're curious about how the company positions itself, you can check it out (*https://oreil.ly/nnVUz*).

 This book isn't here to teach you the fundamentals of Unity. Some of the authors of this book have already written several books on that—from a game development perspective—and you can find those at O'Reilly Media if you're interested. You don't need to learn Unity as a game developer to make use of it for simulation and synthesis with machine learning; in this book we'll teach you *just enough Unity* to be effective at this.

The Unity user interface looks like almost every other professional software package that has 3D features. We've included an example screenshot in Figure 1-1. The interface has panes that can be manipulated, a 3D canvas for working with objects, and lots of settings. We'll come back to the specifics of Unity's user interface later.

You can get a solid overview of its different elements in the Unity documentation (*https://oreil.ly/zN8xU*).

You'll be using Unity for both simulation and synthesis in this book.

Figure 1-1. The Unity user interface

The Unity engine comes with a robust set of tools that allow you to simulate gravity, forces, friction, movement, sensors of various kinds, and more. These tools are the exact set of tools needed to build a modern video game. It turns out that these are also the exact same set of tools needed to create simulations and to synthesize data for machine learning. But you probably already guessed that, given that you're reading our book.

This book was written for Unity 2021 and newer. If you're reading this book in 2023 or beyond, Unity might look slightly different from our screenshots, but the concepts and overall flow shouldn't have changed much. Game engines tend to, by and large, accumulate features rather than remove them, so the most common sorts of changes you'll see are icons looking slightly different and things of that nature. For the latest notes on anything that might have changed, head to our special website for the book (*https://oreil.ly/1efRA*).

PyTorch via Unity ML-Agents

If you're in the machine learning space, you've probably heard of the PyTorch open source project. As one of the most popular platforms and ecosystems for machine learning in both academia and industry, it's nearly ubiquitous. In the simulation and synthesis space, it's no different: PyTorch is one of the go-to frameworks.

In this book, the underlying machine learning that we explore will mostly be done via PyTorch. We won't be getting into the *weeds* of PyTorch, because much of the work we'll be doing with PyTorch will be via the Unity ML-Agents Toolkit. We'll be discussing the ML-Agents Toolkit momentarily, but essentially all you need to remember is that PyTorch is the *engine* that powers what the Unity ML-Agents Toolkit does. It's there all the time, under the hood, and you can tinker with it if you need to, or if you know what you're doing, but most of the time you don't need to touch it at all.

 We're going to spend the rest of this section discussing the Unity ML-Agents Toolkit, so if you need a refresher on PyTorch, we highly recommend the PyTorch website (*https://pytorch.org*), or one of the many excellent books that O'Reilly Media has published on the subject.

PyTorch is a library that provides support for performing computations using data flow graphs. It supports both training and inference using CPUs and GPUs (and other specialized machine learning hardware), and it runs on a huge variety of platforms ranging from serious ML-optimized servers to mobile devices.

 Because most of the work you'll be doing with PyTorch in this book is abstracted away, we will rarely be talking in terms of PyTorch itself. So, while it's in the background of almost everything we're going to explore, your primary interface to it will be via the Unity ML-Agents Toolkit and other tools.

We'll be using PyTorch, via Unity ML-Agents, for all the simulation activities in the book.

Unity ML-Agents Toolkit

The Unity ML-Agents Toolkit (which, against Unity branding, we'll abbreviate to *UnityML* or *ML-Agents* much of the time) is the backbone of the work you'll be doing in this book. ML-Agents was initially released as a bare-bones experimental project and slowly grew to encompass a range of features that enable the Unity engine to serve as the simulation environment for training and exploring intelligent agents and other machine learning applications.

It's an open source project that ships with many exciting and well-considered examples (as shown in Figure 1-2), and it is freely available via its GitHub project (*https://oreil.ly/JPkQ8*).

Figure 1-2. The "hero image" of the Unity ML-Agents Toolkit, showing some of Unity's example characters

If it wasn't obvious, we'll be using ML-Agents for all the simulation activities in the book. We'll show you how to get ML-Agents up and running on your own system in Chapter 2. Don't rush off to install it just yet!

Unity Perception

The Unity Perception package (which we'll abbreviate to *Perception* much of the time) is the tool we'll be using to generate synthetic data. Unity Perception provides a collection of additional features to the Unity Editor that allow you to set scenes up appropriately to create *fake* data.

Like ML-Agents, Perception is an open source project, and you can find it via its GitHub project (*https://oreil.ly/KbvHj*).

The Techniques

The ML-Agents Toolkit supports training using either, or a combination of, *reinforcement learning* and *imitation learning* techniques. Each of these will allow an agent to "learn" a desired behavior through repetitive trial and error—or "reinforcement"—and eventually converge on the ideal behavior for the provided success criteria. What differs between these techniques are the criteria, which are used to assess and optimize agent performance throughout.

Reinforcement Learning

Reinforcement learning (RL) refers to learning processes that employ explicit rewards. It's up to the implementation to award "points" for desirable behaviors and to deduct them for undesirable behaviors.

At this point you may be thinking, *If I have to tell it what to do and what not to do, what's the point of machine learning?* But let's think, as an example, of teaching a bipedal agent to walk. Giving an explicit set of instructions for each state change required to walk—the exact degree of rotation each joint should take, in sequence—would be extensive and complex.

But by giving an agent a few points for moving toward a finish line, lots of points for reaching it, negative points when it falls over, and several hundred thousand attempts to get it right, it will be able to figure out the specifics on its own. So, RL's great strength is in the ability to give goal-centric instructions that require complex behaviors to achieve.

The ML-Agents framework ships with implementations for two different RL algorithms built in: *proximal policy optimization* (PPO) and *soft actor-critic* (SAC).

> Take note of the acronyms for these techniques and algorithms: RL, PPO, and SAC. Memorize them. We'll be using them often throughout the book.

PPO is a powerful, general-purpose RL algorithm that's repeatedly been proven to be highly effective and generally stable across a range of applications. PPO is the default algorithm used in ML-Agents, and it will be used for most of this book. We'll be exploring in more detail how PPO works a little later on.

> Proximal policy optimization was created by the team at OpenAI and debuted in 2017. You can read the original paper on arXiv (*https://oreil.ly/JHfhI*), if you're interested in diving into the details.

SAC is an *off-policy* RL algorithm. We'll get to what that means a little later, but for now, it generally offers a reduction in the number of training cycles needed in return for increased memory requirements. This makes it a better choice for slow training environments when compared to an *on-policy* approach like PPO. We'll be using SAC once or twice in this book, and we'll explore how it works in a little more detail when we get there.

Soft actor-critic was created by the Berkeley Artificial Intelligence Research (BAIR) group and debuted in December 2018. You can read the original release documentation (*https://oreil.ly/7kNmg*) for the details.

Imitation Learning

Similar to RL, *imitation learning* (IL) removes the need to define complex instructions in favor of simply setting objectives. However, IL also removes the need to define explicit objectives or rewards. Instead, a demonstration is given—usually a recording of the agent being manually controlled by a human—and rewards are defined *intrinsically* based on the agent *imitating* the behavior being demonstrated.

This is great for complex domains in which the desirable behaviors are highly specific or the vast majority of possible actions are undesirable. Training with IL is also highly effective for multistage objectives—where an agent needs to achieve intermediate objectives in a certain order to receive a reward.

The ML-Agents framework ships with implementations for two different IL algorithms built in: *behavioral cloning* (BC) and *generative adversarial imitation learning* (GAIL).

BC is an IL algorithm that trains an agent to precisely mimic the demonstrated behavior. Here, BC is only responsible for defining and allocating intrinsic rewards; an existing RL approach such as PPO or SAC is employed for the underlying training process.

GAIL is a generative adversarial approach, applied to IL. In GAIL, two separate models are pitted against each other during training: one is the agent behavior model, which does its best to mimic the given demonstration; the other is a discriminator, which is repeatedly served either a snippet of human-driven demonstrator behavior or agent-driven model behavior and must guess which one it is.

GAIL originated in Jonathan Ho and Stefano Ermon's paper "Generative Adversarial Imitation Learning" (*https://oreil.ly/bokpR*).

As the discriminator gets better at spotting the mimic, the agent model must improve to be able to fool it once again. Likewise, as the agent model improves, the discriminator must establish increasingly strict or nuanced internal criteria to spot the fake. In this back-and-forth, each is forced to iteratively improve.

Behavioral cloning is often the best approach for applications in which it is possible to demonstrate all, or almost all, of the conditions that the agent may find itself in. GAIL is instead able to extrapolate new behaviors, which allows imitation to be learned from limited demonstrations.

BC and GAIL can also be used together, often by employing BC in early training and then allocating the partially trained behavior model to be the agent half of a GAIL model. Starting with BC will often make an agent improve quickly in early training, while switching to GAIL in late training will allow it to develop behaviors beyond those that were demonstrated.

Hybrid Learning

Though RL or IL alone will almost always do the trick, they can be combined. An agent can then be rewarded—and its behavior informed—by both explicitly defined rewards for achieving objectives *and* implicit rewards for effective imitation. The weights of each can even be tuned so that an agent can be trained to prioritize one as the primary objective or both as equal objectives.

In hybrid training, the IL demonstration serves to put the agent on the right path early in training, while explicit RL rewards encourage specific behavior within or beyond that. This is necessary in domains where the ideal agent should outperform the human demonstrator. Because of that early hand-holding, training with RL and IL together can make it significantly faster to train an agent to solve complex problems or navigate a complex environment in a scenario with sparse rewards.

Sparse-reward environments are those in which the agent is rewarded especially infrequently with explicit rewards. In such an environment, the time it takes for an agent to "accidentally" stumble upon a rewardable behavior—and thus receive its first indication of what it should be doing—can waste much of the available training time. But combined with IL, the demonstration can inform on desirable behaviors that work toward explicit rewards.

Together these produce a complex rewards scheme that can encourage highly specific behaviors from an agent, but applications that require this level of complexity for an agent to succeed are few.

Summary of Techniques

This chapter is an introductory survey of concepts and techniques, and you'll be exposed to and use each of the techniques we've looked at here over the course of this book. In doing so, you'll become more familiar with how each of them works in a practical sense.

The gist of it is as follows:

- The Unity ML-Agents Toolkit currently provides a selection of training algorithms across two categories:
  - For reinforcement learning (RL): proximal policy optimization (PPO) and soft actor-critic (SAC)
  - For imitation learning (IL): behavioral cloning (BC) and generative adversarial imitation learning (GAIL)
- These methods can be used independently or together:
  - RL can be used with PPO or SAC alone, or in conjunction with an IL method such as BC.
  - BC can be used alone, as a step on the path to an approach using GAIL, or in conjunction with RL.
- RL techniques require a set of defined rewards.
- IL techniques require some sort of provided demonstration.
- Both RL and IL *learn by doing*.

We'll be touching on or directly using all these techniques across the remainder of the book's exploration of simulation topics.

Projects

This book is a practical, pragmatic work. We want you to get up and running using simulations and synthesis as quickly as possible, and we assume you'd prefer to focus on the implementation whenever possible.

So, while we do explore behind the scenes often, the meat of the book is in the projects we'll be building together.

The practical, project-based side of the book is split between the two domains we discussed earlier: simulation and synthesis.

Simulation Projects

Our simulation projects will be varied: when you're building a simulation environment in Unity, there's a wide range of *ways* in which the agent that exists in the environment can *observe* and *sense* its world.

Some simulation projects will use an agent that observes the world using *vector observations*: that is, numbers. Whatever numbers you might want to send it. Literally anything you like. Realistically, though, vector observations are usually things like the agent's distance from something, or other positional information. But really, any number can be an observation.

Some simulation projects will use an agent that observes the world using *visual observations*: that is, pictures! Because Unity is a game engine, and game engines, like film, have a concept of *cameras*, you can simply (virtually) mount cameras on your agent and just have it exist in the game world. The view from these cameras can then be fed into your machine learning system, allowing the agent to learn about its world based on the camera input.

The simulation examples we'll be looking at using Unity, ML-Agents, and PyTorch include:

- A ball that can roll itself to a target, in Chapter 2 (we know, it sounds too amazing to be true, but it is!)
- A cube that can push a block into a goal area, in Chapter 4
- A simple self-driving car navigating a track, in Chapter 5
- A ball that seeks a coin, trained by imitating human demonstrations, in Chapter 6
- An ballistic launcher agent that can launch a ball at a target, using curriculum learning, in Chapter 8
- A group of cubes that work together to push blocks to goals, in Chapter 9
- Training agents to balance a ball on top of itself, using visual inputs (i.e., cameras) instead of precise measurements, in Chapter 10
- Connecting to and manipulating ML-Agents with, Python, in Chapter 11

Synthesis Projects

Our synthesis projects will be fewer than our simulations because the domain is a little simpler. We focus on building on the material supplied by Unity to showcase the possibilities of simulation.

The synthesis examples we'll be looking at, using Unity and Perception, include:

- A generator for images of randomly thrown and placed dice, in Chapter 3
- Improving the dice image generator by changing the floor and colors of the dice, in Chapter 13
- Generating images of supermarket products to allow for out-of-Unity training on images with complex backdrops and haphazard positioning, in Chapter 14

We won't focus on the actual training process once you've generated your synthesized data, as there are many, many good books and online posts on the subject and we only have so many pages in this book.

Summary and Next Steps

You've taken the first steps, and this chapter contained a bit of the required background material. From here onward, we'll be teaching you by *doing*. This book has the word *practical* in the title for a reason, and we want you to get a feel for simulation and synthesis by building projects of your own.

 You can find the code for every example at our special website for the book (*https://oreil.ly/1efRA*)—we recommend downloading the code only when you need it. We'll also keep the website up-to-date with any changes you should be aware of, so do bookmark it!

In the next chapter, we'll look at how you can create your first simulation, implement an agent to *do something* in it, and train a machine learning system using reinforcement learning.

CHAPTER 2

Creating Your First Simulation

We're going to get started by looking at a simple *simulation environment*: a ball agent that can roll around a platform. As we said earlier, we know it's a lot to handle, but we think you'll be able to cope with the levels of excitement and come through with a better understanding of machine learning and simulation with Unity.

Everybody Remembers Their First Simulation

In this chapter we're going to build a brand-new simulation environment using Unity, create an agent, and then train that agent to accomplish a task in the environment using reinforcement learning. It's going to be a *very* simple simulation environment, but it will serve to demonstrate a number of important things:

- How straightforward it is to assemble a scene in Unity by using a small collection of simple objects
- How to use the Unity Package Manager to import the Unity side of the Unity ML-Agents Toolkit into Unity and set up a Unity project for machine learning
- How to set up a simple agent in your simulation object with the intention of enabling it to accomplish a task
- How to take manual control of your agent to test the simulation environment
- How to start a training run using the command-line tool (CLI) side of the Unity ML-Agents Toolkit, and how to bring up TensorBoard to monitor the training's progress
- How to bring a trained model file back into a Unity simulation environment and run the agent using the trained model

By the end of this chapter, you'll be comfortable enough with Unity and with using the ML-Agents Toolkit to dive into deeper, more complicated problems.

 This chapter and a few of the subsequent ones won't be peeling back the layers on the underlying machine learning algorithms (remember the word *practical* in this book's title?), but we will start to look at the workings of the machine learning algorithms in time, *we promise.*

Our Simulation

Our first simulation is deceptively simple: a small environment with a ball in it, sitting on a floor in a void. The ball will be able to roll around, including falling off the floor and into the void. It will be the only element that's controllable: it will be controllable by both the user (i.e., us, for testing purposes) and the reinforcement learning ML-Agents system.

Thus, the ball will act as our *agent*, and its objective will be to get to the *target* as quickly as possible without falling off the *floor*. The simulation environment we'll build was shown in Figure 2-1.

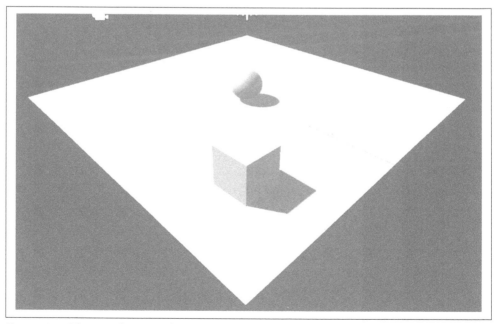

Figure 2-1. The simulation we'll be building

Broadly, the steps to create any simulation environment and train one or more agents to operate within it are as follows:

1. Build the environment in Unity: the environment is a physical simulation that contains objects.

2. Implement the machine learning elements: namely, we need an agent that operates within the environment.

3. Implement the code that will tell the agent how to observe the environment, how to carry out actions within the environment, how to calculate rewards it might receive for acting within the environment, and how to reset itself or the environment when it succeeds or fails at its task.

4. Train the agent in the environment.

We'll be performing each of these four steps in this chapter.

Setting Up

For a rundown and discussion of the tools you'll need for simulation and machine learning, refer back to Chapter 1. This section will give you a quick summary of the bits and pieces you'll need to accomplish *this particular activity*.

Specifically, to work on the activity in this chapter and build the simple simulation environment, you'll need to do the following:

1. *Install Unity 2021 or later.* This book isn't here to teach you the basics of Unity (we wrote a great book on that, if you're keen), but it's worth noting that the way Unity likes to be installed changes more often than the underlying material this book is teaching, so we recommend checking out the Unity Installation Guide on the Unity website (*https://oreil.ly/sEa5n*) for the latest on installing Unity. Hop over there, get the right version of Unity installed, and come back. We'll still be here.

 While the Unity ML-Agents Toolkit works with any version of Unity newer than 2018.4, we recommend that you install the latest 2021 version of Unity. You might find a 2021 LTS version of Unity. LTS stands for Long Term Support, and it is the version of Unity that the Unity team maintains for a designated period of time, with both bug and security fixes. It's a safe bet to base your work on it if you're doing this for production purposes, once you're done learning (if there's such a thing as being done learning). You can learn more about Unity LTS releases in the Unity documentation (*https://oreil.ly/1mtHI*).

2. *Install Python.* You'll need to install a version of Python newer than or equal to Python 3.6.1 and older than (but excluding) Python 3.8. If you don't have a preference or you don't have an existing Python environment, we recommend installing Python 3.7.8. As we discussed in Chapter 1, much of the Unity ML-Agents Toolkit depends on Python.

At the time of this writing, the Unity ML-Agents Toolkit does not support Python 3.8. You'll need to use Python 3.6.1 or newer, or any version of Python 3.7. If you are using Windows, you'll also need the x86-64 version of Python, as the toolkit is not compatible with the x86 version. If you're running on a fancy Apple Silicon macOS device, you might want to run Python under Rosetta 2, but it also might work fine with Apple Silicon builds of Python. Things are changing fast in that respect. Check the book's website (*https://oreil.ly/1efRA*) for the latest on Apple Silicon and Unity for simulation.

To install Python, head to the Python downloads page (*https://oreil.ly/5dPG8*) and grab the installer for your particular operating system. If you don't want to install Python directly in this manner, it's fine to use your operating system's package manager (if it has one), or a comprehensive Python environment (we quite like Anaconda), as long as the *version* of Python you install meets the version and architecture versions that we noted a moment ago.

You'll also need to make sure your Python installation comes with `pip` (or `pip3`), the Python package manager. The Python documentation (*https://oreil.ly/T8c4j*) may help with this, if you're having issues.

We strongly recommend that you use a virtual environment ("venv") for your Unity ML-Agents work. To learn more about creating a venv, you can follow the instructions in the Python documentation (*https://oreil.ly/qQPZj*), or follow the basic steps we outline next.

If you have a preferred way of setting Python up on your machine, just do that. We're not here to tell you how to live your life. If you're comfortable with Python, then realistically all you need to do is make sure you obey the version restrictions of ML-Agents, get the right package installed, and have it available to run when you need it. Python is famously not fragile when it comes to multiple versions, right? (Authors' note: we're Australians, so this should be read with an Aussie accent, and dripping with respectful sarcasm.)

You can create a virtual environment like this:

```
python -m venv UnityMLVEnv
```

We recommend naming it `UnityMLVEnv` or something similar. But the name is your choice.

And you can activate it like this:

```
source UnityMLVEnv/bin/activate
```

3. *Install the Python `mlagents` package.* Once you've got Python and a virtual environment for Unity ML-Agents to live in up and running, install the Python `mlagents` package by issuing the following command from inside the `venv`:

```
pip3 install mlagents
```

Asking `pip`, the Python Package Manager, to fetch and install `mlagents` will also install all the dependencies for `mlagents`, which includes TensorFlow.

4. *Clone or download the Unity ML-Agents Toolkit GitHub repository.* You can clone the repository by issuing the following command:

```
git clone https://github.com/Unity-Technologies/ml-agents.git
```

We largely assume that you're an experienced user of your chosen operating system for development purposes. If you need guidance on accomplishing any of these setup steps, don't despair! We recommend you review the documentation (*https://oreil.ly/xFL3F*) to get up to speed.

With the preceding four steps completed, you've completed the Python-related setup requirements. Next we'll look at the Unity requirements.

Creating the Unity Project

The first step for creating a simulation environment is to create a brand-new Unity project. The Unity project is much like any other development project: it's a collection of files, folders, and *things* that Unity declares to be a project.

 Our screenshots will be from macOS because it's the primary environment we use on a daily basis. All the tools that we'll be using in this book work on macOS, on Windows, and in Linux, so feel free to use your preferred operating system. We'll do our best to point out any glaring differences between macOS and the other operating systems as we go (but there aren't many, as far as what we're doing is concerned). We've tested all the activities on all the supported platforms, and everything worked (on our machines).

To create a project, make sure you've completed all the setup steps, and then do the following:

1. Open the Unity Hub and create a new 3D project. As shown in Figure 2-2, we'll name ours "BallWorld," but feel free to get creative.

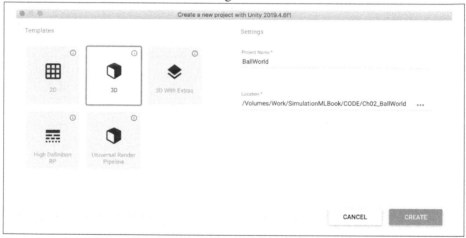

Figure 2-2. Creating the Unity project for our new environment

2. Select the Window menu → Package Manager, and use the Unity Package Manager (*https://oreil.ly/VTwnY*) to install the ML-Agents Toolkit package (`com.unity.ml-agents`), as shown in Figure 2-3.

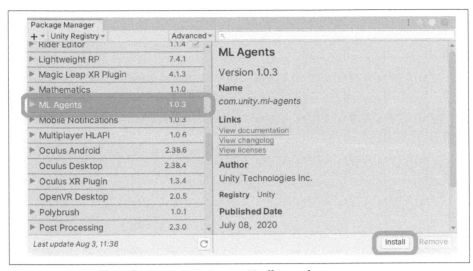

Figure 2-3. Installing the Unity ML-Agents Toolkit package

Like everything these days, Unity has a package manager. It's actually pretty good, but also like everything these days, it can sometimes be a little fragile. If you're having problems, restart Unity and try again, or try the manual installation process explained in the next note.

It might take a few moments for the package to download and install. Once it's finished downloading, you'll see Unity import it, as shown in Figure 2-4.

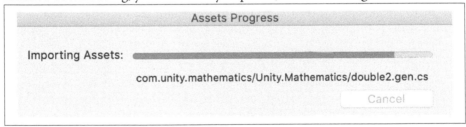

Figure 2-4. The ML-Agents package being imported by Unity

If you want to install the package manually, or if for some reason (such as corporate policy) the Unity Package Manager isn't an option, you can:

a. Open the package manager by selecting the menu named Window → Package Manager.

b. Click the + button in the package manager and select "Add package from disk…".

c. Find the com.unity.ml-agents folder within the copy of the Unity ML-Agents Toolkit you cloned in "Setting Up" on page 19.

d. Select the *package.json* file.

    For more information, check the Unity documentation (*https://oreil.ly/XArSA*) on installing a package from a local folder.

3. Verify that you have an ML Agents folder under Packages in the Project view, as shown in Figure 2-5.

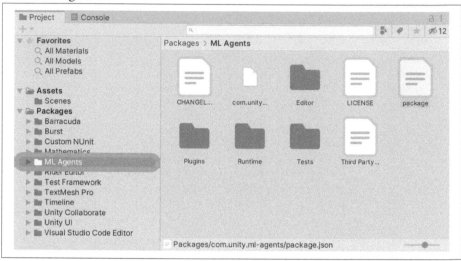

Figure 2-5. The project is ready to go if you can see the ML Agents folder

Your project is ready to go. We recommend you push it to some sort of source control at this point, or duplicate it as a fresh starting point for all your ML-Agents work in this book.

You'll need this basic Unity-powered starting point every time you want to create a fresh simulation environment in Unity. In other words, you'll want a fresh Unity project open with the Unity package installed, and you'll need to do that for each ML-Agents project you work on. The Python setup is effectively a one-off and sets up the Python components available on your machine, but the Unity setup needs to happen for each project you want to work with.

Packages All the Way Down

It might be slightly confusing which component is which, as there are many things with similar names. Let's unpack that a little bit before we move on.

There are effectively three sets of things in play here that you could conceivably refer to as the "ML-Agents package." They are:

- The `mlagents` *Python package*. This is a Python package and we installed it earlier using the Python package manager `pip3`. It's part of the Unity ML-Agents Toolkit and it's distributed via the Python Package Index (*https://pypi.org/project/mlagents*) (which is how you installed it using `pip3` earlier). When we're talking about this *Python package* we'll refer to it as `mlagents`.

- The `com.unity.ml-agents` *Unity package*. You install this package via the Unity Package Manager, as we did in "Creating the Unity Project" on page 22. It's also part of the Unity ML-Agents Toolkit and it's distributed via the Unity Package Manager (which can install it into a Unity project via either the automated process, where you choose it from the list of packages using the Unity Package Manager interface, or manually, where you give the Unity Package Manager a Git URL with a correctly formed Unity package inside it). When we're talking about this *Unity package* we'll refer to it variously as `com.unity.ml-agents`, ML-Agents, the Unity ML-Agents package, or the ML-Agents Toolkit. This is the package that allows you to use features of ML-Agents inside the Unity Editor and in the C# code you'll write in Unity.

> You install the `mlagents` Python package, install the Unity ML-Agents package, and clone a local copy of the ML-Agents repository because each one of these installs a different set of things. The Python package gives you the ability to run certain commands in your terminal that allow you to train agents, the cloned Git repository gives you a useful collection of sample code and resources, and the Unity package gives you the pieces you need to make agents and other ML-Agents (or related) components inside Unity scenes. Each is useful.

- The cloned copy of the *Unity ML-Agents Toolkit GitHub repository*. This is a local copy of the contents of the GitHub repository that we suggest you clone or download as it contains useful documentation, sample files, and such. When we refer to this we'll call it "your local copy of the ML-Agents repository" or something similar.

If you're running Apple Silicon, you're fine to use the Apple Silicon builds of Unity, but you'll need to use Python in an Intel environment. The easiest and laziest way to do this is to run your Terminal app under Rosetta, but there are other ways too. It's beyond the scope of this book to discuss Python on Apple Silicon, but if you're in this position, there are plenty of resources online. Just remember: on macOS, Unity can be either platform, but ML-Agents and Python (for this use case) must be Intel.

The Environment

With the fundamental setup out of the way, it's time to actually start building your simulation environment in the Unity Editor.

This involves creating a scene in Unity that will serve as the simulation environment. The simulation environment we're building has the following requirements:

- A *floor* for the agent to move around on
- A *target* for the agent to seek

We'll also need to create the agent itself, but we'll cover that in "The Agent" on page 29.

The Floor

The floor is where the agent will move around. It exists because our agent exists within the physics simulation engine of Unity, and if there were no floor, it would fall to the ground.

There's nothing special about the concept of a floor in Unity. We've just chosen to use a plane for the floor, but we could use any object that exists in the physics system and is large enough to *be* a floor.

To create the floor, make sure you have a Unity scene open and then follow these steps:

1. Open the GameObject menu → 3D Object → Plane. Click on the new plane you created in the Hierarchy view, and using the Inspector view, set its name to "Floor" or something similar, as shown in Figure 2-6. This is our floor.

2. While the floor is selected, use the Transform Inspector to set its position to (0, 0, 0), its rotation to (0, 0, 0), and its scale to (1, 1, 1), as shown in Figure 2-7. We do this to ensure that the floor is in a sensible position and

orientation, and is of sufficient scale. These values will probably already be the defaults.

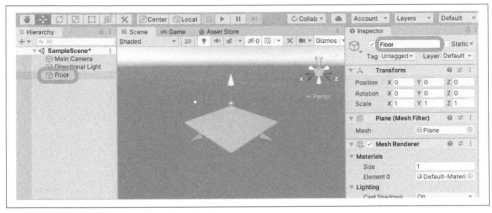

Figure 2-6. Creating and naming the floor

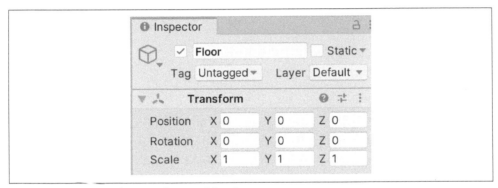

Figure 2-7. Setting the transforms of the floor

 If you need some help creating a Unity scene, check out the Unity documentation (*https://oreil.ly/yrzzq*). The gist is that a scene contains objects, and you can make a new one using the Assets → Create → Scene menu.

That's all we need to do for the floor. We don't need to create an empty void, as Unity conveniently supplies one for us (i.e., every scene is just a void, except for the things you add to it). Don't forget to save the scene you're working in using the File menu.

You can rename the default scene to something other than "SampleScene" by locating it in the Project view, right-clicking on it, and choosing Rename.

The Target

The target is the *thing* that our agent will seek on the floor. Again, Unity has no special concept of a target; we're just calling the cube we're making a target, which is contextually relevant because of the plans we have for this scene and simulation.

To create the target in your scene, follow these steps:

1. Open the GameObject menu → 3D Object → Cube. As with the floor, click on the new cube in the Hierarchy view, and use the Inspector to set its name to "Target" or something similar, as shown in Figure 2-8. This is going to be the target, and as you can see, it's a very compelling target! It will probably be partially embedded in the floor plane.

Figure 2-8. Creating and naming the target

2. While the target is selected, as we did with the floor, use the Transform Inspector to set its position, rotation, and scale. The values in this case should be something like (3, 0.5, 3), (0, 0, 0), and (1, 1, 1), respectively, as shown in Figure 2-9.

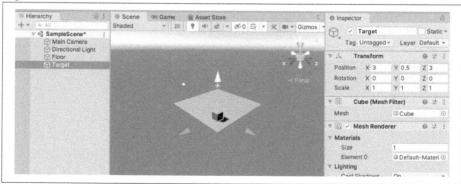

Figure 2-9. The transform for the target and the environment so far

That's all we need to do for the target. At this point, your environment should look similar to Figure 2-9. Don't forget to save your scene again.

The Agent

The next step is to create the agent. The agent is the *thing* that moves around in the environment. It's going to be a sphere that rolls around and seeks the target.

Follow these steps to create the agent:

1. Open the GameObject menu → 3D Object → Sphere. Name the sphere "Agent" or something similar.

2. Use the Inspector and set the transform's position, rotation, and scale to (0, 0.5, 0), (0, 0, 0), and (1, 1, 1), respectively. Your agent should be positioned on the floor similarly to ours, as shown in Figure 2-10.

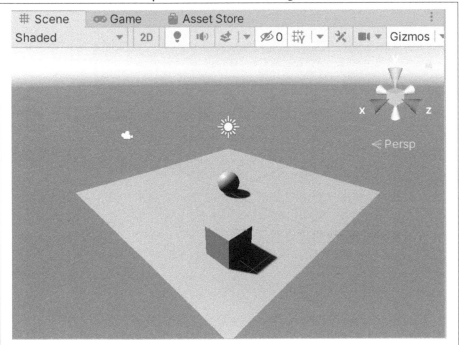

Figure 2-10. The agent in the scene

3. Use the Add Component button at the bottom of the agent's Inspector, shown in Figure 2-11, and add a Rigidbody component to the agent. You don't need to change anything on the Rigidbody component.

Add Component

Figure 2-11. The Add Component button

That's everything for the physical side of the agent. Next, we need to give the agent some logic and facilitate its connection to the machine learning side of things:

1. Select the agent, and add a new Script component via the Inspector's Add Component button, as shown in Figure 2-12. Name the script "BallAgent," and click "Create and Add."

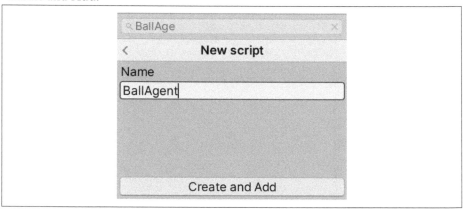

Figure 2-12. Creating the script for the agent

You should see a new Script component attached to your agent in its Inspector, as shown in Figure 2-13.

Figure 2-13. The script is attached to the agent

2. Double-click on the BallAgent script in the Unity Project view to open the script in your code editor.

Basically, an agent that is built using Unity ML-Agents needs to have a script attached to it that tells Unity that its parent class is `Agent`, which is a class supplied by the ML-Agents Unity package. Being a child of `Agent` means we have to implement or override certain methods supplied by the Unity ML-Agents package. Those methods allow us to control and work with the agent for machine learning purposes.

3. Once the script is open, add the following code to the top, below the `using UnityEngine;` line:

```
using Unity.MLAgents;
using Unity.MLAgents.Sensors;
```

These lines import the appropriate bits of the ML-Agents Unity package that we imported, and allow us to use them in code.

4. Find the `Update()` method and delete it. We won't be using it for this simulation.

5. Find the definition of the `BallAgent` class and change it from this:

```
public class BallAgent : MonoBehaviour
```

to this:

```
public class BallAgent : Agent
```

This makes our new class, `BallAgent`, a child of `Agent` (which comes from ML-Agents), instead of the default `MonoBehaviour` (which is the parent of most non-ML Unity objects).

Those are the basics of setting up an agent in a simulation environment with Unity. Next we need to add some logic that provides the ability for our agent to roll about the place (well, the floor). Before we do that, we're going to group the three objects we've made so far.

Save the code in your code editor, and then switch back to the Unity Editor and, in your scene, do the following:

1. Open the GameObject menu → Create Empty to create an empty GameObject.

2. Select the empty GameObject and use the Inspector to name it "Training Area."

When you're renaming something, instead of using the Inspector view, you can simply select it in the Hierarchy view and press your Return/Enter key to enter edit mode for the name in the Hierarchy view. Press Return/Enter again to save your new name.

3. Set the Training Area GameObject's position, rotation, and scale to (0, 0, 0), (0, 0, 0), and (1, 1, 1), respectively.

4. In the Hierarchy, drag the floor, target, and agent into the Training Area. Your Hierarchy should now look like Figure 2-14. Nothing in the scene should change position when you do this.

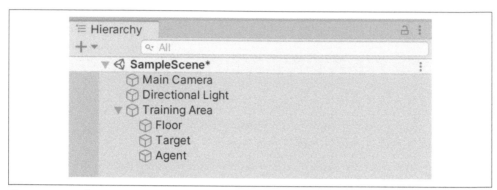

Figure 2-14. The Training Area

Don't forget to save your scene when you're done.

Starting and Stopping the Agent

We're going to train this agent using reinforcement learning. Training for reinforcement learning inside our Unity environment involves running through many *episodes* during which the agent attempts to reach the cube. In each episode, if the agent does something we want it to do, we want to reinforce that behavior by rewarding it, and vice versa if it does something we do not want it to do.

An episode runs until the agent fails the task—in this case, that would be either falling off the floor into the void or running out of a predefined amount of time—or succeeds the task by reaching the target.

At the beginning of each episode, a C# method on the Agent named OnEpisode Begin() is called to initialize the simulation environment for the new episode. This method sets up the environment for the episode. In most cases, you'll be using this to randomize elements of the environment to facilitate the agent learning to succeed in the task under a range of conditions.

For our scenario, at the beginning of an episode the requirements are:

- Make sure the ball agent is somewhere on the floor, and not falling into the abyss.

- Move the target to a random location on the floor.

To fulfill the first requirement, we need to have access to the agent's Rigidbody component. The Rigidbody component is part of what allows Unity to simulate an object in its physics system.

Learn more about the Unity Rigidbody component in the Unity manual (*https://oreil.ly/VqNjd*).

Open up the BallAgent script again. Since we need to reset the agent's velocity (if it's falling into the abyss) and also, eventually, move it around the floor, we need access to its `Rigidbody`:

1. The Rigidbody component we need here is on the same object this script will be attached to (unlike the transform of the target we needed a moment ago), so we can get a reference to it inside our script's `Start()` method.

   First, we'll need somewhere to store it when we get the reference. Add the following above the `Start()` method (inside the class but above, and outside of, the method):

   ```
   Rigidbody rigidBody;
   ```

2. Next, inside the `Start()` method, add the following code to request a reference to the Rigidbody attached to the object that the script is attached to (and to store it in the `rigidBody` variable we created a moment ago):

   ```
   rigidBody = GetComponent<Rigidbody>();
   ```

   To fulfill the second requirement, we need to make sure the code can access the transform of the target so that we can move it to a new random location.

3. Since this script is going to be attached to the agent, not the target, we'll need to acquire the reference to the transform of the target.

   To do this, inside the `BallAgent` class, before the `Start()` method, add a new `public` field of type `Transform`:

   ```
   public Transform Target;
   ```

`public` fields in Unity components will get displayed by the Unity Editor in the Inspector. This means you can visually, or with drag-and-drop, choose which object is used. We didn't need to do this with the `Rigidbody` earlier, because it doesn't need to be exposed to the Unity Editor.

4. Save the script (and leave it open) and switch back to the Unity Editor. Find the script component attached to the agent, look for the newly created Target field in the Inspector, and select the small circular button next to it, as shown in Figure 2-15.

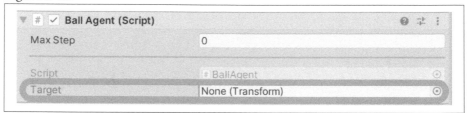

Figure 2-15. Changing the target in the script

5. In the window that appears, double-click on the Target object, as shown in Figure 2-16.

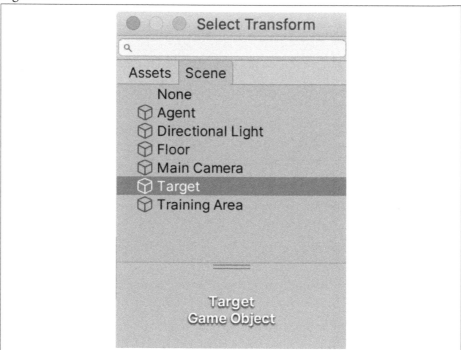

Figure 2-16. Choosing the target

6. Verify that the script component attached to the agent now shows the target's transform in the Target field, as shown in Figure 2-17.

You can also drag the Target object from the Hierarchy view into the slot in the Inspector, if you'd prefer.

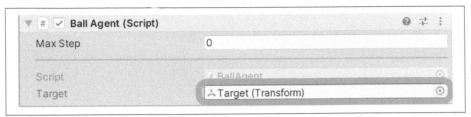

Figure 2-17. Verifying the target's transform is showing in the field

7. Next, switch back to the script's code and implement an empty `OnEpisode Begin()` method inside the class:

```
public override void OnEpisodeBegin()
{

}
```

8. Inside `OnEpisodeBegin()`, add the following code to check if the position of the agent's `Rigidbody` is lower than the floor (which would mean the agent is falling) and, if it is, reset its momentum and move it back onto the floor:

```
if (this.transform.localPosition. y < 0)
{
  this.rigidBody.angularVelocity = Vector3.zero;
  this.rigidBody.velocity = Vector3.zero;
  this.transform.localPosition = new Vector3(0, 0.5f, 0);
}
```

9. And finally, for the first requirement, add some code after the `if` statement to move the target to a new random position:

```
Target.localPosition = new Vector3(Random.value * 8 - 4,
                                   0.5f,
                                   Random.value * 8 - 4);
```

Don't forget to save your code, just in case.

Letting the Agent Observe the Environment

Next, we need to set up the agent to collect *observations* from the simulation environment. We're going to pretend our agent can see its target so that it knows exactly where it is (its objective isn't to figure out where the target is; it's to *reach* the target):

therefore, one of the observations it will have is the exact position of the target. This requires more coding.

Observations are collected by adding *sensors* to our agent. Sensors can be added in code, or by attaching components to things in the Unity scene. For our first simulation, we're going to do it all in code.

In our agent C# code, we need to do the following:

1. Create an empty `CollectObservations()` method:

   ```
   public override void CollectObservations(VectorSensor sensor)
   {

   }
   ```

2. Then, inside the method, add a sensor observation for the agent's own position:

   ```
   sensor.AddObservation(this.transform.localPosition);
   ```

3. We also need to add a sensor observation for the agent's own x and z velocity (we don't care about the y velocity, because the agent can't move up or down):

   ```
   sensor.AddObservation(rigidBody.velocity.x);
   sensor.AddObservation(rigidBody.velocity.z);
   ```

4. And, finally,we need to add an observation for the target's position:

   ```
   sensor.AddObservation(Target.localPosition);
   ```

That's all for the observations!

Letting the Agent Take Actions in the Environment

To achieve its goal of moving toward the target, the agent needs to be able to *move*.

1. First, create an empty `OnActionReceived()` method:

   ```
   public override void OnActionReceived(ActionBuffers actions)
   {

   }
   ```

2. Then, get access to the two continuous actions we need, one for x and one for z, allowing the ball to be controlled in all the directions in which it could roll:

   ```
   var actionX = actions.ContinuousActions[0];
   var actionZ = actions.ContinuousActions[1];
   ```

3. Create a zeroed `Vector3` to serve as a control signal:

   ```
   Vector3 controlSignal = Vector3.zero;
   ```

4. Then, change the x and z components of the control signal to take their values from the X and Z actions:

```
controlSignal.x = actionX;
controlSignal.z = actionZ;
```

5. Finally, using the `Rigidbody` we got a reference to earlier (the component attached to the agent), call the `AddForce()` function that's available on a Unity `Rigidbody` to apply the relevant forces:

```
rigidBody.AddForce(controlSignal * 10);
```

That's it for now! The agent can now be controlled by the machine learning system. Don't forget to save your code.

> The reason we create the `controlSignal` `Vector3` by using `Vector3.zero` initially is because we want the y component to be 0. We could've achieved the same by creating an entirely empty `Vector3`, and then assigning 0 to `controlSignal.y`.

Giving the Agent Rewards for Its Behavior

A fundamental component of reinforcement learning, as we mentioned in Chapter 1, is *rewards*. Reinforcement learning requires the reward signals in order to guide the agent to the optimal policy—that is, to do what we want it to do, or as close as possible to that. The *reinforcement* of reinforcement learning occurs by using reward signals to guide the agent toward the desired behavior (i.e., the optimal policy).

Inside your `OnActionReceived` method, after the existing code you just wrote, do the following:

1. Store the distance to the target:

```
float distanceToTarget = Vector3.Distance
    (this.transform.localPosition, Target.localPosition);
```

2. Check if the distance to the target is close enough that you have reached the target, and if it is, assign a reward of 1.0:

```
if (distanceToTarget < 1.42f)
{
    SetReward(1.0f);
}
```

3. After assigning the reward, *inside* the `if` statement, because the target was reached, call `EndEpisode()` to finish the current training episode:

```
EndEpisode();
```

4. Now check if the agent has fallen off the platform and, if it has, end the episode then as well (no reward applies in this case):

```
if (this.transform.localPosition.y < 0)
{
  EndEpisode();
}
```

With that done, you'll want to save your code and return to the Unity Editor.

Finishing Touches for the Agent

An agent doesn't just require a script extending Agent; it also requires a few support scripts and settings in the Unity Editor. The ML-Agents package that we installed in Unity earlier brought along the scripts we need.

To add them to your agent, in the Unity Editor with your scene open, do the following:

1. Select the agent in the Hierarchy, and click the Add Component button at the bottom of its Inspector.

2. Search for, and add, a Decision Requester component, as shown in Figure 2-18. Verify that it's added correctly by looking for the component in the agent's Inspector, as shown in Figure 2-19.

Figure 2-18. Adding a Decision Requester

Figure 2-19. The Decision Requester component is visible in the agent's Inspector

3. Use the slider to change the Decision Period to 10.

4. Use the Add Component button again and add a Behavior Parameters component to the agent.

5. Verify that the Behavior Parameters component was added successfully, and update Behavior Name to "BallAgent," Vector Observation Space Size to 8, Continuous Actions to 2, and Discrete Branches to 0, as shown in Figure 2-20.

We set the Vector Observation Space Size to 8 because there are eight values being provided as observations. They are:

- The three components of the vector representing the position of the target
- The three components of the vector representing the position of the agent
- The single value representing the agent's X velocity
- The single value representing the agent's Z velocity

Check back to "Letting the Agent Observe the Environment" on page 35, when we added each observation in code, for a refresher of the eight values we're sending as observations.

Similarly, we set Continuous Actions to 2 because there are two actions. They are:

- The force being applied on the x-axis
- The force being applied on the z-axis

Again, check back to "Letting the Agent Take Actions in the Environment" on page 36, when we added the OnActionReceived method for the code representing two actions.

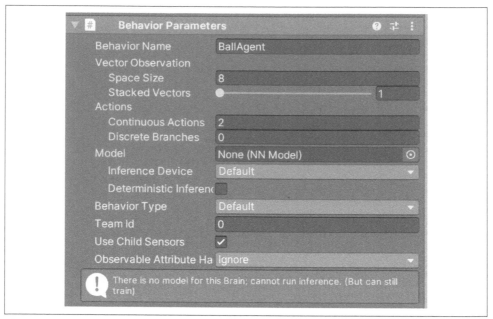

Figure 2-20. Setting up the Behavior Parameters

It's a good time to save your scene too.

Providing a Manual Control System for the Agent

One of the joys of building simulation environments for machine learning using a game engine is that you can take control of the agents in the simulation and test out the agent's ability to exist in the environment, and even whether the goal is achievable.

To do this, we extend the Heuristic() method. Open your agent's C# code again and follow these steps:

1. Implement an empty Heuristic() method:

```
public override void Heuristic(in ActionBuffers actionsOut)
{

}
```

The in keyword is a parameter modifier in C#. This means it causes the arguments to be passed by reference. In this case, this effectively means you're working directly with the actions of the agent, and not a copy of it that's then passed somewhere else.

2. Inside, add the following code, mapping the 0 index action to the horizontal input of Unity's input system and the 1 index action to the vertical input (matching the way we mapped the x and z actions earlier, in "Letting the Agent Take Actions in the Environment" on page 36):

```
var continuousActionsOut = actionsOut.ContinuousActions;
continuousActionsOut[0] = Input.GetAxis("Horizontal");
continuousActionsOut[1] = Input.GetAxis("Vertical");
```

That's it. You'll want to save your code and return to the Unity Editor. Your manual control system is hooked up.

How do you *use* this control system? We're glad you asked. To use the manual control system, you need to do the following:

1. Select the agent in the Hierarchy, and use the Inspector to set the Behavior Type to Heuristic Only.
2. Press the Play button in Unity. You can now use the arrow keys on your keyboard to control the agent. The agent should reset as expected if it falls into the void.

You can change the keys that are connected to the Horizontal and Vertical axes that we're connecting to the actions arrow using Unity:

1. Open the Edit menu → Project Settings… and select Input Manager in the sidebar of the Project Settings view.
2. Find the Horizontal and Vertical axes and the associated Positive and Negative buttons, and change the mappings at your leisure, as shown in Figure 2-21.

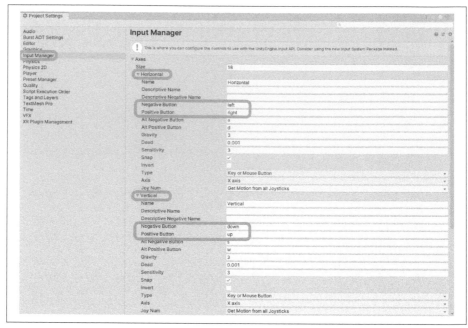

Figure 2-21. Changing the keys mapped to input axes in Unity

You should save your scene now, as well.

Training with the Simulation

Training the simulation is a multistep process, and it involves the creation of a configuration file using some provided Unity ML-Agents scripts, and quite some time depending on the power of your machine. To train, we'll be using Python and the terminal, but first we need to do a little setup.

Specifically, we need to create a YAML file to serve as the hyperparameters for our training. Then we'll run the training using the `mlagent-learn` command from the `mlagents` Python package.

> YAML is a useful storage configuration format and is designed to be as human-readable as possible. You can learn more about YAML from Wikipedia (*https://oreil.ly/XzIKU*).

So, to train your ball agent, follow these steps:

1. Create a new file named *BallAgent.yaml*, and include the following hyperparameters and values:

```
behaviors:
  BallAgent:
    trainer_type: ppo
    hyperparameters:
      batch_size: 10
      buffer_size: 100
      learning_rate: 3.0e-4
      beta: 5.0e-4
      epsilon: 0.2
      lambd: 0.99
      num_epoch: 3
      learning_rate_schedule: linear
    network_settings:
      normalize: false
      hidden_units: 128
      num_layers: 2
    reward_signals:
      extrinsic:
        gamma: 0.99
        strength: 1.0
    max_steps: 500000
    time_horizon: 64
    summary_freq: 10000
```

2. Save the new YAML file somewhere sensible. We like to put it in a *config/* directory near where we keep the Unity project, but there's no need to keep it inside the Unity project (although you can if you want to).

 We're only using a very small batch and buffer size because this is such a simple simulation for training in: there's not that many inputs and outputs, so making the batch and buffer sizes small speeds up the training. A more complex simulation environment, reward system, set of observations would warrant a different set of hyperparameter values. We'll talk a little more about the potential hyperparameters later, in Chapter 12.

3. Next, in your terminal, inside the venv we created in "Setting Up" on page 19, fire up the training process by running the following command:

```
mlagents-learn config/BallAgent.yaml --run-id=BallAgent
```

Replace *config/BallAgent.yaml* with the path to the configuration file we just created.

4. Once the command is up and running, you should see something that looks like Figure 2-22. At this point, you can press the Play button in Unity.

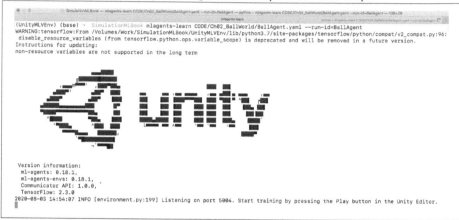

Figure 2-22. The ML-Agents process begins training

5. You'll know the training process is working when you see output that looks like Figure 2-23.

If you're running a fancy Apple Silicon-powered macOS machine, you might want to run all of this under Rosetta 2.

Figure 2-23. The ML-Agents process during training

Monitoring the Training with TensorBoard

While it may not look it, the `mlagents-learn` command is using PyTorch under the hood. PyTorch under the hood means you can use the amazing suite of Python machine learning tools: this doesn't mean much for such a simple simulation, but we can at least discuss how to take a look at what's going on under the hood during the training via TensorBoard.

 Despite TensorBoard originating as part of the TensorFlow project, which is a different framework from PyTorch and was originally developed by a totally different team, TensorBoard has become a more generic support tool for machine learning frameworks and works with many other tools, including PyTorch.

Follow these steps to monitor the training process via TensorBoard:

1. Open an additional terminal and change the directory to the location where the Unity ML-Agents Toolkit is installed.

2. Activate your venv, and execute the following command:

```
tensorboard --logdir=results --port=6006
```

 If you have issues starting TensorBoard, try installing a fresh copy using the command `pip3 install tensorboard` (don't forget that you'll need to be inside your venv!).

3. Once TensorBoard is up and running, you can open your web browser and go to the following URL: *http://localhost:6006*.

4. From this browser instance of TensorBoard, you can monitor the training process, as shown in Figure 2-24. Of particular relevance at this point in your simulation journey are the `cumulative_reward` and `value_estimate` statistics, as they show how well the agent is performing the task (based on its reward). If `cumulative_reward` and `value_estimate` are approaching `1.0`, it's likely that the agent has solved the problem of reaching the target (because the maximum reward the agent can earn is `1.0`).

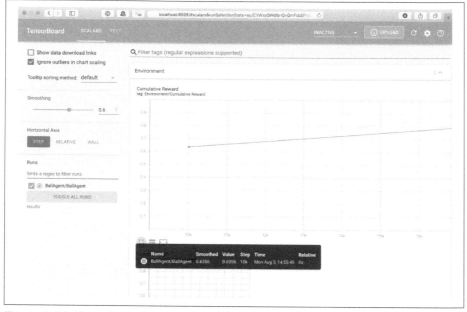

Figure 2-24. TensorBoard monitoring the training

When the Training Is Complete

Eventually, the training process will complete and will save a *model file*. The training process will display a "Saved Model" message when this occurs.

Once the model file is saved, follow these steps to bring it into Unity and run the simulation using the model (instead of using the simulation to train) to watch your agent in action with the trained model:

1. Locate the model file (it will be named *BallAgent.onnx* or *BallAgent.nn*, or similar), as shown in Figure 2-25.

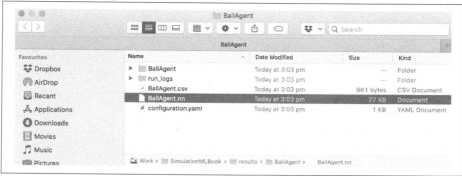

Figure 2-25. The saved model file

2. Move the model file into the Unity project, either using your file manager or by dragging it into the Unity Project view. You should see the *.onnx* file in Unity, as shown in Figure 2-26.

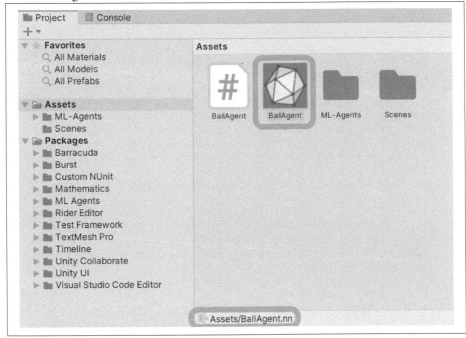

Figure 2-26. The model in Unity

The *.onnx* file that you generated here (and will generate in many other chapters in this book) is an Open Neural Network Exchange (ONNX) format file. ONNX is an open format for storing machine learning models and provides a common set of operators and a common file format to enable AI developers to use models with a variety of frameworks, tools, runtimes, and compilers. It's an exciting open standard for machine learning, and you're using it here!

3. Select the agent in Unity, and drag the *.onnx* or *.nn* file from the Project view to the Model component in the Inspector. Your agent's Inspector should look like Figure 2-27.

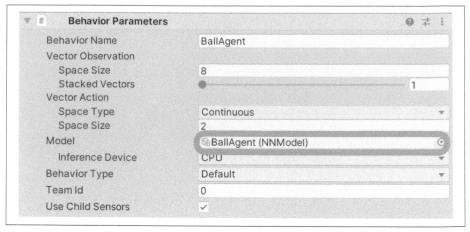

Figure 2-27. Attaching the trained model to the agent in Unity

You can also use the circular button next to the model field in the Inspector to select from the *.onnx* or *.nn* files available in the project (you'll only have one file to choose from right now, though!).

4. Run the simulation by pressing the Play button in Unity.

You should see your agent repeatedly achieving its goal! Great success.

What's It All Mean?

In this chapter, you built a very simple simulation environment in which a single agent is equipped to learn how to roll itself to a target (and ideally not roll itself off the edge of the world).

This agent was able to observe its environment because `BallAgent` was given *observations* about:

- Its own position
- Its own x velocity
- Its own z velocity
- The target's position

It's important to remember that the observations provided are all an agent can know about its environment and the changes of state therein.

We turned a simple sphere object in Unity into an agent by attaching a Script component to it that extends the `Agent` class. If we hadn't done that, the sphere would not be an agent.

Like how humans have senses that provide information about the world as we interact with it (sight, smell, touch, hearing, and taste) and the state of our own bodies (proprioception, interoception, and vestibular sense), agents need the same to determine their own state at different points in time and to observe how changes in their own state affect the state of the parts of their environment that relate to their objectives.

For a ball that needs to seek a cube, knowing its position, speed, and objective position is sufficient. It doesn't need to be told, for example, that there is a floor that ends at a certain point. This is because:

- A direct path to the target from any other point on the floor will never lead off the sides.
- The agent will learn from experience that going past a certain distance in each direction results in the episode ending without a reward.

Other types of agents may require many more or complex observations. As we'll see a bit later, ML-Agents has some built-in utilities for hooking agents up with cameras or LIDAR-like depth sensors, but you can pass whatever information you like to an agent. Observations can be anything you can boil down into a number or a numerical array to pass into the `AddObservation` method.

It's important that an agent is given only enough observations to figure out what it is supposed to do. Extra or redundant information may seem like it would help the agent figure out its task more quickly, but in reality it will give it more work to do to figure out which observations are important and correlate with success.

Maybe the most impressive thing about an agent is that it doesn't even know what its observations *are*; it just gets passed numbers with no field names or context. It learns what it needs to by observing how these numbers change as a result of various *actions*.

Actions are the instructions an agent can follow to effect change in their environment. The `BallAgent` had the ability to add or remove force—and therefore roll or brake—in either of two directions. Together this allows for complete movement along a 2D plane, as shown in Figure 2-28.

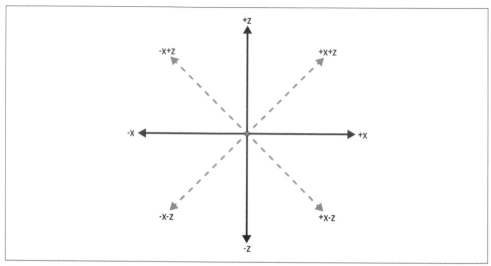

Figure 2-28. Range of movement given two axes of potential force

But actions can be anything that enacts change in the environment, from physical movement of the agent (e.g., roll ball, move joint, flap wings, turn wheels), to high-level actions (e.g., walk forward one meter, stand up, turn around 180 degrees), to changes in the environment (e.g., pick up object agent is standing on, open door in front of agent). The granularity and extent of the actions an agent should be given access to will depend on the specific task you wish it to learn.

For example, if you want an agent to learn to walk, you probably don't want its action to be something like "walk forward." Because then you'll have to write code to make it walk, and it won't need to learn. But if you want your agent to learn how to complete a maze, you might provide coded instructions for movement so that it doesn't have to learn how to walk and *then* learn how the maze works.

 Think back to how we implemented the OnActionReceived method on BallAgent by explicitly adding force in the required direction. It didn't need to learn how to add force to its own RigidBody; instead, it learned when it is appropriate to *decide* to move along either axis. Thus, any actions you wish to give an agent will need to be implemented by you; what the agent is learning is *when* and *in what order* to trigger the actions you give it to choose between.

An agent's job is to use the observations it has to assess the state of the environment in order to decide on the best response, and then execute the required series of actions. We guide the agent to select the desired response to various environmental states—and therefore work toward our intended objectives for the agent—using *rewards*. In the case of `BallAgent`, there is only one reward: +1.0 when the agent reaches the target.

Rewards are simply points awarded to or taken from the agent when certain conditions are met. Some rewards are intrinsic, such as in imitation learning where rewards are given automatically for similarity to example behavior. In reinforcement learning, explicit rewards must be defined.

These rewards are the only feedback an agent will receive about its behavior, so the rewards and the trigger conditions must be carefully decided. Over time, an agent will generally optimize for the behavior that has historically gotten it the most points, and this means a poorly designed rewards scheme can result in unexpected behavior.

For example, say we decided to help `BallAgent` along by giving it points for *approaching* the target. This might speed up training, as the time it takes for the agent to receive its first reward and get a hint of what it should be doing will be much earlier than if it is only rewarded for reaching the target.

So, you decide that for this agent that starts out some distance away from the target (say, 10 units), you will reward it for each step based on how close it is to the target. When it has reached the target, the reward will be +10.0; when it is one unit away, it will receive +9.0, and so on. At the first step of the episode, it will not have moved and will receive +0.0.

After some training, the average rewards the agent receives for each episode are high, so you end training. You start the agent up in inference mode and you see that during each episode, the agent approaches the object and then circles around it without touching it until the episode reaches its length limit and ends. What went wrong?

You have a think and realize you've fallen into an easy trap in rewards design: you've made the agent optimize for the wrong thing. Three factors have come together to create this mess:

- Though an agent does consider how much it has to gain from potential actions at each step, it will tend to optimize for *the most points it can get in a whole episode*.

- In an ideal episode, `BallAgent` will go straight toward the target and reach it. Assuming it rolls about one unit per step, the agent will receive steadily increasing rewards: +0.0 in the first step, +1.0 in the second, all the way up to +10.0 when the agent reaches the goal, and *the episode ends after 10 steps with a reward of 55.0.*

- If the `BallAgent` instead approaches to one unit away from the target, it will receive the same rewards for the first nine steps of the simulation (totaling 45.0). Then, circling the target at this distance, it will receive +9.0 for each step the simulation allows it to continue. With `max_steps=500000` in our hyperparameters file, this behavior will continue for the remaining 499,991 steps and *the episode will forcibly end after half a million steps, with a reward of 4,499,964.0.*

You can see how the agent—given only reward points to go by—might think circling is the preferred behavior rather than touching the target.

So there you have it: simulation is built upon three main concepts—observations, actions, and rewards. With these three things, all manner of intelligent behavior can be learned by a simulated agent. An agent uses experience of observations it has collected, actions it has taken, and rewards it has received as it explores the environment it is placed in. At first, actions will be random, then will become more targeted as rewards are received and lessons are therefore learned about what the desirable behaviors are in the current scenario. During *training*, this behavior model of the agent is ever-changing, updating as reward feedback is received, but once training is over (when the agent runs in inference mode), it is locked in place and that will be the behavior the agent exhibits forever.

This model, which acts as a mapping of observations to the actions that will yield the highest rewards in that moment, is called a *policy*. This is the conventional term for the behavior model in reinforcement learning, but it's also a class name in ML-Agents. The `Policy` class abstracts the decision-making process in a way that lets you swap what's making the decision. That is what allows switching between heuristic control—which allowed you to control the agent with Unity's input system earlier—and control via a neural network, as seen in "When the Training Is Complete" on page 46.

Coming Up Next

Simulation-based machine learning with ML-Agents is explored further throughout Part II of this book, beginning with our next simulation activity in Chapter 4. There we'll build on what you've learned here to create a more complex simulation environment, with an agent that knows a lot more about its situation than the rolling ball in this example.

You'll learn how to feed multiple kinds of observations into your agent, and take advantage of the game engine to send *visual* input into your agent instead of raw numbers.

We'll also look at how you can speed up the training process in more complex situations, by duplicating the simulation environment and training in parallel across many similar agents so that the neural network model can receive far more experiences. Exciting, right?

CHAPTER 3

Creating Your First Synthesized Data

This chapter introduces synthesis, the second pillar of this book, as discussed in Chapter 1. Here the focus is on the tools and process you'll be using to synthesize data for machine learning, and how it ties into the work you've done so far for simulation as well as how it's quite different.

By the end of this chapter, you'll be generating the *world's most disappointing synthesized data*! But you'll be prepared to make *far more interesting data* in future chapters. We promise. Stick with us.

As we mentioned in "Unity" on page 6, the primary tool we'll be using for our initial foray into synthesis is a Unity package called *Perception*.

 We're not going to be doing quite as much synthesis in this book as we do simulation. This is simply because there's not as much to learn: simulation is a tremendously wide field with many different approaches that you can take, while synthesis with Unity mostly boils down to the different kinds of randomizations that you want to perform in order to generate the data you need. We'll teach you everything you need to know, but there will be fewer activities.

Unity Perception

Unity's Perception package turns the Unity game engine into a tool for generating synthetic datasets—primarily images—for use in ML workflows that are primarily outside of Unity.

The Perception Framework provides an array of useful tools, ranging from dataset capture, to object labeling, image capture, and beyond. You can create straightforward object–label associations and have them fed directly to whatever part of an

ML toolchain you require. Perception can even help you generate bounding boxes and semantic segmentation masks, as well as scene generation and beyond. It's really powerful.

The Perception Framework is an open source project and freely available via its GitHub project (*https://oreil.ly/x0tKg*). An example of its features is shown in Figure 3-1.

Figure 3-1. Unity's Perception Framework

We'll be using the Unity Perception package, which plugs into the Unity Editor (just like Unity ML-Agents does), for everything in this chapter, as well as later on in Chapter 13.

The Process

The overall workflow we'll use for all the synthetic data we generate through the examples in this book is as follows:

1. We'll determine a *scenario* that requires a large volume of data, typically for training.

2. We'll create a *scene*, or a number of scenes, in Unity, laying out the objects that we want to be involved in our simulated data.

3. We'll use *randomizers* to alter the parameters of the scene in order to vary data as needed.

4. Finally, we'll specify *ground truth* and *labels* for our data, and *generate* the data.

Unlike for simulation, Unity isn't the beginning and the end of the work you do for synthesis. In simulations, using ML-Agents you build a scene in Unity to act as your simulation, and the agents related to your simulation will exist and act in and on that scene. And, ultimately, the trained version of your agents (which hopefully perfect whatever task you've given them) are also used in that scene (of course, you can then take what you and they have learned and put their *brain* in something else, but that's beyond the scope of this book).

For synthesis, we're just using Unity and the Perception package as a tool to generate lots of data. Realistically, because Unity is a visual development environment, the kind of data most suited to this is visual data (images). Just as with simulations, you'll use Unity to build some sort of environment or world, but you'll then use a Unity camera to take thousands and thousands of pictures of that world and export them to your filesystem. Once you've got the pictures, you'll do the actual machine learning somewhere else, using PyTorch, TensorFlow, Create ML, or whatever training system you like. In this chapter, we'll be working through the setup for generating data, and the first two steps of the aforementioned workflow.

The ML-Agents Toolkit pipeline includes the training, and the Perception pipeline does the training. Got it?

Using Unity Perception

To explore Unity's Perception package, we will work through a simple activity that highlights the workflow. Examples of the sorts of images we'll be generating are shown in Figure 3-2.

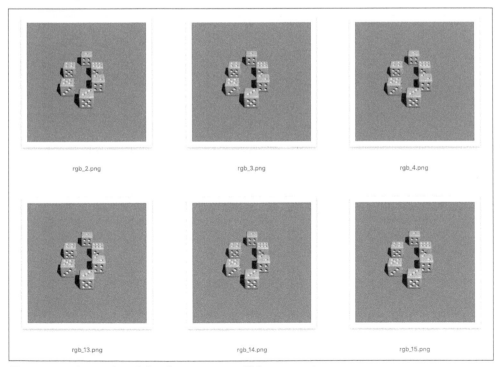

Figure 3-2. Examples of the dice images we'll be generating

Eventually, we'll generate images of dice, with the camera at different angles, the background in different colors, and the dice in different color combinations (the randomizers that we mentioned in "The Process" on page 54). We'll do everything prior to adding the randomizers in this chapter.

For now, however, we'll be setting up a scene and preparing to add randomization. We won't be adding actual randomizers yet, though. That will come later, in Chapter 13.

Creating the Unity Project

As with many of our practical scenarios, the first step for creating synthetic data with Unity is to create a brand-new Unity project:

1. Open the Unity Hub and create a new 3D "URP" project. As shown in Figure 3-3, we'll name ours "SimpleDice," but the name isn't important for the functionality. The choice of project template ("Universal Render Pipeline" or "URP") is what's important.

Figure 3-3. Creating a URP project in Unity Hub

We're not going to create a "3D Project," as we did in the previous chapter, because we need to use Unity's Universal Render Pipeline. The Universal Render Pipeline (URP) is a scriptable graphics pipeline that creates a different workflow for game developers.

Because one of the core things we need to do as part of generating our synthetic data is output images, we're going to use the URP. Perception uses an event that the URP generates when a frame has completed rendering, at a project-wide level, and we'll be using that event to output an image.

Don't want to think about it? Don't worry about it! We just need certain features from a different rendering pipeline in order to use Unity Perception. And we don't need those features for ML-Agents.

Just remember, you'll likely want to use the URP when you're building projects around Unity's Perception features, and the easiest way to do that is to start from the provided URP template in the Unity Hub.

If you want to learn about Unity's different rendering pipelines, head over to the Unity documentation (*https://oreil.ly/ waDBl*).

2. Once the project has loaded, you'll want to delete the example assets that are added by the URP template, as shown in Figure 3-4. Only delete the parent object named "Example Assets" and the children below it. Leave the camera, light, and "Post-process Volume" in place.

For some reason, the easiest way to create a new URP project is to create one that comes with a sample environment. We're not sure why, either.

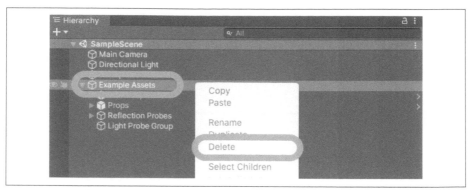

Figure 3-4. Deleting the example assets

3. Next, we want to install the Perception package. Select the Window menu →
   Package Manager, and use the Unity Package Manager to install the Perception
   package by choosing the "+" menu → "Add package from git URL" and entering
   `com.unity.perception`, as shown in Figures 3-5 and 3-6.

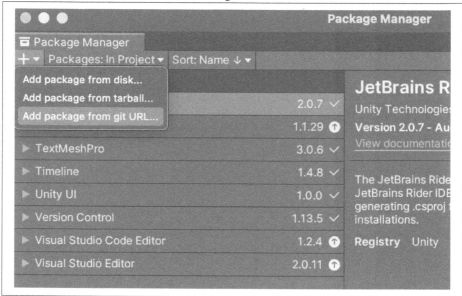

Figure 3-5. Adding a package from Git

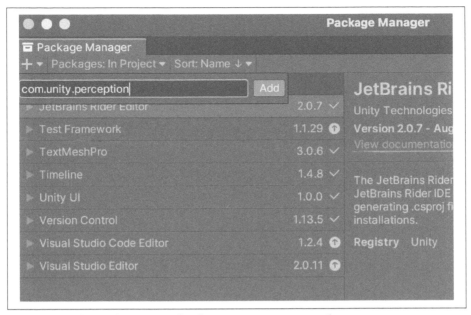

Figure 3-6. The package name for the Unity Perception package

It might take a few moments for the package to download and install, so be patient. Once it's finished downloading, you'll see Unity import it, as shown in Figure 3-7. You can then close the Package Manager window.

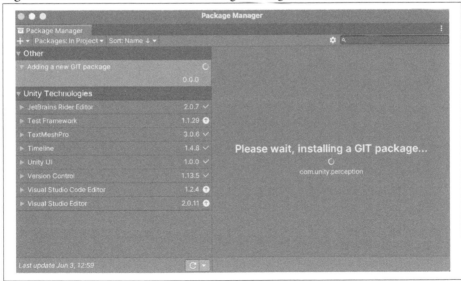

Figure 3-7. The Unity Perception package being loaded by Unity

4. Next, select the ForwardRenderer asset in the Project pane, as shown in Figure 3-8 (you'll find it in the *Settings* folder).

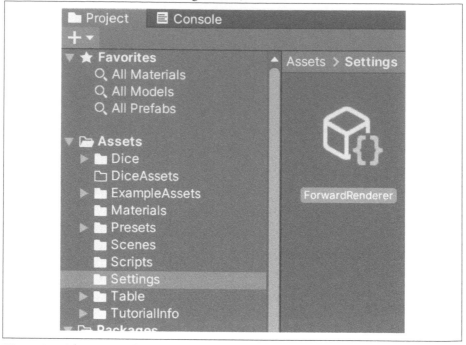

Figure 3-8. The ForwardRenderer asset

5. In its Inspector, click Add Renderer Feature, and then click Ground Truth Renderer Feature, as shown in Figure 3-9.

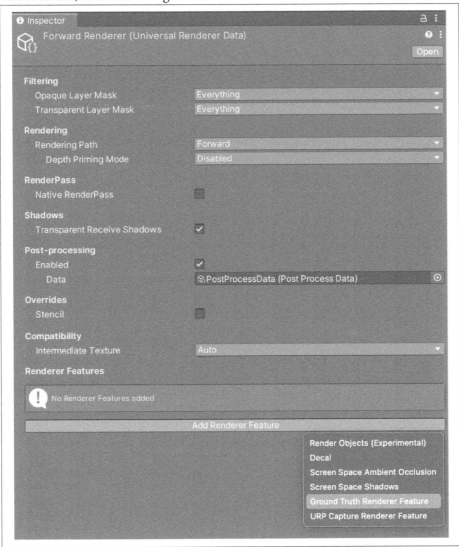

Figure 3-9. Adding a ground truth renderer

Your project is largely ready to go at this point. This is a good, clean starting point for all your work using Unity's Perception Framework, so we recommend pushing it to some sort of source control, or duplicating it, so that you have a fresh starting point each time.

Creating a Scene

Sometimes it's good to create a scene! This is one of those times. The scene we're going to build is very simple: it's some dice! The dice will be sitting on a plane, and we'll take in-engine images of the dice to generate our synthetic data (which will be synthetic images of dice).

Let's get started!

Getting the Dice Models

First, we'll need the dice models we're going to use. You could make your own if you wanted, but in the book's resources (*https://oreil.ly/9WmyP*), you can download a Unity package that contains dice models we made for you:

1. Download the *Dice.unitypackage* file (*https://oreil.ly/1efRA*) and import it into Unity by double-clicking on it, then clicking Import All in Unity.

2. Once the models are imported, verify that they're visible in the Project pane of the Unity Editor, as shown in Figure 3-10.

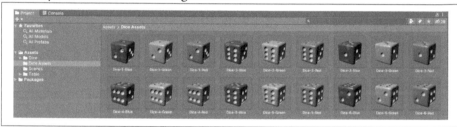

Figure 3-10. The dice assets in the Unity Editor

That's it! You're ready to make a scene.

A Very Simple Scene

With the scene open, first we need to add a floor and some dice:

1. Create a floor by adding a plane to the scene in the Hierarchy and renaming it "Floor," as shown in Figure 3-11.

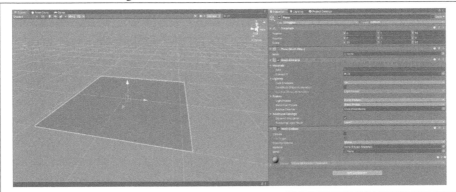

Figure 3-11. The initial scene, with a floor

2. Drag some of the dice from the Project pane (you'll find them in the *Dice* folder, in a subfolder named *Prefabs*) into the Scene or Hierarchy view, and position them on the floor. The absolute specifics don't hugely matter right now, but if you'd like to duplicate our scene, you can see it in Figure 3-12.

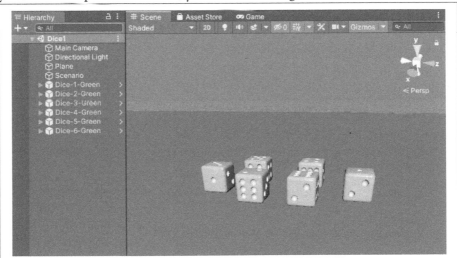

Figure 3-12. The dice in the scene

3. Position the camera so that it's showing the dice from a slightly elevated angle. You can verify this by looking at the Game view while you reposition the camera. Ours is shown in Figure 3-13.

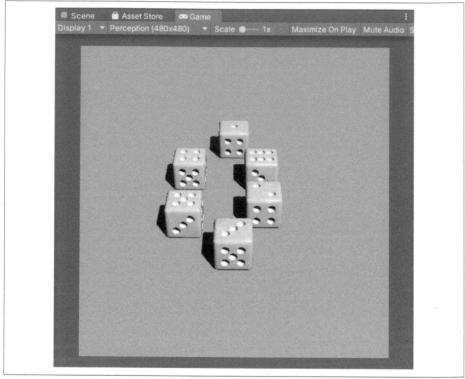

Figure 3-13. A good perspective on the dice

4. Use the drop-down menu at the top of the Game view, as shown in Figure 3-14, to add a named resolution (ours is called Perception) and set the resolution of the camera to 480x480. Because we'll be using the Main Camera (which is the only camera) to render the images, the resolution here controls the size of the images we'll be rendering and saving to disk.

 If you can't find the drop-down menu, make sure you're looking on the Game view. The Scene view does not have the menu you need.

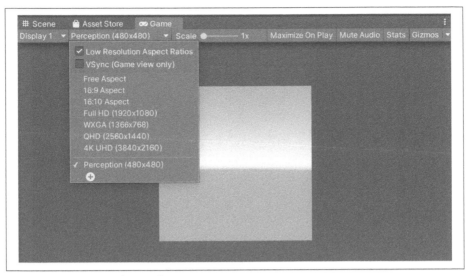

Figure 3-14. Setting the resolution

Save your scene before continuing.

Next, we need to create a means to control our synthesis scenario. We'll do this by creating an "empty" GameObject that lives in our scene, with some special components that are supplied by the Unity Perception Framework attached to it. Here are the steps to do this:

1. Create a new empty GameObject in the Hierarchy view, and name it "Scenario" or something similar.

 Our Scenario GameObject is "empty" in the sense that it doesn't map to a visual component that you can see in the scene. It exists in the scene, but it is not visible in the scene. If we added a visual component to it (e.g., something that was a mesh, like a cube), it would be visible. To control a scenario, you don't need any visible components, though.

2. Select the new Scenario object in the Hierarchy, and then use the Add Component button in its Inspector, shown in Figure 3-15, to add a Fixed Length Scenario component to this new GameObject, as shown in Figure 3-16.

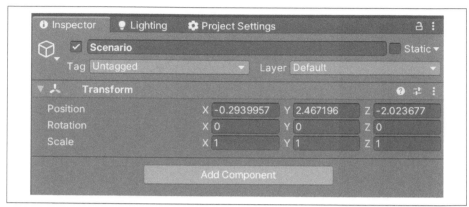

Figure 3-15. The Add Component button

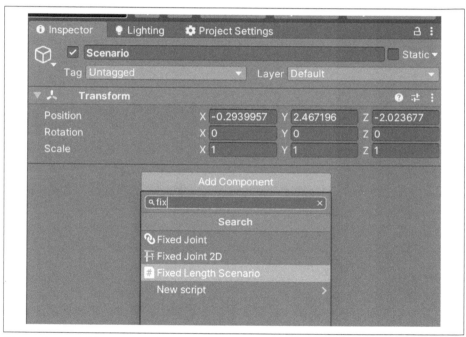

Figure 3-16. Adding a Fixed Length Scenario component

3. Leave the Fixed Length Scenario parameters and settings alone for now. The Total Iterations parameter is, effectively, the number of images in our scene that will be saved to disk when we run the scenario.

If you don't have a Fixed Length Scenario component available, review the steps listed previously for importing the Perception package. This asset comes from the Perception package.

The Fixed Length Scenario component is used to control the execution flow of the scene by coordinating all the necessary random elements.

Now we need to modify the Main Camera to allow it to be used for Perception:

1. Select the Main Camera, and use its Inspector to add a Perception Camera component.

2. Leave the parameters of the Perception Camera at their defaults, as shown in Figure 3-17. We'll come back to the specifics of this shortly, but if you want, you can modify the Output Base Folder to point to where you'd like the rendered images to be saved.

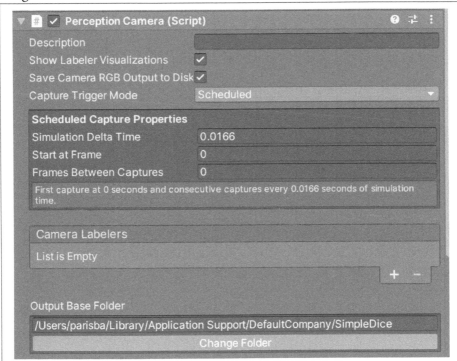

Figure 3-17. A new Perception Camera component

If you start seeing errors or warnings related to asynchronous shader compilation in the Unity Editor's Console pane when you add the Perception Camera component, don't worry too much! If this occurs, select the Edit menu → Project Settings… → Editor, and in the Shader Compilation settings, find and disable Asynchronous Shader Compilation.

The Perception Camera component allows us to modify and control the parameters of the synthetic frames that are being captured from the camera, how they're annotated, and how the labels we'll ultimately provide relate to ground truth.

Don't forget to save your scene again.

Preparing for Synthesis

When you generate a synthesized image, you can also generate different kinds of *ground truth* with it.

Perception provides a range of different *labelers*, which control the types of ground truth you can generate alongside each captured image:

- 3D bounding boxes
- 2D bounding boxes
- Object counts
- Object metadata/information
- Semantic segmentation maps

Ground truth refers to information that we know is true. For example, because we're making the images of dice, we know they are definitely dice. That they are dice is a piece of ground truth.

Because we're going to be generating images of dice with different numbers facing up, we're interested in the object metadata/information labeler. Unity refers to this in the Unity Editor as RenderedObjectInfoLabeler.

To add a labeler for this project, do the following in your scene:

1. Select the Main Camera in the Hierarchy pane, and find the Perception Camera component attached to it.
2. Click the + button in the Camera Labelers section of the Perception Camera, as shown in Figure 3-18.

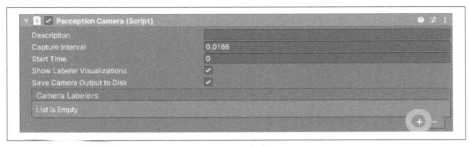

Figure 3-18. The + button in the Camera Labelers section

3. From the list that appears, select RenderedObjectInfoLabeler, as shown in Figure 3-19.

Figure 3-19. Adding a RenderedObjectInfoLabeler

4. Verify that a labeler has been added, as shown in Figure 3-20.

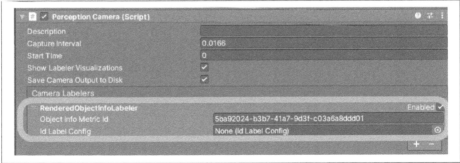

Figure 3-20. The RenderedObjectInfoLabeler on our Perception Camera, which is on our Main Camera

To use the labeler, we need to create some labels:

1. In the Project pane, right-click and choose Create → Perception → ID Label Config, as shown in Figure 3-21.

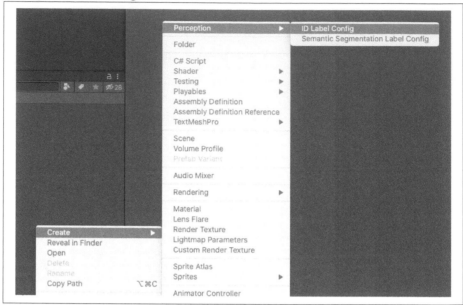

Figure 3-21. Creating a new ID Label Config

2. Find the new asset that was created (it will likely be named `IdLabelConfig` or something similar) and rename it `DiceLabels` or something similarly obvious.

3. Select this asset in the Project pane, and use the Add New Label button in its Inspector pane to create six labels. When you're done, your list of labels should resemble ours, shown in Figure 3-22.

Figure 3-22. The six labels have been created

4. Select the Main Camera in the Hierarchy again, find the Id Label Config field in the Camera Labelers section of the Perception Camera component attached to it, and either drag the DiceLabels asset you just made from the Project pane to the field, or click the field and select the asset. It should look like Figure 3-23 once it's in place.

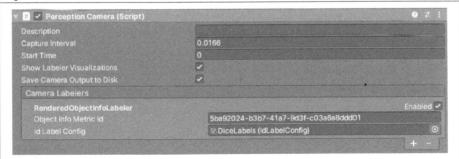

Figure 3-23. The Perception Camera is set up

Once again, you'll need to save your scene before continuing.

Testing the Scenario

Now is a good time to test your scenario, without any random elements applied. Follow these steps to test the scenario and check that everything we've done so far is working correctly:

1. Run the scene using Unity's Play button. It might take a while.

2. The scene should generate as many pictures as are specified in the Total Iterations parameter of the Fixed Length Scenario component that we added to the scenario GameObject; it should then exit play mode automatically. Again, it might take a little while, and it could appear like the Unity Editor has hung.

3. To verify that everything worked, when Unity is responsive again (and play mode has ended), select the Main Camera in the Hierarchy and locate the Perception Camera component. It will have a new Show Folder button, as shown in Figure 3-24.

4. Click the Show Folder button. This will open the location where the images are stored on your local machine.

   At this point, you should find a folder with 100 pictures generated from the scene's camera. They'll all be identical, as shown in Figure 3-25. If you've made it this far and everything's working, you're ready to continue!

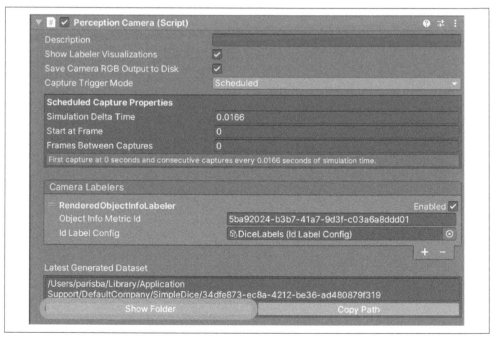

Figure 3-24. The Show Folder button, after a successful run

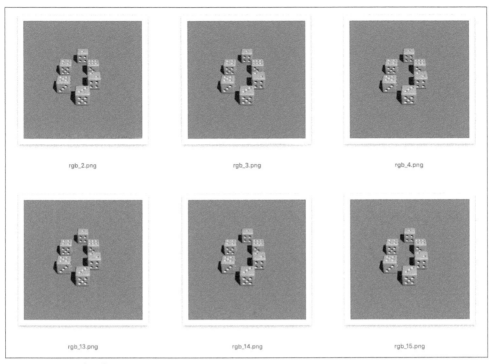

rgb_2.png   rgb_3.png   rgb_4.png

rgb_13.png   rgb_14.png   rgb_15.png

Figure 3-25. The dice images

Great! You've actually synthesized some data—it just so happens that every image you've synthesized is the same, there's no change each time an image is saved, and our labels are not really being used.

Setting Up Our Labels

The labels we created represent which side of the dice is facing upward. In order to make that information available in a format that matches the images we're outputting, we need to attach it to the prefabs:

1. Open the prefab for Dice-Black-Side1 (the black dice, with the side showing one pip facing up) by double-clicking on it in the Project pane.

2. When the prefab is open, as shown in Figure 3-26, select the root object in its Hierarchy (in this case "Dice-Black-Side1") and use the Add Component button in its Inspector to add a Labeling component, as shown in Figure 3-27.

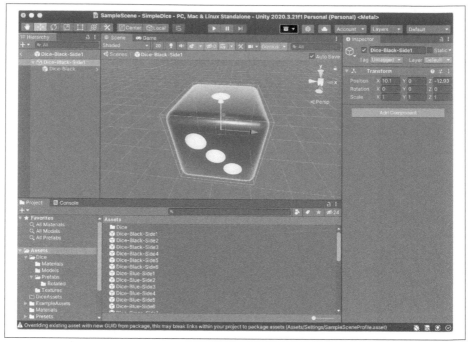

Figure 3-26. Opening a prefab

Figure 3-27. Adding a Labeling component

3. Expand the DiceLabels section found in the Inspector for the new component, and click the Add to Labels button next to the label representing the side that is facing up (this one should be "one"), as shown in Figure 3-28.

4. Back out of the dice prefab, and repeat this process for all the dice prefabs (there should be 30 in total, made up of 5 different colors, each with 6 pips facing up). You should apply the label number corresponding with the face that's upward for each dice.

Figure 3-28. Adding a specific label

Checking the Labels

We'll work more with labels later, but you can quickly check that they work by doing the following:

1. Select the Main Camera in the Hierarchy, add a new BoundingBox2D labeler, and connect it to the set of labels we created earlier, as shown in Figure 3-29.

Figure 3-29. Adding a new labeler to the camera

2. Run the project and look at the Game view. In addition to it saving out image files as normal, you'll see it drawing boxes around each of the labeled objects, as shown in Figure 3-30.

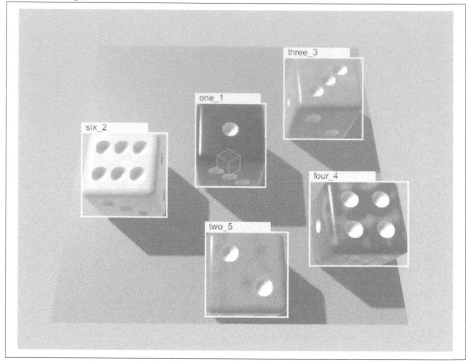

Figure 3-30. Bounding boxes being drawn

We'll make more use of the labels in later chapters, when we start working with randomizers.

What's Next?

So far, we've built a scene and we've connected all the necessary plumbing to make Unity Perception work:

- We've created a project using the URP pipeline, which is required to create simulated image data using Unity Perception.

- We've added a Perception Camera component to the camera in the scene that we want to use to generate images.

- We've added a Fixed Length Scenario component to an otherwise empty object in the scene, allowing us to manage the overall generation of images.

- We've identified where images get saved to when the image synthesis process is run.
- We've created some labels as ground truth for our dice synthesis, and applied them to the relevant dice prefabs we're using.

Later, in Chapter 13, we'll take this further by adding randomizers to our scene, which will change the position, size, and other elements of the dice, as well as elements of the scene itself, so that every image we generate is different. Later still, in Chapter 14, we'll take a look at exploring the synthesized data we've generated and how to make use of it.

PART II

Simulating Worlds for Fun and Profit

CHAPTER 4

Creating a More Advanced Simulation

So far, you've been introduced to the basics of simulation and the basics of synthesis. It's time to dive in a bit further and do some more simulation. Back in Chapter 2, we built a simple simulation environment that showed you how easy it is to assemble a scene in Unity and use it to train an agent.

In this chapter, we're going to build on the things you've already learned and create a slightly more advanced simulation using the same fundamental principles. The simulation environment we're going to build is shown in Figure 4-1.

Figure 4-1. The simulation we'll be building

This simulation will consist of a cube, which will again serve as our *agent*. The agent's *goal* will be to *push a block into a goal* area as quickly as possible.

By the end of this chapter, you'll have continued to solidify your Unity skills for assembling simulation environments, and have a better handle on the components and features of the ML-Agents Toolkit.

Setting Up the Block Pusher

For a full rundown and discussion of the tools you'll need for simulation and machine learning, refer back to Chapter 1. This section will give you a quick summary of the bits and pieces you'll need to accomplish *this particular activity*.

Specifically, here we will do the following:

1. Create a new Unity project and set it up for use with ML-Agents.
2. Create the environment for our block pusher in a scene in that Unity project.
3. Implement the necessary code to make our block pushing agent function in the environment and be trainable using reinforcement learning.
4. And finally, train our agent in the environment and see how it runs.

Creating the Unity Project

Once again, we'll be creating a brand-new Unity project for this simulation:

1. Open the Unity Hub and create a new 3D project. We'll name ours "Block-Pusher."
2. Install the ML-Agents Toolkit package. Refer back to Chapter 2 for instructions.

That's all! You're ready to go ahead and make the environment for the block pusher agent to live in.

The Environment

With our empty Unity project ready to go with ML-Agents, the next step is to create the simulation environment. In addition to the *agent* itself, our simulation environment for this chapter has the following requirements:

- A *floor* for the agent to move around on
- A *block* for the agent to push around
- A set of outer *walls* to prevent the agent from falling into the void

- A *goal* area for the agent to push the block into

In the following few sections, we'll create each of these pieces in the Unity Editor.

The Floor

The floor is where our agent and the block it pushes will live. The floor is very similar to the one created in Chapter 2, but here we'll also be building walls around it. With the new Unity project open in the editor, we'll create a new scene and create the floor for our agent (and the block it pushes) to live on:

1. Open the GameObject menu → 3D Object → Cube. Click on the cube that you've created in the Hierarchy view, and as before set its name to "Floor" or something similar.

2. With the new floor selected, set its position to something suitable, and its scale to (20, 0.35, 20) or something similar, so that it's a big flat floor with a bit of thickness to it, as shown in Figure 4-2.

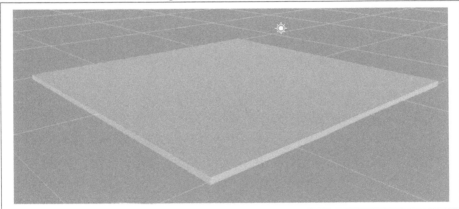

Figure 4-2. The floor for our simulation

 The floor is the center of existence for this world. By centering the world on the floor, the floor's position doesn't really matter.

We want our floor to have a little more character this time, so we're going to give it some color:

1. Open the Assets menu → Create → Material to create a new material asset in the project (you can see it in the Project view). Rename the material to

"Material_Floor" or something similar by right-clicking and selecting Rename (or pressing Return while the material is selected).

2. Ensure that the new material is selected in the Project view and use the Inspector to set the albedo color to something fancy. We recommend a nice orange color, but anything is fine. Your Inspector should look something like Figure 4-3.

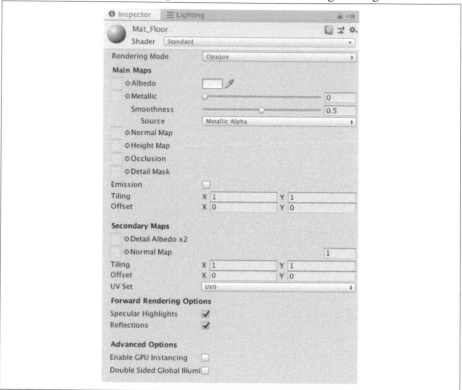

Figure 4-3. The floor material

3. Select the floor in the Hierarchy view and drag the new material from the Project view directly onto either the floor's entry in the Project view, or the empty space at the bottom of the floor's Inspector. The floor should change color in the Scene view, and the Inspector for the floor should have a new component, as shown in Figure 4-4.

Figure 4-4. The Inspector for the floor, showing the new Material component

That's it for the floor! Make sure you save the scene before continuing.

The Walls

Next, we need to create some walls around the floor. Unlike in Chapter 2, we don't want the agent to ever have the possibility of falling off the floor.

To create walls, we'll once again be using our old, versatile friend, the cube. Back in the Unity scene where you made the floor a moment ago, do the following:

1. Create a new cube in the scene. Make it the same scale on the x-axis as the floor (so probably about 20), 1 unit high on the y-axis, and around 0.25 on the z-axis. It should look something like Figure 4-5.

Figure 4-5. The first wall

2. Create a new material for the walls, give it a nice color, and apply it to the wall you've created. Ours is shown in Figure 4-6.

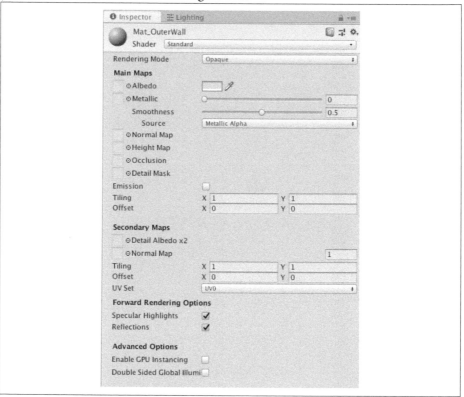

Figure 4-6. The new wall material

3. Rename the cube "Wall" or something similar, and duplicate it once. These will be our walls on one axis. Don't worry about moving them to the right position just yet.

4. Duplicate one of the walls again and, using the Inspector, rotate it 90 degrees on the y-axis. Once it's there, duplicate it.

You can switch to the move tool by pressing the W key on your keyboard.

5. Position the walls by using the move tool while each wall is selected (in either the Scene view or the Hierarchy view) and holding the V key on your keyboard to enter vertex snapping mode. While the V key is held, mouse over the different vertices in the wall's mesh. Mouse over one of the outer bottom-corner vertices of a wall, and then click and drag on the move handle to snap it to the appropriate upper-corner vertex on the floor. This process is shown in Figure 4-7.

Figure 4-7. Vertex-snapping on the corner

You can switch between different views in the Scene view using the widget in the upper-right corner, shown in Figure 4-8.

Figure 4-8. The scene widget

6. Repeat this for each wall segment. Some of the wall segments will overlap and intersect each other, and that's fine.

When you're done, your walls should look like Figure 4-9. As always, save your scene before you continue.

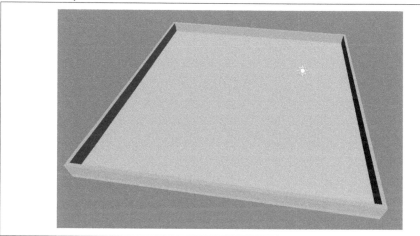

Figure 4-9. The four final walls

The Block

The block, at this phase, is the simplest element that we need to create in the editor. Like many of us, it exists to be pushed around (in this case, by the agent). We'll add the block in the Unity scene:

1. Add a new cube to the scene, and rename it "Block."

2. Use the Inspector to add a Rigidbody component to the agent, setting its mass to 10 and its drag to 4, and freezing its rotation on all three axes, as shown in Figure 4-10.

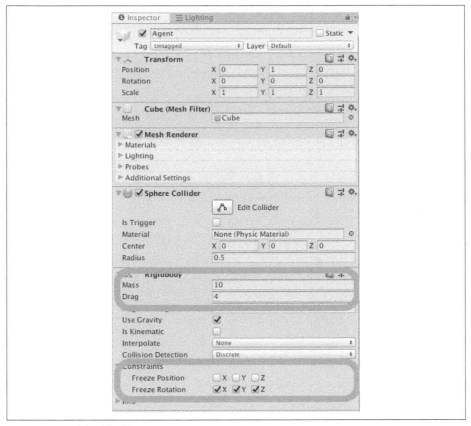

Figure 4-10. The block's parameters

3. Position the block somewhere on the floor. Anywhere is fine.

 If you're having trouble positioning the block precisely on the floor, you can use the move tool in vertex snapping mode, like you did for the walls, and snap the agent to one of the corners of the floor (where it will be intersecting with the walls). Then use the directional move tool (by clicking and dragging on the arrows coming out of the agent while it's in move mode) or the Inspector to move it to the desired location.

The Goal

The goal is the location in the scene where the agent needs to push the block. It's less of a physical thing and more of a concept. But concepts can't be represented in video game engines, so how do we implement it? That's a great question, dear reader! We make a plane—a flat area—that we set to a specific color so that the watching human (i.e., us) can tell where the goal area is. The color won't be used by the agent at all, it's just for us.

The agent will use the collider we add, which is a big volume of space that exists above the colored ground area, and using C# code, we can know when something is inside that volume (hence the name "collider").

Follow these steps to create the goal and its collider:

1. Create a new plane in the scene and rename it "Goal" or something similar.

2. Create a new material for the goal and apply it. We recommend you use a color that will stand out, since this is the goal area that we want the agent to push the cube into. Apply the new material to the goal.

3. Use the same trick with vertex snapping that you used earlier in "The Walls" on page 85 to position the goal using the Rect tool (accessible using T on your keyboard) or via the tools selector, shown in Figure 4-11. Position the goal roughly as shown in Figure 4-12.

Figure 4-11. The tool selector

Figure 4-12. The goal in position

4. Using the inspector, remove the Mesh Collider component from the goal, and use the Add Component button to add a Box Collider component instead.

5. With the goal selected in the Hierarchy, click the Edit Collider button in the Box Collider component of the goal's Inspector (shown in Figure 4-13.)

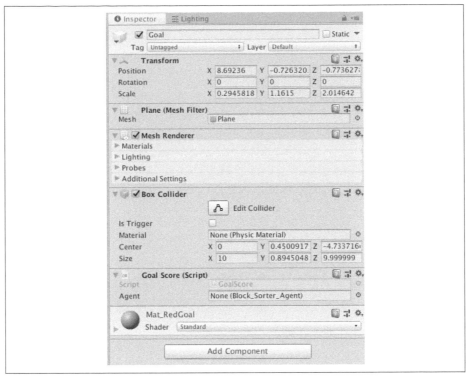

Figure 4-13. Edit Collider button

6. Use the small green square handles to size the collider of the goal so that it encompasses more of the environment's volume, so if the agent enters the collider it will be detected. Ours is shown in Figure 4-14, but this is not a science; you just need to make it big! You might find it easier just to increase the Box Collider component's size on its y-axis using the Inspector.

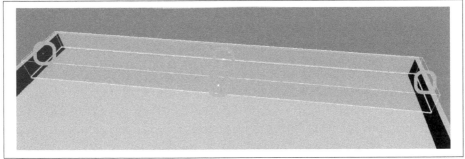

Figure 4-14. Our large collider, showing the handles

As before, don't forget to save the scene.

The Agent

Finally (almost), we need to create the agent itself. Our agent is going to be a cube, with the appropriate script (which we'll also create) attached to it, just like we did with the ball agent in Chapter 2.

Still in the Unity Editor, do the following in your scene:

1. Create a new cube and name it "Agent" or something similar.
2. In the agent's Inspector, select the Add Component button and add a new script. Name it something like "BlockSorterAgent."
3. Open the newly created script and add the following import statements:

   ```
   using Unity.MLAgents;
   using Unity.MLAgents.Actuators;
   using Unity.MLAgents.Sensors;
   ```
4. Update the class to be a child of Agent.
5. Now you need some properties, starting with a handle for the floor and environment (we'll get back to assigning these shortly). These go inside the class, before any methods:

   ```
   public GameObject floor;
   public GameObject env;
   ```
6. You also need something to represent the bounds of the floor:

   ```
   public Bounds areaBounds;
   ```
7. And you need something to represent the goal area and the block that needs to be pushed to the goal:

   ```
   public GameObject goal;
   public GameObject block;
   ```
8. Now add some Rigidbodys to store the body of the block and the agent:

   ```
   Rigidbody blockRigidbody;
   Rigidbody agentRigidbody;
   ```

When the agent is initialized, we need to do a few things, so the first thing we'll make is the Initialize() function:

1. Add the Initialize() function:

   ```
   public override void Initialize()
   {

   }
   ```

2. Inside, get a handle on the agent and block's `Rigidbody`s:

```
agentRigidbody = GetComponent<Rigidbody>();
blockRigidbody = block.GetComponent<Rigidbody>();
```

3. And finally, for the `Initialize()` function, get a handle on the bounds of the floor:

```
areaBounds = floor.GetComponent<Collider>().bounds;
```

Next, we want to be able to randomly position the agent within the floor when it spawns (and for each training run), so we'll make a `GetRandomStartPosition()` method. This method is entirely ours, and isn't implementing a required piece of ML-Agents (like the methods we override):

1. Add the `GetRandomStartPosition()` method:

```
public Vector3 GetRandomStartPosition()
{

}
```

We'll call this method whenever we want to position something randomly within the floor that's in our simulation. It will return a random usable position on the floor.

2. Inside `GetRandomStartPosition()`, get a handle on the bounds of the floor and the goal:

```
Bounds floorBounds = floor.GetComponent<Collider>().bounds;
Bounds goalBounds = goal.GetComponent<Collider>().bounds;
```

3. Now create someplace to store the new point on the floor (we'll return to this in a bit):

```
Vector3 pointOnFloor;
```

4. Now, make a timer so that you can see if this process takes too long for some reason:

```
var watchdogTimer = System.Diagnostics.Stopwatch.StartNew();
```

5. Next, add a variable to store a margin. We'll use this to add and remove a small buffer from the random position that is picked:

```
float margin = 1.0f;
```

6. Now start a `do-while` that continues picking a random point if it picks one that is *inside the goal's bounds*:

```
do
{

} while (goalBounds.Contains(pointOnFloor));
```

7. Inside the do, check if the timer has gone on too long, and throw an exception if it did:

```
if (watchdogTimer.ElapsedMilliseconds > 30)
{
    throw new System.TimeoutException
        ("Took too long to find a point on the floor!");
}
```

8. Then, still inside the do, but below the if statement, pick a point on the top face of the floor:

```
pointOnFloor = new Vector3(
    Random.Range(floorBounds.min.x + margin, floorBounds.max.x - margin),
    floorBounds.max.y,
    Random.Range(floorBounds.min.z + margin, floorBounds.max.z - margin)
);
```

Add and remove the margin so that the box is always on the floor, and not in the walls or in space.

9. After the do-while, return the pointOnFloor that you created:

```
return pointOnFloor;
```

That's it for GetRandomStartPosition(). Next, we need a function to call when the agent gets the block to the goal. We'll use this function to reward the agent for doing the right thing, reinforcing the policy that we want:

1. Create the GoalScored() function:

```
public void GoalScored()
{

}
```

2. Add a call to AddReward():

```
AddReward(5f);
```

3. And add a call to EndEpisode():

```
EndEpisode();
```

Next, we'll implement OnEpisodeBegin(),the function that's called when each training or inference *episode* begins:

1. First, we'll put the function in place:

```
public override void OnEpisodeBegin()
{

}
```

2. And we'll get a random rotation and angle:
   ```
   var rotation = Random.Range(0, 4);
   var rotationAngle = rotation * 90f;
   ```

3. Now we'll get a random start position for the block, using the function we created:
   ```
   block.transform.position = GetRandomStartPosition();
   ```

4. We'll set the block's velocity and angular velocity, using its `Rigidbody`:
   ```
   blockRigidbody.velocity = Vector3.zero;
   blockRigidbody.angularVelocity = Vector3.zero;
   ```

5. We'll get a random start position for the agent:
   ```
   transform.position = GetRandomStartPosition();
   ```

6. And we'll set the agent's velocity and angular velocity, using its `Rigidbody` as well:
   ```
   agentRigidbody.velocity = Vector3.zero;
   agentRigidbody.angularVelocity = Vector3.zero;
   ```

7. Finally, we'll rotate the whole environment. We do this so that the agent doesn't learn the side that always has the goal:
   ```
   //env.transform.Rotate(new Vector3(0f, rotationAngle, 0f));
   ```

And that's it for the `OnEpisodeBegin()` function. Save your code.

Next, we're going to implement the `Heuristic()` function so that we can manually control the agent if we want to:

1. Create the function `Heuristic()`:
   ```
   public override void Heuristic(in ActionBuffers actionsOut)
   {

   }
   ```

Manual control of the agent here is entirely unrelated to the training process. It just exists so that we can verify the agent can move in the environment appropriately.

2. Get a handle on the actions that the Unity ML-Agents Toolkit sends, and set the action to 0 so that you know you'll always end up with a valid action or 0 by the end of the call to `Heuristic()`:
   ```
   var discreteActionsOut = actionsOut.DiscreteActions;
   discreteActionsOut[0] = 0;
   ```

3. Then, for each key—D, W, A, and S—check if it's being used, and send the appropriate action:

```
if(Input.GetKey(KeyCode.D))
{
    discreteActionsOut[0] = 3;
}
else if(Input.GetKey(KeyCode.W))
{
    discreteActionsOut[0] = 1;
}
else if (Input.GetKey(KeyCode.A))
{
    discreteActionsOut[0] = 4;
}
else if (Input.GetKey(KeyCode.S))
{
    discreteActionsOut[0] = 2;
}
```

 These numbers are totally arbitrary. As long as they stay consistent and don't overlap, it doesn't matter what they are. One number consistently represents one direction (which corresponds to a keypress when under human control).

And that's all for the Heuristic() function.

Next, we need to implement the MoveAgent() function, which will allow the ML-Agents framework to control the agent for both training and inference purposes:

1. First, we'll implement the function:

```
public void MoveAgent(ActionSegment<int> act)
{

}
```

2. Then, inside, we'll zero out the direction and rotation that will be used for the movement:

```
var direction = Vector3.zero;
var rotation = Vector3.zero;
```

3. And we'll assign the action coming in from the Unity ML-Agents Toolkit to something a little more readable:

```
var action = act[0];
```

4. Now we'll switch on that action and set the direction or rotation appropriately:

```
switch (action)
{
    case 1:
        direction = transform.forward * 1f;
        break;
    case 2:
        direction = transform.forward * -1f;
        break;
    case 3:
        rotation = transform.up * 1f;
        break;
    case 4:
        rotation = transform.up * -1f;
        break;
    case 5:
        direction = transform.right * -0.75f;
        break;
    case 6:
        direction = transform.right * 0.75f;
        break;
}
```

5. Then, outside the switch, we'll act on any rotation:

```
transform.Rotate(rotation, Time.fixedDeltaTime * 200f);
```

6. And we'll also act on any direction, by applying a force to the agent's Rigidbody:

```
agentRigidbody.AddForce(direction * 1, ForceMode.VelocityChange);
```

And that's all for MoveAgent(). Again, save your code.

Finally, for now, we need to implement the OnActionReceived() function, which doesn't do much more than pass the received action on to our MoveAgent() function:

1. Create the function:

```
public override void OnActionReceived(ActionBuffers actions)
{

}
```

2. Call your own MoveAgent() function, passing in the discrete actions:

```
MoveAgent(actions.DiscreteActions);
```

3. And punish the agent by setting a negative reward based on the step:

```
SetReward(-1f / MaxStep);
```

This negative reward will hopefully encourage the agent to economize its movement and take as few moves as possible in order to maximize its reward and achieve the goal we want from it.

That's everything for now. Make sure your code is saved before you continue.

The Environment

We need to do a little more administrative work in setting up the environment before we continue, so switch back to your scene in the Unity Editor. We'll start by creating a GameObject to hold the walls in, just to keep the Hierarchy clean:

1. Right-click on the Hierarchy view and choose Create Empty. Rename the empty GameObject "Walls," as shown in Figure 4-15.

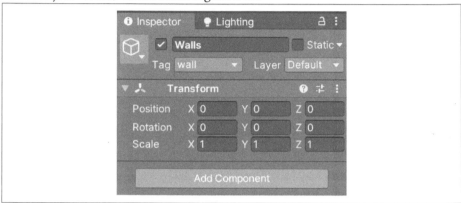

Figure 4-15. The walls object, named

2. Select all four walls (you can hold your Shift key and click them one by one, or hold Shift after clicking the first one and then click the last one) and drag them under the new walls object. It should look like Figure 4-16.

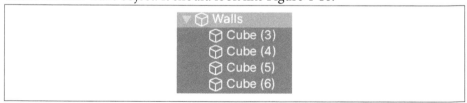

Figure 4-16. The walls are nicely encapsulated

Now we'll create an empty GameObject in which to hold the entire environment:

1. Right-click in the Hierarchy view and choose Create Empty. Rename the empty GameObject "Environment."

2. In the Hierarchy view, drag the walls object we just made, plus the agent, floor, block, and goal, into the new environment object. It should look like Figure 4-17 at this point.

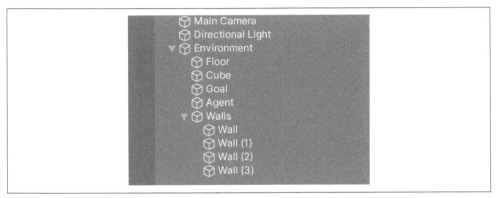

Figure 4-17. The environment, encapsulated

Next, we need to configure some things on our agent:

1. Select the agent in the Hierarchy view, and scroll down to the script you added in the Inspector view. Drag the floor object from the Hierarchy view into the Floor slot in the Inspector.

2. Do the same for the overall environment GameObject, the goal, and the block. Set the Max Steps to 5000 in the editor so that the agent doesn't take forever to push a block to the goal. Your Inspector should look like Figure 4-18.

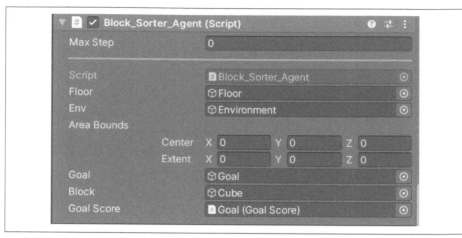

Figure 4-18. The agent script properties

3. Now, using the Add Component button in the Inspector for the agent, add a DecisionRequester script and set its Decision Period to 5, as shown in Figure 4-19.

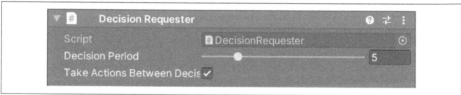

Figure 4-19. The Decision Requester component, added to the agent and appropriately configured

4. Add two Ray Perception Sensor 3D components, each with three detectable tags: block, goal, and wall, with the settings shown in Figure 4-20.

Back in "Letting the Agent Observe the Environment" on page 35, we said you can add observations via code or via components. There we did it all via code. Here we're going to do it all via components. The components in question are the Ray Perception Sensor 3D components that we just added.

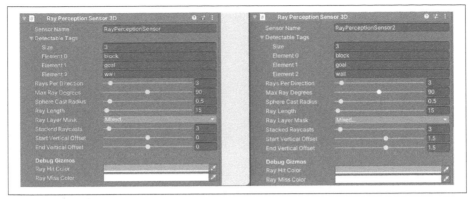

Figure 4-20. The two Ray Perception sensors

We don't even have a CollectObservations method in our agent this time, because all the observations are collected via the Ray Perception Sensor 3D components that we add in the editor.

5. We'll need to add the tags we just used to the objects we actually want to tag. The tags allow us to refer to objects based on what they're tagged with, so if something is tagged with "wall," we can treat it as a wall, and so on. Select the block in the Hierarchy, and use the Inspector to add a new tag, as shown in Figure 4-21.

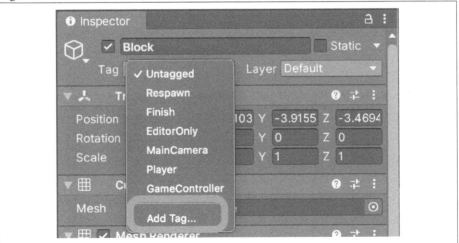

Figure 4-21. Adding a new tag

6. Name the new tag "block," as shown in Figure 4-22.

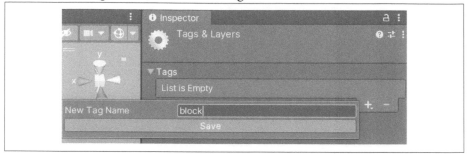

Figure 4-22. Naming a new tag

7. And finally, attach the new tag to the block, as shown in Figure 4-23.

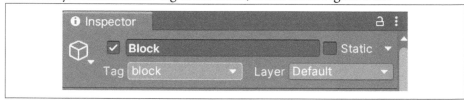

Figure 4-23. Attaching the tag to an object

8. Repeat this for the goal, using a "goal" tag, and for all the wall components, using a "wall" tag. With these in place, the Ray Perception Sensor 3D components we added will only "see" things tagged with "block," "goal," or "wall." As shown in Figure 4-24, we've added two layers of Ray Perception sensors, which case a line out from the object they're attached to and report back on the first thing that line hits (in this case, only if it's a wall, a goal, or a block). We've added two that are staggered at different angles. They'll only be visible in the Unity Editor.

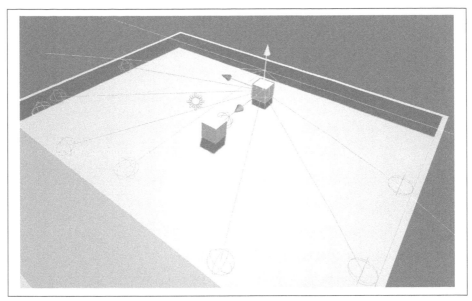

Figure 4-24. The Ray Perception Sensor 3D components

9. Finally, add a Behavior Parameters component, using the Add Component button. Name the behavior "Push" and set the parameters as shown in Figure 4-25.

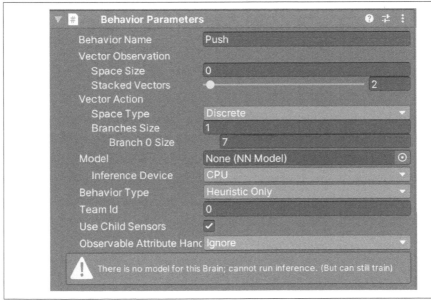

Figure 4-25. The Behavior Parameters for the agent

Save your scene in the Unity Editor. Now we'll do some configuration on our block:

1. Add a new script to the block, named something like "GoalScore."
2. Open the script, and add a property to refer to the agent:

   ```
   public Block_Sorter_Agent agent;
   ```

   The type of the property you create here should match the class name for the class attached to the agent.

 You don't need to change the parentage to Agent or import any ML-Agents components this time, as this script isn't an agent. It's just a regular script.

3. Add an OnCollisionEnter() function:

   ```
   private void OnCollisionEnter(Collision collision)
   {

   }
   ```

4. Inside OnCollisionEnter(), add the following code:

   ```
   if(collision.gameObject.CompareTag("goal"))
   {
       agent.GoalScored();
   }
   ```

5. Save the script and return to Unity, and with the block selected in the Hierarchy, drag the agent from the Hierarchy into the Agent slot in the new GoalScore script. This is shown in Figure 4-26.

Figure 4-26. The GoalScore script

Don't forget to save the scene again.

Training and Testing

With everything built in both Unity and C# scripts, it's time to train the agent and see how the simulation works. We'll be following the same process we followed in "Training with the Simulation" on page 42: creating a new YAML file to serve as the hyperparameters for our training.

Here's how to set up the hyperparameters:

1. Create a new YAML file to serve as the hyperparameters for the training. Ours is called *Push.yaml* and includes the following hyperparameters and values:

```
behaviors:
  Push:
    trainer_type: ppo
    hyperparameters:
      batch_size: 10
      buffer_size: 100
      learning_rate: 3.0e-4
      beta: 5.0e-4
      epsilon: 0.2
      lambd: 0.99
      num_epoch: 3
      learning_rate_schedule: linear
    network_settings:
      normalize: false
      hidden_units: 128
      num_layers: 2
    reward_signals:
      extrinsic:
        gamma: 0.99
        strength: 1.0
    max_steps: 500000
    time_horizon: 64
    summary_freq: 10000
```

2. Next, inside the venv we created earlier in "Setting Up" on page 19, fire up the training process by running the following command in your terminal:

```
mlagents-learn _config/Push.yaml_ --run-id=PushAgent1
```

 Replace *config/Push.yaml* with the path to the configuration file you just created.

3. Once the command is up and running, you should see something that looks like
   Figure 4-27. At this point, you can press the Play button in Unity.

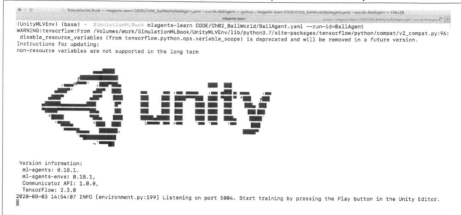

Figure 4-27. The ML-Agents process begins training

You'll know the training process is working when you see output that looks like
Figure 4-28.

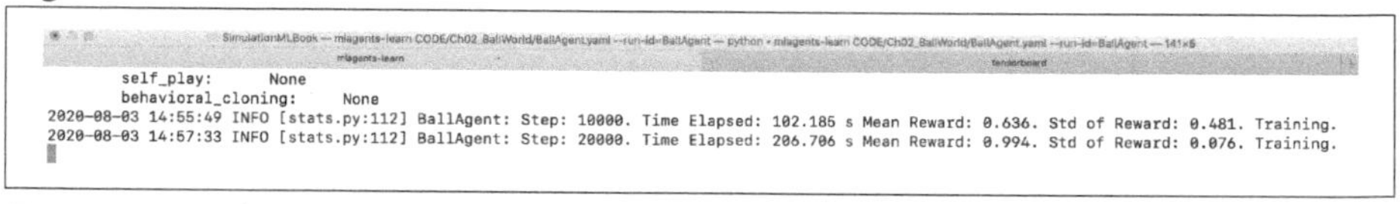

Figure 4-28. The ML-Agents process during training

When the training is complete, refer back to "When the Training Is Complete" on
page 46 for a refresher on how to fine the *.nn* or *.onnx* file that's been generated.

Use the model to run the agent, and watch it go!

CHAPTER 5

Creating a Self-Driving Car

The two simulations you've built so far have been fairly abstract concepts—balls that roll around a plane in a void, cubes that push other cubes around, and such—but simulation for machine learning is genuinely, practically useful (we promise). In this chapter, we're going to make a very simple self-driving car in Unity and train it to drive using reinforcement learning. It's not going to be practical in the sense that you can load up the ensuing trained model into a real, physical car, but it demonstrates that what you can do in a simulated environment can go beyond the abstract.

Your time has come! You basically, for the good of the world, are going to build your own self-driving car (Figure 5-1).

Figure 5-1. The self-driving car on its track. In his yurt. With his iPad.

Our self-driving car is only going to exist in a beautiful void of its own, instead of the pesky real world—so we get to avoid all those nasty ethical quandaries, such as what to do if there's a human in front of us (we'll tackle that, a little bit, later in the book).

Our car is going to learn how to drive, and not much else. Ready?

Creating the Environment

The first thing we need to make is the beautiful void our car exists in. It's going to consist of a few things, the most important of which is the track the car will navigate. After we build the track, we'll create the car itself, and then set everything up to work with the machine learning system.

The key pieces of the world are the track, the thing the car drives around, and the car itself. That's it. It's a pretty simple self-driving car, we admit.

We'll do this work in the Unity Editor, in a scene, as we've done with our simulations so far. It will involve assembling the world our car lives in, and the car itself. A key difference between this and the earlier activities is that we'll provide a downloadable set of assets with which to construct the car's track.

Before you move on, do the following:

1. Create a new 3D Unity project (ours is named "SimpleCar"), as shown in Figure 5-2.

Figure 5-2. Creating a new 3D project in the Unity Hub

2. Import the Unity ML-Agents package into the Unity project (see "Creating the Unity Project" on page 22).

3. Make sure your Python environment is ready to go (see "Setting Up" on page 19).

The Track

The first thing we're going to make is the track. Our track is going to be nice and simple, since we want to make sure it's very obvious how our self-driving car works. There will be two basic pieces: a straight piece, as shown in Figure 5-3, and a corner piece, as shown in Figure 5-4.

Figure 5-3. The straight piece of our track

Figure 5-4. The corner piece of our track

Each piece of the track is made up of a floor and some barrier walls. Let's make the straight piece now:

1. Create a new plane. Name it "Track," and tag it with "track."

2. Create a material in the Project view, name it something like "TrackMaterial" so you know what it's for, and give it a nice color for a road. Ours is black, but feel free to get creative. Assign this material to the track plane.

3. Create a new cube, and using the Inspector set its scale to (1, 1, 10), making it long and thin. Position the cube along one edge of the plane with the snap tools you've previously used.

4. Create a material in the Project view, name it something like "WallMaterial," and give it a nice color. Assign this material to the cube.

5. Duplicate the cube, and move it to the other side of the plane. Your piece should look like Figure 5-5.

Figure 5-5. The straight piece

6. Name the two wall pieces some variant of "Wall," and assign them the tag "wall."

7. Create an empty GameObject, name it some variant of "Track_Piece," and make it the parent of the track plane and the two walls, as shown in Figure 5-6.

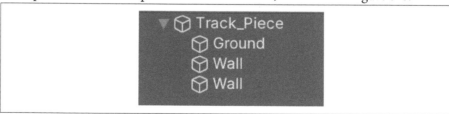

Figure 5-6. The track piece in the Hierarchy

8. Next, select the track piece parent object, then choose the Assets menu → Create → Prefab, as shown in Figure 5-7.

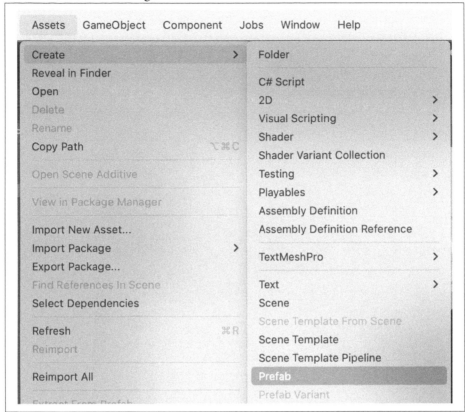

Figure 5-7. Creating a prefab using the Assets menu

You'll now have a track prefab in your Project pane, which is a duplicatable piece of track. You can modify the prefab once and update all uses of it. We'll be assembling our track using this prefab shortly.

 You can also click and drag from the parent object in the Hierarchy into the Project pane to create a prefab.

Next, we'll make the corner piece:

1. In the scene, create another new plane. Name it "CornerTrack," and tag it with "track" (use the same track tag as the previous piece). Assign the previously created track material to it.

2. Create a new cube, and using the Inspector, set its scale to (1, 1, 10), making it long and thin. Position the cube along one edge of the plane with the snap tools you've previously used. Assign the previously created wall material to it.

3. Duplicate the cube and move it to one side of the plane, making a corner. Your piece should look like Figure 5-8.

Figure 5-8. The corner piece so far

4. Create a new cube and place it in the opposing corner, as shown in Figure 5-9.

Figure 5-9. The opposite corner, finalizing the corner piece

5. Name the three wall pieces some variant of "Wall," and assign all three of them the tag "wall," the same as the walls in the previous piece.

6. Create an empty GameObject, name it some variant of "Corner Piece," and make it the parent of the track plane and the three walls, as shown in Figure 5-10.

Figure 5-10. The hierarchy of the corner piece

7. Next, select the corner piece parent object, then choose the Assets menu → Create → Prefab.

You'll now have a corner prefab in your Project pane, alongside the track prefab. Ours are shown in Figure 5-11, with the materials they use.

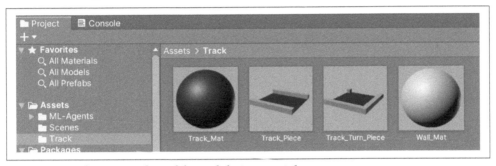

Figure 5-11. The two track prefabs and their materials

If you're comfortable with Unity, you can make your own track pieces however you want! It's beyond the scope of this book to teach you how, but it's a good learning exercise. We recommend trying Blender, the fantastic open source 3D modeling tool. If you have Blender and Unity installed on the same machine and you drag a *.blend* file into Unity, you can use the file directly within Unity, and any changes you make and save in Blender will be reflected automatically.

Use Unity's tools, as you did with the snapping in earlier activities, to place the pieces next to each other to lay out a track. Ours is shown in Figure 5-12, but it doesn't hugely matter what yours looks like right now. All you need to do is make a track of similar complexity to ours.

Figure 5-12. Our training track

 If you don't feel comfortable making your own track, you can find a premade one in the assets available for this book. After you've downloaded the assets, you can use the track by opening the file *CarPremadeTrack.unitypackage* and importing it into your Unity project.

The Car

Next, naturally, we need a car. Our car does not need to be complex, and it won't be rigged or animated in any way (i.e., the wheels won't move, the lights won't work). It could even be shaped like a cube, but for fun, we'll make it look like a car.

To get the car and get it into the scene, follow these steps:

1. Download a nice car from Sketchfab, as shown in Figure 5-13. The one we used is available here (*https://oreil.ly/puzjd*), but any car is fine.

Simple Car Low Poly
3D Model

Figure 5-13. The car we're going to use

2. Import the car into your Unity project by dropping the *.blend* file into the Assets view.

3. Next, create an empty GameObject in the Hierarchy, and name it "Car."

4. Add a Rigidbody component to the car, as shown in Figure 5-14.

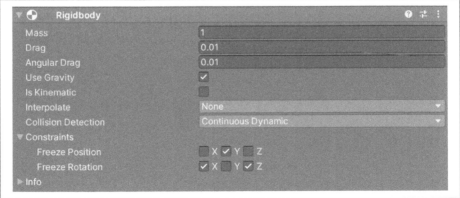

Figure 5-14. The car's Rigidbody component

5. Add a Box Collider to the car, as shown in Figure 5-15.

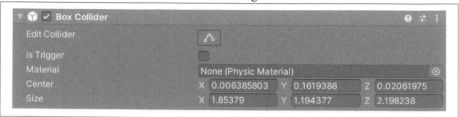

Figure 5-15. The car's Box Collider

6. Drag the newly added car model inside the car GameObject, as shown in Figure 5-16. Make sure the car model *inside* the GameObject is positioned at (0,0,0).

Figure 5-16. The car's GameObject, with the model inside it

Make sure the Rigidbody and Box Collider components are attached to the uppermost car GameObject (the one you created), and not to the internal GameObject that's created by adding the model to the scene.

7. Position the car GameObject on the track, centered, at a location to be your starting spot (it doesn't matter specifically where it is). Ours is shown in Figure 5-17.

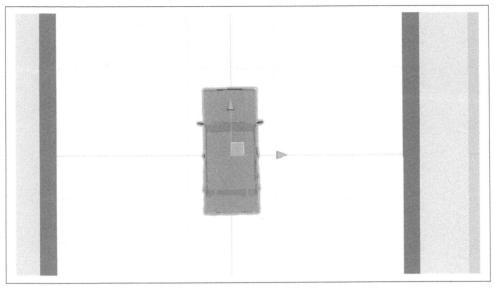

Figure 5-17. The car on the track, in its starting position

That's everything for the environment in the scene, so don't forget to save it.

Setting Up for ML

Next, we need to set the project up to be an ML simulation. We'll do this, as we have before, by installing the ML-Agents Unity package, and adding some components to the GameObjects in the Unity Editor:

1. Use the Unity Package Manager to install the Unity ML-Agents Toolkit. Refer back to Chapter 2 if you need a reminder on how to do this.

2. Once it's installed, add a Behavior Parameters component to the car's GameObject, as shown in Figure 5-18.

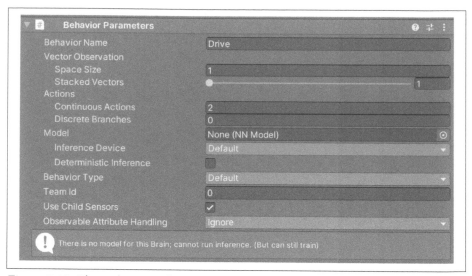

Figure 5-18. The car's new Behavior Parameters component

3. Next, add a Decision Requester component to the car's GameObject, as shown in Figure 5-19.

Figure 5-19. The Decision Requester component, added to the car

You should probably save your Unity scene at this point. With that done, it's time to make the car's script:

1. Create a new script in the Unity Editor by adding a component to the car's GameObject. Name it "CarAgent," or something similar.

2. Open the newly created CarAgent script asset, and inside, import the appropriate pieces of the Unity ML-Agents Toolkit in addition to the boilerplate imports:

```
using Unity.MLAgents;
using Unity.MLAgents.Sensors;
```

3. Update the CarAgent to inherit from Agent, removing all the boilerplate code provided by Unity:

```
public class CarAgent : Agent
{
}
```

As with the previous simulations, in order to be an agent, our car needs to inherit from Agent, which comes from the Unity ML-Agents package.

4. Add a few variables:

```
public float speed = 10f;
public float torque = 10f;

public int progressScore = 0;

private Transform trackTransform;
```

We'll be storing the speed and torque of the car so that we can tweak them, as well as a progressScore. This allows us to display and use the score (progress along the track) if we wish to.

We'll also create a place to store the trackTransform, which we'll update based on where on the track the car is. The Transform type represents a position in the 3D scene you've created, and is a type that comes from Unity.

5. Implement the Heuristic() method so that the car can be tested and controlled by you, a human, as needed:

```
public override void Heuristic(float[] actionsOut)
{
    actionsOut[0] = Input.GetAxis("Horizontal");
    actionsOut[1] = Input.GetAxis("Vertical");
}
```

This Heuristic() method is very similar to what we've done in earlier simulations: it allows us to take the two elements of the actionsOut array and assign them to Unity's input system on the Horizontal and Vertical axes, respectively. Whatever keys are assigned to Horizontal and Vertical axes in the Unity input system will control what goes into actionsOut.

 We're using Unity's "Classic" input system here. It's technically been superceded by a new input system, but as with most things in game engines, nothing is ever removed, and there's no advantage to the added complexity of using the new input system here. You can learn about the Classic input system in the Unity documentation (*https://oreil.ly/RimPC*), and find out about the Input Manager (*https://oreil.ly/EDMPw*), which allows you to configure what keys are assigned to the axes.

You can choose which keys are assigned to the axes by choosing the Edit menu → Project Settings, and choosing Input Manager from the sidebar of the resulting dialog. By default, the arrow keys on the keyboard will be assigned.

6. Create a `PerformMove()` method that takes three floats—for horizontal movement, vertical movement, and delta time—and translates and rotates the car appropriately:

```
private void PerformMove(float h, float v, float d)
{
    float distance = speed * v;
    float rotation = h * torque * 90f;

    transform.Translate(distance * d * Vector3.forward);
    transform.Rotate(0f, rotation * d, 0f);
}
```

We'll be using this `PerformMove()` method to move the car, either via human control or the machine learning *brain*. The only thing happening here is that we call `Translate` and `Rotate` on the transform (the position) of the car (because this script is attached to the car agent in the scene, as a component), in order to move it:

1. Override the `OnActionReceived()` method, which is a required part of being an `Agent` via the Unity ML-Agents framework:

```
public override void OnActionReceived(float[] vectorAction)
{
    float horizontal = vectorAction[0];
    float vertical = vectorAction[1];

    PerformMove(horizontal, vertical, Time.fixedDeltaTime);
}
```

Our `OnActionReceived()` method uses the two `vectorAction` actions received from the ML-Agents framework, mapping to horizontal and vertical, gets the last or current premoving position, and calls the `PerformMove()` function that we created a moment ago to action the move.

We'll be adding some reward functionality to this method shortly, but we'll leave it as is for now.

2. Next, implement `CollectObservations()`, another override of an ML-Agents framework method:

```
public override void CollectObservations(VectorSensor vectorSensor)
{
    float angle = Vector3.SignedAngle
        (trackTransform.forward, transform.forward, Vector3.up);
    vectorSensor.AddObservation(angle / 180f);
}
```

CollectObservations() is used to supply information about the environment to the ML-Agents system. Observations are the information the agent knows about the world it lives in, and it's entirely up to you as to how much information you supply.

In the car agent's case, the only thing we're doing in CollectObservations() is comparing the direction of the car with the track's direction. This uses the track Transform that we created earlier, which holds the current position of the car. This initial observation gives the car something to work with: it needs to minimize this angle in order to follow the track. It's a signed angle, between -180 and 180, in order to tell the car whether it needs to steer left or right.

Now we'll briefly jump back to the Unity Editor to add some additional observations via components. As we've said before, not all observations have to arrive via code; some can be added via components in the Unity Editor. Save your code and return to your Unity scene:

1. Select the agent's parent object in the Hierarchy, and use the Add Component button in the Inspector to add two Ray Perception Sensor 3D components.

2. Give them sensible names (e.g., "RayPerceptionSensor1," "RayPerceptionSensor2").

3. Set one of them to the parameters shown in Figure 5-20.

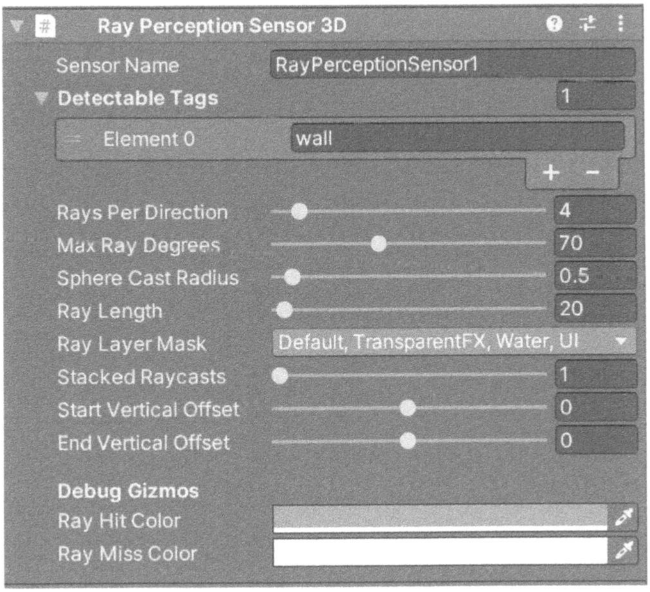

Figure 5-20. The first of two Ray Perception Sensor 3D components

This sensor sends four rays out from either side of the car and one from the front, as shown in Figure 5-21.

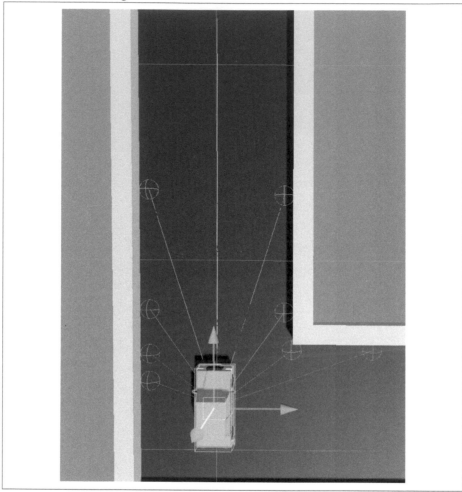

Figure 5-21. The first sensor's raycasts

4. Set the other Ray Perception Sensor 3D component to the parameters shown in Figure 5-22.

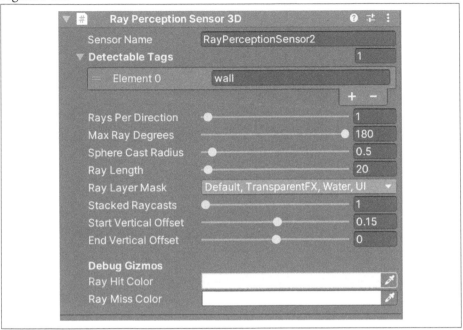

Figure 5-22. *The second of two Ray Perception Sensor 3D components*

 It's important that both of these sensors are set to only detect things tagged with "wall."

This sensor sends one ray out from the front of the car and one directly from the back, as shown in Figure 5-23.

 If we didn't override CollectObservations() and implement it in code, we could still exclusively supply observations to our agent via components in the editor if we wanted to.

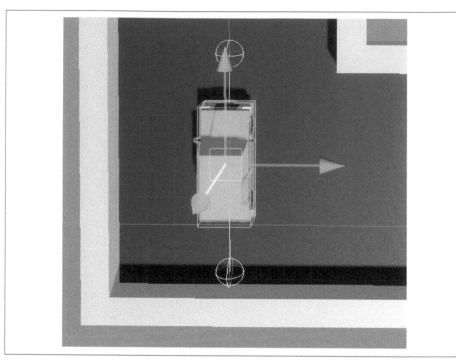

Figure 5-23. The second sensor's raycasts

5. Save the scene, and return to the agent script in your code editor.

Now we'll implement our own function, named `TrackProgress()`. It will be used to figure out a reward system:

```
private int TrackProgress()
{
    int reward = 0;
    var carCenter = transform.position + Vector3.up;

    // Where am I?
    if (Physics.Raycast(carCenter, Vector3.down, out var hit, 2f))
    {
        var newHit = hit.transform;

        // Am I on a new spot?
        if (trackTransform != null && newHit != trackTransform)
        {
            float angle = Vector3.Angle
                (trackTransform.forward, newHit.position - trackTransform.position);
            reward = (angle < 90f) ? 1 : -1;
        }

        trackTransform = newHit;
```

```
    }
        return reward;
    }
```

`TrackProgress()` will return 1 if we're moving in a forward direction to a new part of the road, `-1` if we move backward, and 0 in other situations.

It does this by employing the following logic:

- It casts a ray from the middle of the car object down into the ground.
- Using the information from that ray, it knows which tile of the track the car is currently on.
- If the current tile is not the same as the last one, it calculates the angle between the direction of the tile and the position of the car (with respect to the tile).
- If that angle is less than 90 degrees, it moved forward; otherwise, it went backward.

It's important to provide the car with the ability to know whether it's progressing; otherwise, it won't know when to be rewarded. That's what this function is for. Next, we need to create some new methods:

1. First we need to implement `OnEpisodeBegin()`, another override of the ML-Agents framework:

   ```
   public override void OnEpisodeBegin()
   {
       transform.localPosition = Vector3.zero;
       transform.localRotation = Quaternion.identity;
   }
   ```

   We're not doing much here: just setting the car's local position and rotation to zero and identity, respectively. This function is called at the beginning of each episode, hence we're using it to reset the car's local position and rotation.

2. The next method to implement is `OnCollisionEnter()`, which we'll use to make sure that the car agent is penalized accordingly for colliding with the walls:

   ```
   private void OnCollisionEnter(Collision collision)
   {
       if (collision.gameObject.CompareTag("wall"))
       {
           SetReward(-1f);
           EndEpisode();
       }
   }
   ```

   `OnCollisionEnter()` is a standard part of Unity objects, and is called whenever something collides with another object in the scene. In this case, we check to see if the thing that was collided with is tagged with "wall." We'll tag the objects in the environment with "wall," and some other useful tags, shortly in the Unity Editor. If the car agent does collide with a wall, it's penalized with a -1 reward, and the `EndEpisode()` function, which is part of ML-Agents, is called to start a new episode.

3. Next, we'll add an `Initialize()` method, which calls `TrackProgress()` for the first time:

```
public override void Initialize()
{
    TrackProgress();
}
```

`Initialize()` is part of Unity, and is called when an object is first instantiated.

4. Returning to `OnActionReceived()`, at the end of the previous code we wrote, after the call to `PerformMove()`, we'll add some more code:

```
var lastPos = transform.position;

int reward = TrackProgress();

var dirMoved = transform.position - lastPos;
float angle = Vector3.Angle(dirMoved, trackTransform.forward);
float bonus = (1f - angle / 90f)
    * Mathf.Clamp01(vertical) * Time.fixedDeltaTime;
AddReward(bonus + reward);

progressScore += reward;
```

This code first stores the position before the car moves, and then calls `Track Progress()` to check if the tile we're on has changed.

Using those two pieces of information, we compute a vector, `dirMoved`, that represents the direction we moved in, and we use that to get the angle between the current track piece and the agent.

Because the angle we get is between 0 and 180 degrees, it's easier if we map it to something smaller: 0–2. We do that by dividing it by 90. Subtracting this from 1 gives a small bonus (that decreases while the angle increases). If our angle is greater than 90 degrees, it becomes negative.

The result is multiplied by the vertical speed (which is positive), and thus we have a reward. We multiply the whole thing by the time (`Time.fixedDeltaTime`) so that we only get one reward per second, at the most.

Don't forget to save the code in your code editor, and the scene in the Unity Editor.

Training the Simulation

With everything built, we're going to set things up to train, and then we'll see how our simple self-driving car works in practice. The first step is to set the behavior to heuristic so that we can test the car using keyboard controls, then we'll move to training.

To set your car agent's behavior type to heuristic, open the scene in the Unity Editor, select the agent in the Hierarchy and change the behavior type to Heuristic as shown in Figure 5-24, then play the scene in Unity.

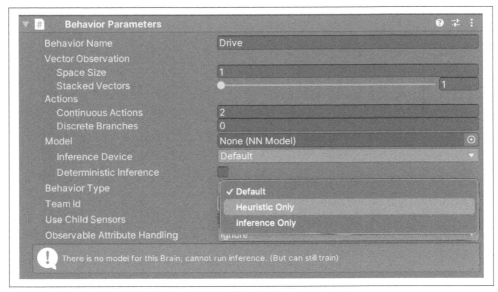

Figure 5-24. Setting the behavior type to Heuristic

You'll be able to use your keyboard (arrow and WASD keys, in all likelihood—unless you modified them in the Unity input system) to drive the car around the track. Amazing, right?

 It will probably be quite difficult to drive well.

Training

As with the previous chapters, training a simulation requires a configuration file and some ML-Agents scripts to read them:

1. First, we'll need the customary YAML file to serve as the hyperparameters for our training. Create a new file named *CarAgent.yaml*, and include the following hyperparameters and values:

```
behaviors:
  CarDrive:
    trainer_type: ppo
    hyperparameters:
      batch_size: 1024
      buffer_size: 10240
      learning_rate: 3.0e-4
      beta: 5.0e-3
      epsilon: 0.2
      lambd: 0.95
      num_epoch: 3
      learning_rate_schedule: linear
    network_settings:
      normalize: false
      hidden_units: 128
      num_layers: 2
      vis_encode_type: simple
    reward_signals:
      extrinsic:
        gamma: 0.99
        strength: 1.0
    keep_checkpoints: 5
    max_steps: 1.0e6
    time_horizon: 64
    summary_freq: 10000
    threaded: true
```

2. Next, select the car agent in the Hierarchy panel, and choose Default from the Behavior Type drop-down menu in the Behavior Parameters component, as shown in Figure 5-25.

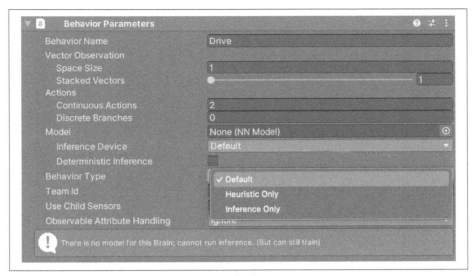

Figure 5-25. Setting Behavior Type to Default

3. With that, you're ready to train. Fire up the virtual environment we created earlier and start the training process by running the following command in your terminal:

```
mlagents-learn config/CarAgent.yaml --run-id=CarAgent1
```

You will need to replace the path to the YAML file with the path to the configuration file that was created a moment ago.

Once your system has executed `mlagents-learn`, you should see something that looks a lot like Figure 5-26. Press the Play button in the Unity Editor.

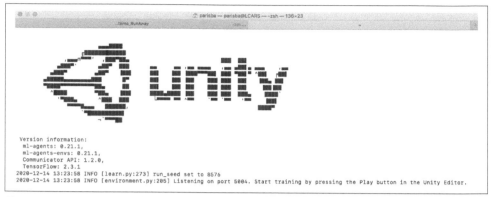

Figure 5-26. Getting ready to start training the car

The training will run for `1.0e6` steps (also known as `1,000,000` steps). You can monitor the training with TensorBoard if you'd like. Refer back to "Monitoring the Training with TensorBoard" on page 45 for details on that.

When the Training Is Complete

Eventually the training will complete, and you will have an *.onnx* or *.nn* file, as shown in Figure 5-27.

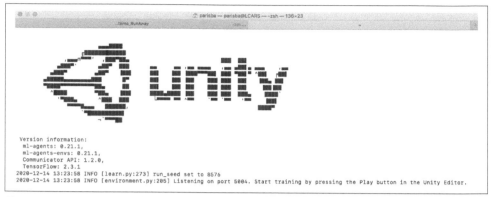

Figure 5-27. The .onnx file is written out when training is completed

Next, we need to attach the newly trained machine learning model (stored in the *.nn* or *.onnx* file) to the agent:

1. Drag the new model file into the Project pane in the Unity Editor and then attach it to your agent, as shown in Figure 5-28.

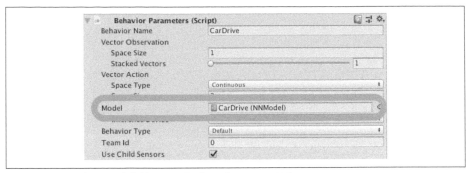

Figure 5-28. The model file attached in the Unity Editor

2. Run the project, and watch your self-driving car self-drive itself around your track! Amazing.

CHAPTER 6

Introducing Imitation Learning

In this chapter, we're going to look at imitation learning (IL). Imitation learning is slightly different from other forms of machine learning because the intent of IL isn't to achieve a specific goal. Instead, the intent is to copy the behavior of something else. That something else? Probably a human.

To explore IL, we'll be making another ball-based agent that can roll around, and we'll be training it to seek and pick up a coin (a classic video game–style pickup). But instead of training it to do what we want by reinforcing the behavior using reward signals, we'll train it using our own human brains.

This means that, initially, we'll be moving the agent around ourselves, using the keyboard, just like when we've used the heuristic behavior to control agents in previous chapters. The difference is that while we drive the agent around this time, ML-Agents will be watching us, and once we've finished, we'll use IL to let the agent work out how to copy our behavior.

IL not only lets you create more humanlike behaviors, it can also be used to essentially jump-start training. Some tasks have very high initial learning curves, and training to get over these early hurdles can be quite slow. If a human can show the agent how to do a task, the agent can use that as guidance when getting started and then optimize the approach from there. Luckily for us, humans are pretty good at plenty of things, and IL lets you take advantage of this. A disadvantage of IL is that it's not as good at finding novel approaches and can often peak earlier than other approaches. It's only as good as the demonstrations it has been given.

The main advantage of IL is that you can very quickly get results with far less training than other machine learning techniques. We won't have to set up any reward structure for this scenario, as the reward signal will automatically be how closely it matches our behavior, instead of something more explicit. We will look at using rewards together with IL later, in Chapter 7.

In this chapter, we'll be using a specific IL approach called behavioral cloning (BC), which is relatively straightforward to implement using Unity and ML-Agents, but has more limitations than other techniques. We'll touch on those limitations as we encounter them.

 Unity also supports an IL technique called generative adversarial imitation learning (GAIL). We will be using GAIL in Chapter 7.

Simulation Environment

Our IL simulation environment will be fairly simple and abstract. You can see an image of our version in Figure 6-1. Our environment will have a large plane for our ground, a ball to serve as our agent, and a flattened cylinder as our goal coin (trust us, it's a coin!).

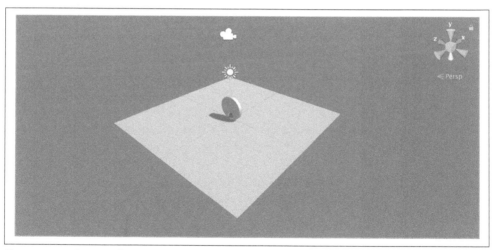

Figure 6-1. The simulation we'll be building

To build the simulation environment, we need to:

- Make the ground
- Make the goal
- Make the agent

Let's get cracking:

1. Create a new 3D Unity project using the Unity Hub. Ours is named "Imitation-LearningBall."
2. Import the Unity ML-Agents package.
3. Make sure your Python environment is ready to go.

Once you've done this, continue on to build the environment.

Creating the Ground

First we will need our ground to exist, for without a ground it would be very hard for our ball to roll anywhere. After creating a new Unity project, importing the Unity ML-Agents package, and getting into an empty scene, you'll need to:

1. Create a plane, name it "Ground," and make sure its position is (0, 0, 0).

   Now that our ground is correctly positioned, we will quickly give it a different appearance so that it is slightly easier for us to distinguish from the other soon-to-exist elements of our environment.

2. Create a material in the Project view, name it something like "GroundMaterial," and give it a nice color that looks like the ground (we recommend a nice grass-like green) by changing the albedo property.

3. Assign the material to the ground plane by dragging it onto it.

When you're done, you should have something similar to Figure 6-2.

Figure 6-2. The ground plane for our IL scenario

Our ground is ready, so it's time to make the goal. Don't forget to save your scene before continuing.

Creating the Goal

Our goal for this scenario is going to be a large gold coin. What more could a rolling ball desire? (If it is good enough for Mario, it is good enough for our ball!)

To create the coin, open your Unity scene and do the following:

1. Create a new cylinder and name it "Goal."

2. Use the Inspector and change the goal's position to (0, 0.75, 0), its rotation to (0, 0, 90), and its scale to (1.5, 0.1, 1.5).

This gives us a nice flat disk, but it doesn't look much like a coin, so let's change that by giving it a little pizazz with a material:

1. Create a new material, and name it something related to a Goal Coin.

2. Use the Inspector, and set the new material's albedo color to a nice golden yellow.

3. Still in the material's Inspector, drag the Metallic slider all the way to the right until it reads 1.0, and drag the Smoothness slider to around 0.3.

4. Drag the new material onto the goal object in the scene or the Hierarchy to apply it.

When you're done, you should have a coin that looks similar to Figure 6-3. Aren't video games amazing?

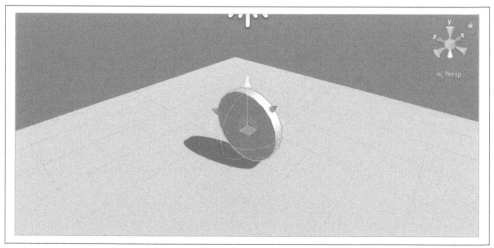

Figure 6-3. The goal coin for our IL scenario

Of course, it isn't really a video game coin *unless* it slowly spins. This has nothing to do with any aspect of machine learning or the simulation, but we feel it's very important:

1. Select the coin in the Hierarchy.

2. In the Inspector, click on the Add Component button.

3. Select the New Script option in the drop-down menu.

4. Name the script "CoinSpin" and press Return.

5. Open the *CoinSpin.cs* script in your code editor.

6. Replace the code in that file with the following code:

```
using System.Collections;
using System.Collections.Generic;
using UnityEngine;

public class CoinSpin : Monobehavior
{
    public float speed = 10;
    void Update()
    {
        var rotationRate = Time.deltaTime * speed;
        transform.Rotate(Vector3.left * rotationRate);
    }
}
```

There is a `speed` float variable that is exposed in the Inspector in the Unity Editor (because it was set to `public` in the code) if you want to make the coin spin faster or slower.

Now if we play the scene in Unity, the goal coin will slowly spin around. Perfection.

 Making the coin spin or coloring it a shiny gold isn't at all necessary for training. However, because humans will need to be the ones driving the ball around initially, it's worth spending a little bit of time making things more clearly delineated and interesting to look at. Humans don't like looking at abstract white shapes much, and adding a bit of fun is rarely a bad idea, even if the computer doesn't care.

The final thing we need to do is set the coin up to handle the situation when it collides with the ball.

When you create one of Unity's predefined polyhedrons (like the cylinder we fashioned into a coin), it comes with a collider, which lets us know when things collide with it. By default, Unity treats the collider like a solid object, but we don't want that.

We don't want the ball to bounce off the coin, we want it to pass through it, and notify us that that's what happened.

To do this, we need to convert our collider to a trigger volume:

1. Select the coin in the Hierarchy.
2. Inside the Inspector, locate the Capsule Collider section.
3. Tick the Is Trigger tickbox to make it a trigger.

Now when things collide with the coin, instead of hitting it like a wall, we will be informed that something hit it, but there will be no physics effect.

We still need an easy way to let the ball know it hit the coin instead of something else. As we did in Chapter 5, we will use the Unity Editor's tags for this. Tags let you quickly flag certain objects in a scene with additional metadata, and while there are other ways of achieving the same effect, tags are very lightweight and convenient:

1. Select the coin in the Hierarchy.
2. Inside the Inspector, select the Tag drop-down menu, as shown in Figure 6-4.

Figure 6-4. The initial list of tags

There are a few predefined tags, but we don't want these so we will have to make our own:

1. Select the Add Tag option from the drop-down menu. This will open the Tag editor, allowing us to create new tags.

2. Click the + button to create a new tag.

3. Name the tag "Goal."

4. Select the coin in the Hierarchy and open the Tag drop-down menu from the Inspector.

5. Select the newly created "Goal" tag, as shown in Figure 6-5.

Figure 6-5. The modified list of tags

Now our coin is tagged as a goal, which we can use later to differentiate between objects. Our goal coin is complete! Don't forget to save.

The Name's Ball, Agent Ball

Time to make our ball agent. We know, it's always very exciting to ponder any form of orb, and our ball agent is no exception. At this point we will just be setting up the physical properties of our ball, not the ML elements.

In the Unity Editor, do the following:

1. Create a new sphere in the Hierarchy, and name it "Ball."

2. Use the Inspector, and set the ball's position to (0, 0.25, 0) and its scale to (0.5, 0.5, 0.5).

3. Use the ball's Inspector to add a Rigidbody component. You don't need to modify any of its parameters.

Now we have a ball created and placed in the scene, and we have given it a Rigidbody, so it exists in the physics system.

 The Rigidbody is the component that allows the ball to participate in Unity's physics system, and gives it various physical properties such as its mass.

Finally, we want to give the ball agent a different appearance:

1. Create a new material in the Assets pane.

2. Rename it "Ball_Mat."

3. Download the book's assets from the book's website (*https://oreil.ly/1efRA*) and locate the file *ball_texture.png*. Drag that files into the Project pane in Unity.

4. Select the ball material.

5. Drag the ball texture from the Assets section into the Albedo field in the Inspector.

6. Drag the material from the assets onto the ball in the scene.

Now our ball in Figure 6-6 is ready and looking good. Feel free to make your own texture for the ball if you prefer.

Figure 6-6. Our ball with its new material applied

Don't forget to save your scene before continuing.

The Camera

Even though the camera is not used in the training (we'll get to that later, in Chapter 10), as humans we will need to be able to see the environment when we are driving the ball around, so we need to position the camera somewhere we're comfortable with.

There are no real rules here, and whatever camera angle and position you feel works best for you is where you should settle. However, if you want the entire ground in view at all times, you can use the following settings in the Unity Editor:

1. Select the Main Camera in the Hierarchy.

2. In the Inspector, change the position of the camera to 0, 5, 0.

3. In the Inspector, set the rotation to 90, 0, 0.

4. In the Inspector, find the Camera component section.

5. Set the Field of View to 90.

Now you should be able to have a top-down view of the entire ground and anything on it, as shown in Figure 6-7.

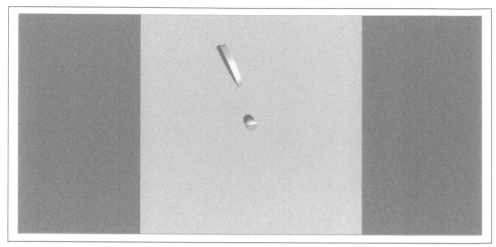

Figure 6-7. The top-down all-seeing camera

Again, don't forget to save the scene.

Building the Simulation

With the majority of our environment set up and configured, we can now turn to the simulation and training side of things.

We will be doing multiple things here, most of which relate to our ball (soon to be an agent).

The steps we'll take here should be starting to become familiar, but in case you're feeling rusty, we will be:

- Configuring the ball to be an agent
- Writing heuristic control code, allowing us to drive the ball
- Writing code to generate observations
- Writing code to reset the environment on success or failure

Because we're using IL instead of RL, we won't be using rewards in this scenario. This means you won't see us provide any rewards, positive or negative.

 We could include rewards if we wanted, but it wouldn't have any impact on this particular scenario, so we won't bother. In the next chapter, when we look at GAIL approaches to IL, we will investigate combining rewards and imitation further.

Agent Components

Our ball is going to need to be an agent, but currently it's just a ball with an inferiority complex, so let's fix that. In your scene, in the Unity Editor, do the following:

1. Select the ball in the Hierarchy.
2. In the Inspector, click on the Add Component button.
3. Add a Decision Requestor component.
4. Change the Decision Period to 10.

This will add a bunch of other components. Some are necessary, but others aren't needed, so we'll make some tweaks:

1. In the Inspector, inside the Behavior Parameters component, change the Behavior Name to "RollingBall."
2. Change the Vector Observations Space Size to 8 instead of 1.
3. Change the Continuous Actions to 2.

These means we have set our agent up to have eight observations and two control actions, but none of this allows for heuristic control. Let's add that now. These will be new steps, compared to what we've done in the past:

1. In the ball agent's Inspector, click on the Add Component button.
2. Add a Demonstration Recorder component.
3. Set the Demonstration Name to "RollerDemo."
4. Set the Demonstration Director to Assets/Demos.

The Demonstration Recorder is a component that allows the ML-Agents system to watch what we do when we drive the ball around, and record it to a file at the directory we set earlier. That file will then be used in training.

Finally, we need to set up an agent script. Because the Decision Requestor component requires an agent script, it added a default version for us, but we want a custom one:

1. In the Inspector, click the Add Component button.
2. Add a new script called "Roller" to the ball.
3. Open *Roller.cs* in your code editor.

Now we'll configure the ball to be an agent. We will be doing some basic setup here and then adding more in later sections:

1. Add the following imports to the top of the *Roller.cs* file:

```
using UnityEngine;
using Unity.MLAgents;
using Unity.MLAgents.Sensors;
```

   These give us the basic ML components we will be using as well as access to the UnityEngine library, which we will need for generating some random numbers.

2. Modify the class definition of `Roller`:

```
public class Roller : Agent
```

3. Add the following instance variables to `Roller`:

```
public float speed = 10;
public Transform goal;

private Rigidbody body;
private bool victory = false;
```

4. Replace the `Start` method with the following:

```
void Start()
{
    body = GetComponent<Rigidbody>();
}
```

   We did a few things here: first we made `Roller` a subclass of `Agent`, which means we can get a default agent that Unity added for us. Then we set up four different properties we will need.

   The `speed` and `goal` are public and are intended to be set in the Inspector, and we will do this in a moment. These control how fast the ball moves and what `GameObject` it should be aiming for as its goal.

   The `body` keeps track of the physics Rigidbody component so that we can add and remove forces to it as necessary.

   And the `victory` will be used to determine if we have hit the goal or not.

5. In the Inspector, drag the goal coin from the scene into the goal slot in the Roller component.

6. In the Inspector, delete the default Agent component that Unity added.

With that all done, you should now have ML-Agents components on your ball agent that look similar to Figure 6-8.

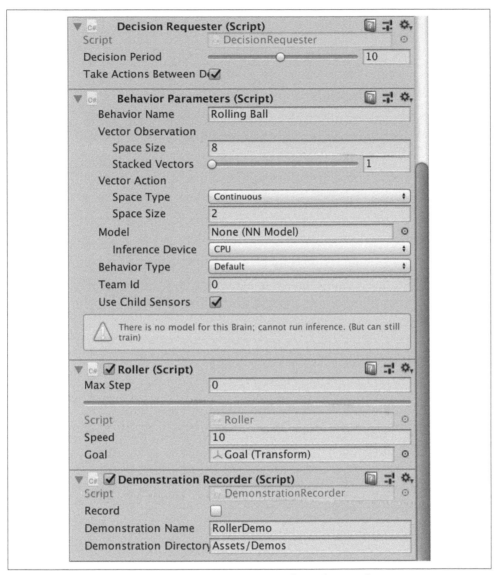

Figure 6-8. Our ball with its Agent components configured correctly

Depending on your particular version of ML-Agents it may not have installed the same components automatically. If that is the case, you will want a Decision Requestor, a Behavior Parameters, and a Demonstration Recorder component. You will also need our custom agent script Roller.

Don't forget to save everything.

Adding Heuristic Controls

As we will be driving the ball around to generate training behavior, we need some way to move the ball directly, which (as usual) we can do using heuristic controls:

1. Open *Roller.cs*.

2. Add the following method to the class:

```
public override void Heuristic(in ActionBuffers actionsOut)
{
    var continuousActionsOut = actionsOut.ContinuousActions;

    continuousActionsOut[0] = Input.GetAxis("Horizontal");
    continuousActionsOut[1] = Input.GetAxis("Vertical");
}
```

This method gets called by ML-Agents when it is time for the agent to take an action, except now we are intercepting that and providing our own actions.

We are using the default Unity input system to get 0 - 1 normalized horizontal and vertical values to give our ball. By default these map to the standard WASD or arrow-key control scheme in games, which is perfect for us.

Now we need to be able to configure the agent and its goal for each episode.

3. Add the following method to the class:

```
public override void OnEpisodeBegin()
{
    victory = false;
    body.angularVelocity = Vector3.zero;
    body.velocity = Vector3.zero;
    this.transform.position = new Vector3(0, 0.25f, 0);

    var position = UnityEngine.Random.insideUnitCircle * 3;
    goal.position = new Vector3(position.x, 0.75f, position.y);
}
```

This accomplishes a few things. First, we set the victory flag back to false, not that it has changed yet. Then we remove all forces from our ball and set it back to the center of the ground.

Finally, we generate a random position on a circle of radius 3 (which maps well to the size of our ground) and set the goal to that position. The only thing that remains before we can drive the ball around ourselves is to add the action code.

4. Add the following method to the class:

```
public override void OnActionReceived(ActionBuffers actions)
{
    var continuousActions = actions.ContinuousActions;

    Vector3 controlSignal = Vector3.zero;

    controlSignal.x = continuousActions[0];
    controlSignal.z = continuousActions[1];

    body.AddForce(controlSignal * speed);

    if (victory)
    {
        EndEpisode();
    }
    else if (this.transform.localPosition.y < 0)
    {
        EndEpisode();
    }
}
```

Here we are getting the horizontal and vertical components of the action values and using them to add a small force to the physics body of our ball. This essentially pushes it in the direction of the action values, using Unity's physics system.

 You can learn more about AddForce() in the Unity documentation (*https://oreil.ly/mbUOy*).

Then we do a quick check to see if we've won (which we can't yet) or if we've fallen off the edge. If so, we end the episode and reset everything back to how it was before.

With that done, we save our work and return to the Unity Editor so that we can test our code.

5. In the Inspector, in the Behavior Parameters script, change the Behavior Type setting to be Heuristic.

6. Play the scene.

You can now drive the ball around using your keyboard. If you fall off the edge of the world, the environment should be reset. Huzzah!

You might notice that Unity is warning you about the number of observations not matching the values set, and we'll fix that next. It's happening because we're not yet providing all the observations we intend to, and we told Unity to expect eight when we configured the Vector Observations Space Size in the Behavior Parameters component on the agent in the Unity Editor.

As always, remember to save the scene.

Observations and Goals

Although we can drive our ball around perfectly well, it has no understanding of its world, so it would have no capacity to learn.

To give the ball agent an understanding of the world, it needs observations. As with every simulated agent we've built so far, the observations are what the agent knows about the world it's in.

While we are doing that, we should also handle what happens when we hit the coin and how we hit the coin:

1. Open *Roller.cs*.

2. Add the following method:

```
public override void CollectObservations(VectorSensor sensor)
{
    sensor.AddObservation(goal.position);
    sensor.AddObservation(this.transform.position);

    sensor.AddObservation(body.velocity.x);
    sensor.AddObservation(body.velocity.z);
}
```

This method is called by ML-Agents when it needs to collect observations for the agent. Our observations are fairly simple for this scenario: we are passing over the position of the goal and ourselves (x and z positions). We're also passing over the horizontal and vertical velocities of the ball.

That concludes the observations, and it's now time to add in the collisions.

3. Add the following method to *Roller.cs*:

```
void OnTriggerEnter(Collider other)
{
    if (other.CompareTag("Goal"))
    {
        victory = true;
    }
}
```

`OnTriggerEnter` is a built-in Unity function that gets called when an object enters the trigger volume (such as that of our coin).

Here we are just checking if what we collided with is tagged as a "goal," which our coin is, and if it is, we tell it to set a flag that we have achieved our goal.

Save your script. Now, if we jump back into Unity and play the scene, we can drive the ball around, pick up the coins, and reset the episode.

We are ready to start generating some training data and perform some learning.

 While we are using the Unity physics system to let us know when collisions happen, this can lead to some weird results in more complex scenarios. The timing of events that lets the agent associate actions, observations, and rewards means you can't always rely on `OnTriggerEnter` firing off when you need it to for training. In this case, our example is simple, and this lets us delve a bit more into the Unity physics system, so we think it's worth it. For the most part, however, doing distance checking is advised.

Generating Data and Training

With our scene set up correctly, we can generate some training data. It's time to show a robot how to drive a ball into coins.

Creating Training Data

Helpfully, Unity has made it trivial to record our actions: all we need to do is set a flag. The hard bit will be being good at driving the ball around.

 It is important here that you try your best at the game. The agent will be learning directly from you, so if you are bad, the agent will be bad. The *ML-Apple* won't fall far from the *You-Tree*.

1. Select the ball in the Hierarchy.

2. In the Inspector, find the Demonstration Recorder component.

3. Set the Record toggle to be on. We are ready to record.

4. Play the scene.

5. Drive the ball around with your keyboard, and make sure you pick up the coin a few times.

6. Stop the scene when you are happy with it. We recommend trying to pick up the coin about 20 times.

You should see that once that is done, there is a new folder called *Demos* in the *Assets* directory. Inside that folder, you should see a file called *RollerDemo*. If you select it in the Inspector in the Unity Editor, it will tell you relevant information, like what sort of actions and observations were recorded, as shown in Figure 6-9.

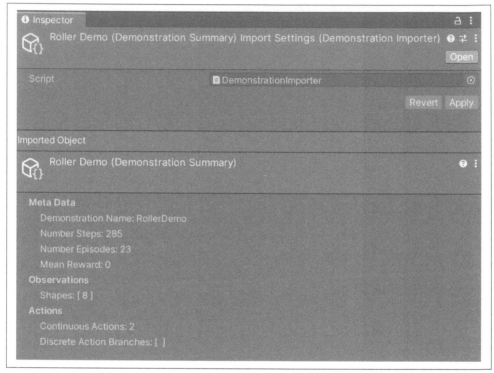

Figure 6-9. Inspecting our demo recording

If you do multiple training runs, you will see multiple demo files all named numerically increasing values, like *RollerDemo_0*, *RollerDemo_1*, and so on. These will be our training data.

Configuring for Training

With our training data written, we now need to make our YAML configuration file. Everyone loves YAML.

Most of this file will be based on Chapter 2, so we won't be going into too much detail here. We will be talking about the parts specific to the IL, though:

1. Create a config folder at the project root.

2. Inside that folder, create a new text file.

3. Name it *RollerBallIL.yaml*.

4. Add the following YAML to that file:

```
behaviors:
  RollerBall:
    trainer_type: ppo
    hyperparameters:
      batch_size: 10
      buffer_size: 100
      learning_rate: 3.0e-4
      beta: 5.0e-4
      epsilon: 0.2
      lambd: 0.99
      num_epoch: 3
      learning_rate_schedule: linear
    network_settings:
      normalize: false
      hidden_units: 128
      num_layers: 2
    reward_signals:
      extrinsic:
        gamma: 0.99
        strength: 1.0
    max_steps: 500000
    time_horizon: 64
    summary_freq: 10000

    # behavior cloning
    behavioral_cloning:
      demo_path: ./Assets/Demos/RollerDemo.demo
      strength: 0.5
      steps: 150000
      batch_size: 512
      num_epoch: 3
```

Most of this is identical to the earlier YAML files we made, with the main difference being the behavioral_cloning section. Those are the specific parameters for behavioral cloning (or BC), the IL technique we are using.

Currently, they're fairly generic because of the simplicity of our simulation. However, of particular interest is the strength setting, which controls the learning rate of the BC relative to normal PPO training. Essentially, strength is saying how strongly the BC influences and controls the training; setting this too high means it might overfit to you, but if you set it too low, it won't learn enough.

As with all configuration parameters, the best way to see their impact is to change them and see what it does to the training.

Another interesting property is the demo_path. This points to the demonstration recording we made earlier. If you changed the name of your demo, or want to use a different demo than the first run, make sure to change the demo_path variable to match. You might need to give it an absolute path, depending on your system (e.g., */Volumes/Work/Sims/IL/RollerDemo.demo*).

> It is easy to type these parameters incorrectly in the YAML file. It might be easier to copy them directly from our code at GitHub (*https://oreil.ly/u43u2*).

Begin Training

It's almost time to do the *machine* part of machine learning, *finally*. Almost. First, we have to do some setup in the Unity Editor:

1. Select the ball inside the Hierarchy.

2. In the Inspector, find the Behavior Parameter component.

3. Set the Behavior Type to Default.

4. In the Inspector, find the Demonstration Recorder component.

5. Toggle off the Record setting. Now our agent is ready to be controlled by Python.

6. Open the Terminal.

7. Navigate to the Unity project root.

8. Run the following command:

```
mlagents-learn config/rollerball_config.yaml --run-id=RollerBall
```

After a brief moment, you should see something similar to Figure 6-10, which means we can start things up in Unity.

Figure 6-10. Python ML-Agents is ready to train

9. Go back to Unity.

10. Play the scene.

    You should see the ball zipping off on its own, attempting to learn how you drive.

11. Go get a very tall cup of coffee, or maybe read a book for a bit. It's OK, we'll wait.

Once this process ends, our training is finished and we can test it.

 If you want a pretrained machine learning model, check out the one we made over on GitHub (*https://oreil.ly/nwupp*).

Running with Our Trained Model

Time to take our IL-trained model out for a spin.

First, as usual, we need to locate the neural net ML-Agents created for us: by default it will be in the results folder in the project root. Inside there will be another folder named *Roller Ball*, and inside that there will be a file named *Rolling Ball.onnx*, which is our trained neural net.

Follow these steps to run the ball agent with the trained model:

1. Drag the *.onnx* file into Unity's Assets pane.

2. Select the ball in the Hierarchy.

3. In the Inspector, locate the Behavior Parameters component.

4. Add the *.onnx* file into the Model slot.

5. Set the Behavior Type to Inference Only.

6. Play the scene in Unity.

Now you should see the ball rolling around collecting coins and, if you drive like we do, often falling off the edge. Hopefully you're a better teacher to the ball than we are.

Congratulations, you trained an agent using imitation learning!

Understanding and Using Imitation Learning

Imitation learning is useful for making an agent behave like a human (somewhat); however, in practice, it's more likely to be used as part of a multistage, multitechnique training process to help an agent along, particularly in *early training*.

For further information on the multiple techniques possible, refer back to "The Techniques" on page 9.

When you're considering a simulation, you're trying to make something that's going to be an efficient simulation: you want early training to be as successful as possible.

In reinforcement learning, an agent has absolutely no idea what it's doing, even slightly, until it gets its first reward. IL lets you shortcut the process and use a human to demonstrate a "good behavior" to start with, and then either continue with IL, or switch to RL to continue training, with the difficult early training out of the way, as quickly as possible.

After the early training, you can continue with IL to generate an agent with more organic, "humanlike" behavior (whatever that means in the context of your simulations), or swap to another technique, such as the aforementioned RL, to rapidly generate new experiences and improve upon the demonstrated human behaviors.

For example, the car that we created in Chapter 5, which was trained solely using RL, could instead have an initial training phase using IL in which human demonstrations of driving the track are used to inform its driving behavior, and then a second training phase—largely identical to the one we actually used in Chapter 5—using RL on top of this. This approach would likely yield both faster training time overall, and a slightly more human feel to the car's approach to driving the course.

CHAPTER 7

Advanced Imitation Learning

In this chapter, we're going to look at imitation learning (IL) using generative adversarial imitation learning (GAIL). We could use GAIL in an almost identical fashion to what we did when we used IL for behavioral cloning (BC), but that wouldn't really be showing you anything new other than changing the configuration YAML file.

With our simulations so far, we've done the basics, built upon them, and created a simple self-driving car, all using reinforcement learning. And in the previous chapter, we used IL to train an agent using human behavior. The IL we used for behavioral cloning attempted to maximize its similarity to our provided training data.

IL is not the only BC technique we can use. This time, we'll use GAIL. GAIL can help improve the training of our agent, allowing it to essentially jump over the early hurdles in the learning process and let it focus on improving itself from then on.

 BC and GAIL can also be combined so that you can hopefully extract the benefits of both and mitigate the weaknesses of either. Toward the end of this chapter, we'll cover how you can combine GAIL and BC, but for now the focus will be on GAIL.

Meet GAIL

Before we start working on a GAIL-based activity with Unity and ML-Agents, we're going to unpack a little bit of what makes GAIL tick.

GAIL is, as its name implies, an adversarial approach to imitation learning and is based on a type of machine learning network called a *GAN*: a generative adversarial network. A GAN effectively plays two trained models, named a *discriminator* and a *generator*, against each other. The discriminator model judges how well the generator is copying some desired training data or behavior, and the feedback from the discriminator is used by the generator to direct and hopefully improve its actions.

These actions and behaviors are then fed back into the discriminator so that it learns more about the scenario. The discriminator is learning the rules and rewards of the scenario based on the actions taken by the generator and the provided demonstrations.

> GAIL is a much newer approach to imitation learning than BC, but that doesn't necessarily mean it is better; it is just different. Machine learning as a field is constantly in flux.

The natural question that arises, then, is *When should I use GAIL, and when should I use BC?* As with most things in machine learning, the answer isn't simple. In general, choosing which to use depends more on the scenario you are intending to use. Just to confuse things, you can also combine them to (often) get better results than when using them in isolation.

> Academic research around GAIL often talks about inverse reinforcement learning and model-free learning, and other very fancy-sounding terms.
>
> These basically mean that GAIL doesn't have an intrinsic understanding of the world; it has to figure out both the rules of the scenario and the actions to maximize the scenario rewards.
>
> As such, it does quite well when it's just thrown into the deep end and has to work things out with minimal assistance.

If you have a lot of human-generated training data that covers the gamut of possible changes in the environment, BC with IL will generally do better than GAIL.

If you only have a little bit of human-generated data, GAIL will be able to extrapolate better from this to work out the best approach. GAIL also tends to work better than BC when combined with extrinsic rewards as defined by humans (using the AddReward function in ML-Agents).

It's often very tricky to work out the correct reward structure for your simulations when you're using reinforcement learning. Using GAIL helps with this, because it operates without knowledge of exactly what your scenario is and somewhat has to work out what you want. It does this by relying on the information contained in the demonstration data. In complex scenarios where designing a good reward structure is difficult, you may be able to use GAIL to work out the scenario based on what you did even if you aren't able to essentially explain why what you are doing is good.

GAIL is a bit more flexible than BC with IL, but that isn't why we are using it here; we are using it because GAIL works better when combined with extrinsic rewards. BC with IL is better when you have demonstrated exactly what to do, and GAIL is better when you have only provided partial information as demos.

 Essentially, inside GAIL there are two wolves: the first wolf is working to better understand the world it is in, and the second wolf is performing actions it hopes will please the first wolf.

Do What I Say and Do

There's an old proverb, "Do what I say, not what I do," that always comes to mind when training ML-Agents agents.

We basically just set up some rewards and tell the agent to figure it out from there. If we did this with children as they were growing up, it would be considered a pretty bad form of imparting knowledge, so instead we tend to show them what to do a few times, and then present them with the rules and let them improve from there.

Almost anytime you, as a human, are trained, you will generally be shown the correct way of doing it a few times before you're expected to do it by yourself.

This is what we are going to attempt to reproduce here; we want to use GAIL to kick-start the training of our agent. We want to show the correct approach a few times and then let it work out the best approach from then on.

A GAIL Scenario

For this scenario we are going to use a problem and environment similar to the activity we did earlier, when we trained an agent using IL for BC in Chapter 6. Our activity concerned an environment with the following:

- A goal area
- A ball, acting as the agent, that needed to move to the goal

It looked like Figure 7-1.

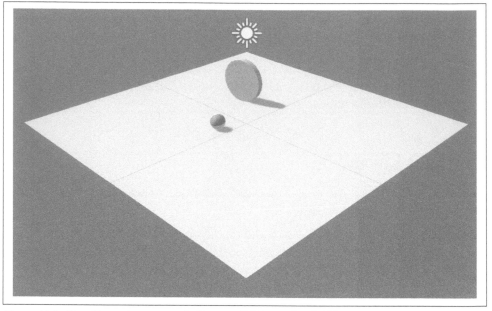

Figure 7-1. Our IL environment, before modifying it for GAIL

If the ball falls off the world, it ends the episode unsuccessfully; if the ball reaches the goal, it ends the episode successfully.

For our activity with GAIL, we're going to use the same environment with a small addition:

- There will be a "key" that the agent needs to reach before the goal is unlocked.
- Touching the goal without first having touched the key will do nothing.

At this point, you can either duplicate the Unity project you made for Chapter 6, or just straight-up modify it. We're choosing to duplicate the scene inside the project, so we open the Unity Editor and do the following:

1. Select the scene in the Project pane, as shown in Figure 7-2.

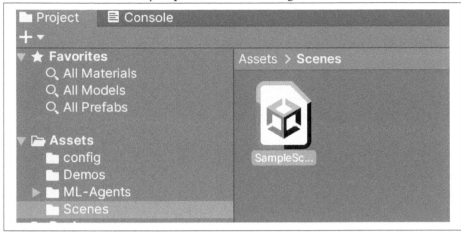

Figure 7-2. Selecting the scene in the Project pane

2. Select the Edit menu → Duplicate, as shown in Figure 7-3.

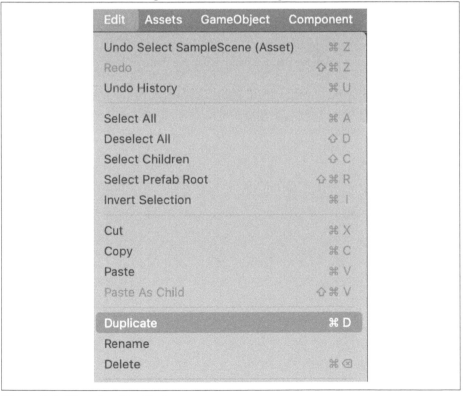

Figure 7-3. Choosing Duplicate

3. Rename the duplicated scene "GAIL" or something similar.

Make sure the new scene is open and ready to go. Then it's time to add the key:

1. Add a new cube to the project hierarchy.
2. Rename this cube "key."

The cube will be partially embedded in the ground, but that's OK for now. The next step is to modify the agent and the agent's scripts.

 If you haven't worked through Chapter 6, we highly suggest you do that before trying this.

Modifying the Agent's Actions

Our agent as it currently exists only uses the training data in the demonstrations we recorded for it earlier—it has no reward structure otherwise set up.

Having no rewards is great for BC with IL, but it's not what we're after for this activity with GAIL. We want the agent to use the training data to help start learning and then have the values from the rewards be the component the agent optimizes for.

 Because we're working in the same project as we did with BC-based IL, we are going to be modifying the roller agent class directly (which will impact the function of the scene we made in the previous chapter), but if you want to keep it as is, you can duplicate that file or create a new C# file to be your new agent.

Just remember to hook it up to your agent in the scene and remove the old one.

1. Open *Roller.cs*.
2. Add the following member variables to the class:

   ```
   public Transform key;
   private bool hasKey = false;
   ```

The first of these two variables, key, will be used so that we have a reference to the key object in the scene, and the second will be used to know if we have picked up the key.

Now we could use some GameObject-specific information on the key itself to know whether it's been hit and do that instead of having another variable lying around, but this isn't such a huge savings to be bothered by it.

3. Replace the OnActionReceived method with the following code:

```
var continuousActions = actions.ContinuousActions;
Vector3 control = Vector3.zero;
control.x = continuousActions[0];
control.z = continuousActions[1];

body.AddForce(control * speed);

if (transform.position.y < 0.4f)
{
  AddReward(-1f);
  EndEpisode();
}

var keyDistance = Vector3.Distance(transform.position, key.position);
if (keyDistance < 1.2f)
{
  hasKey = true;
  key.gameObject.SetActive(false);
}
if (hasKey)
{
  if (Vector3.Distance(transform.position, goal.position) < 1.2f)
  {
    AddReward(1f);
    EndEpisode();
  }
}
```

The first part of this works similarly to our earlier code: it applies a force based on the movement action values. We are still resetting the environment if the agent rolls off the edge of the plane, but now we are punishing it for doing so.

Next, we work out if we have touched the key. If we have touched it, we deactivate the key (so that it no longer appears in the scene) and flag the key as found.

Finally, we do something similar but with the goal instead of the key, and if we have the key, we give a reward and end the episode.

We are using a distance value here, 1.2 units, to work out whether we are close enough. We chose that number because it is just a teensy bit bigger than the combined center distance to center distance of a unit sphere up against a unit cube. We are doing this because it is nice and simple code to show off. It isn't perfect, however:

what we are crudely doing is drawing a sphere around the agent of radius 0.6 and seeing if anything is inside.

 Unity has a built-in method to do exactly that: `Physics.Overlap Sphere`, which lets you define a center point and radius and see what `colliders` are inside that imaginary sphere. We aren't using that method because it looks a little bit clunky, and to properly determine *what* you hit you should be using tags, which we'd need to set up. As such, we are keeping it simple and doing a distance check, but the built-in methods do have a lot of flexibility in letting you define collision layer masks, and if we had a more complex example, that's what we'd do.

If you are curious, here are the basics of an `OverlapSphere` call. To work out what you hit or to filter the collisions to only relevant ones is an exercise, as they say, left to the reader:

```
var colliders = Physics.OverlapSphere(transform.position,
  0.5f);
foreach(var collider in colliders)
{
   Debug.Log($"Hit {collider.gameObject.name}");
}
```

Those are our modified actions; now on to the observations. Don't forget to save your code.

Modifying the Observations

Working with observations is probably quite familiar by now, and we'll be doing it all by passing observations to ML-Agents via the `CollectObservations()` function. The core changes to the observations from the IL-powered version are the additition of information about the key, and the status of the key.

With your code open, replace the `CollectObservations` method with the following code:

```
sensor.AddObservation(body.velocity.x);
sensor.AddObservation(body.velocity.z);

Vector3 goalHeading = goal.position - transform.position;
var goalDirection = goalHeading / goalHeading.magnitude;
sensor.AddObservation(goalDirection.x);
sensor.AddObservation(goalDirection.z);

sensor.AddObservation(hasKey);
if (hasKey)
{
  sensor.AddObservation(0);
```

```
    sensor.AddObservation(0);
  }
  else
  {
    Vector3 keyHeading = key.position - this.transform.position;
    var keyDirection = keyHeading / keyHeading.magnitude;
    sensor.AddObservation(keyDirection.x);
    sensor.AddObservation(keyDirection.z);
  }
```

This is not conceptually hugely different from what we had before; we are just tracking more things.

We still have our velocity and the direction to the goal, but we are adding a new observation of whether we have the key or not, and the direction to the key. If the key has been picked up, we don't bother working out its direction; we just send over zero, which is about as close as we can get to not sending over an observation.

The reason we do this is because we have to send over the same number of observations each time.

All of this code changes the number of observations being sent over to the agent, as compared to the previous IL-powered version. We'll fix that shortly.

Resetting the Agent

For our final bit of code, we need to update the `OnEpisodeBegin()` function to appropriately reset everything. Specifically, we now need to reset the state and status of the key.

Replace the `OnEpisodeBegin` method body with the following code:

```
body.angularVelocity = Vector3.zero;
body.velocity = Vector3.zero;
transform.position = new Vector3(0, 0.5f, 0);
transform.rotation = Quaternion.identity;

hasKey = false;
key.gameObject.SetActive(true);

var keyPos = UnityEngine.Random.insideUnitCircle * 3.5f;
key.position = new Vector3(keyPos.x, 0.5f, keyPos.y);
var goalPos = UnityEngine.Random.insideUnitCircle * 3.5f;
goal.position = new Vector3(goalPos.x, 0.5f, goalPos.y);
```

As with the observations, this isn't hugely different from before: we are still resetting the agent back to the center and removing all forces on it, and we are still picking a random point and moving the goal to that. However, we are also flagging us as not having the key, ensuring that the key game object is active in the scene, and finally moving it to a random position.

With that change, our code is done. We don't have to touch the heuristic code because nothing there has changed. Don't forget to save before you return to the Unity Editor.

Updating the Agent Properties

Our agent's code has changed a fair bit, so a lot of the component values set in the Inspector are no longer correct for this agent; let's fix that. In the Unity Editor, with your scene open:

1. Select the agent in the Hierarchy.
2. In the Inspector, find the Agent component.
3. Drag the key game object from the Hierarchy into the Key field in the Inspector.
4. In the Inspector, find the Behavior Parameters component.
5. Set the space size of the observations to 7.

With that, our agent is now correctly coded and configured. Let's give it some training data next.

Demonstration Time

This slightly modified world is no longer the same as the ones we previously used, so we should create some new demonstration data for the agent:

1. Select the agent in the Hierarchy.
2. In the Inspector, find the Behavior component.
3. Change the Type from Default to Heuristic.
4. In the Heuristic Recorder component, set it to Record.
5. Play the scenario.
6. Do your best to record some demonstration data.

 You might be wondering why are we bothering to record new demonstration data considering we already did that back when we were using BC. We are doing this because that data has no rewards as part of it, which means GAIL will never be able to associate the actions and the reward. If we used the old data, we would be training GAIL without any extrinsic reward. This will work, but it isn't the point of this chapter and very likely isn't going to give you the results you are after.

Once you feel you have enough data recorded, stop the scene. You should now have some data you can use to feed into GAIL.

 If you select the demonstration file that was created, inside the Unity Inspector you can see the average reward we were getting. It also shows some other information, but the mean reward is the main thing we care about here. If it is too low, it might not be a particularly good demonstration file.

Next up, training.

Training with GAIL

If you guessed, "Do I just set some weird settings in a YAML file to enable GAIL?" you'd be correct, so once again it is time for another exciting round of *Let's Edit Some Magic Numbers in YAML!* In the case of GAIL, the relevant bits we want to play around with are all part of the reward settings.

For this scenario, we are going to be using the same training configuration file we used earlier on when we had BC, but we will be making some changes. First up, we will want to make a new configuration file:

1. Duplicate *rollerball_config.yaml* and name it *rollerball_gail_config.yaml*.

   Next, you need to remove the BC-relevant sections of the configuration.

2. Delete the `behavioral_cloning` line and all lines below and indented from it.

   Finally, we want to add in GAIL.

3. Under the `reward_signals` section, add a new section for GAIL:

   ```
   gail:
     strength: 0.01
     demo_path: ./Assets/Demos/RollerDemoGail.demo
   ```

There are a few different GAIL parameters we can tweak; here we are only setting two, and only one of them is required.

The required one is `demo_path`, which is pointing to the demo file we created just a moment ago. We have also set `strength`, which has a default value of 1, and we are setting it well below that because `strength` is used by GAIL to scale the reward signal.

We are setting it so low because we have less-than-optimal demonstration data and are planning on the extrinsic reward signal being the main indicator of what action to take. If we gave it a stronger signal, it would learn more like our demonstration file and less like the optimal play for the scenario.

Other settings we can configure here for GAIL (but are leaving at their defaults) include the size of the discriminator, the learning rate, and the gamma, among others.

We don't need any of these here, so we are leaving them at their default settings, but if you are interested in them, the official docs (*https://oreil.ly/6w9DO*) have a description of them all should GAIL not be working the way you want.

 Because of how GAIL was designed, it has the habit of introducing various biases (*https://oreil.ly/gNIgb*) into the agent; that is to say, it often tries to extend the episode length even if this is in direct conflict with the goals of the scenario.

Due to this, if during training you find your agent basically hanging around and not completing the task at hand, you very likely need to lower the GAIL reward signal to prevent it from overpowering the extrinsic reward.

When done, the finished YAML file should look like the following:

```
behaviors:
  rolleragent_gail:
    trainer_type: ppo
    hyperparameters:
      batch_size: 10
      buffer_size: 100
      learning_rate: 3.0e-4
      beta: 5.0e-4
      epsilon: 0.2
      lambd: 0.99
      num_epoch: 3
      learning_rate_schedule: linear
    network_settings:
      normalize: false
      hidden_units: 128
      num_layers: 2
    reward_signals:
      extrinsic:
        gamma: 0.99
        strength: 1.0
      gail:
        strength: 0.01
        demo_path: ./Assets/Demos/RollerDemoGail.demo
        use_actions: true
    max_steps: 500000
    time_horizon: 64
    summary_freq: 10000
```

With our configuration file configured, it's time to start the actual training:

1. Select the agent inside Unity.
2. In the Inspector, inside the Behavior Parameters component, change the Behavior Type to Default.
3. In the Inspector, inside the Demonstration Recorder, untick the Record box.
4. In the command line, run the following command:

   ```
   mlagents-learn config/rolleragent_gail_config.yaml
     --run-id=rolleragent_gail
   ```

5. Once that has started, go back to Unity and press Play.

The agent should now be training. Take a quick (or not so quick) coffee break, and we will return once that finishes.

Running It and Beyond

Once our training has finished, we can run it like we've been doing so far:

1. Add the trained *.onnx* model file into Unity.
2. Select the agent inside Unity.
3. In the Inspector, inside the Behavior Parameters component, change the Behavior Type to Inference Only.
4. Drag the model file into the model slot.
5. Click Play, and sit back and enjoy watching your agent roll about, picking up cubes.

In the case of our agent, after being trained for 500,000 iterations it was getting an average reward score of 0.99, which is about as perfect as could ever be expected.

When compared to our demo file, its average reward was 0.95, so the agent has edged us out, which is what we expected: the student has become the master.

Now we've covered the basics of combining GAIL with extrinsic reward factors, but before we move on to other topics and chapters, it is a good time to talk about combining GAIL. In this example we combined GAIL with extrinsic rewards, but we can also combine it with imitation learning and behavioral cloning as well. To do so, all we have to do is add the BC configuration elements back into the YAML config file.

The trick, however, comes from balancing the relative strength values of extrinsic, GAIL, and BC rewards.

For this scenario, we tried a variety of different values of all three, tweaked other configuration settings, and even tried limiting the BC to the first part of the training, but we didn't see any significant improvement in the training. In one case, when attempting to best blend the various elements, we ended up with an agent that was so bad its average reward was -0.4, which means most of the time it just fell clean off the edge of the ground; our just GAIL or just BC both worked great.

It may well be that in this scenario it is simple enough that such adjustments don't provide enough value, or maybe we just haven't found the right values to make it all click.

Unity found in its Pyramid example (*https://oreil.ly/dP67X*) that when training with the combination of different techniques, the agent trained faster and better than with any other approach done by itself.

There definitely is something that makes sense about combining different approaches; after all, it isn't that different from how we learn. We try and combine many different techniques to get the best outcome we can when we are growing up, so why should an agent be any different? There is a great amount of potential in imitation learning, and because it is relatively easy to add into your training, it is well worth checking out.

CHAPTER 8
Introducing Curriculum Learning

Think back to your first few days in school. What strange times they were…the teacher standing at the front of the class presenting you all with a quadratic equation and asking you to solve it.

"What is the value of x?" you find yourself being asked.

Confused, you have no idea what's going on; it's your first day, after all.

Still you take a guess: "Three." The teacher stares at you before pronouncing you exceptionally wrong. You are sent home.

The next day this repeats. The teacher gives you another quadratic equation; you once again fail and are sent home. Day after day this happens: you show up and are given an equation, you take a guess, get it exceptionally wrong, and are then sent home.

One day you guess and the teacher says, "Wrong, but close."

Finally, some progress.

You are still sent home.

The next day this repeats, and the next and the next, again and again. Each time you are guessing closer and closer. Each time you get sent home, and each time you show up the next day and guess again.

Finally you start to piece it together, you start to understand the individual parts that make up the equations, the way they interact, the way they influence the value of x. When asked, this time things are different. You respond, "x is -1 plus or minus root 2," and you are confident in your answer. Your teacher slowly nods. "Correct."

You've been at school now for 600 years, but you finally know how to solve a quadratic equation. You are sent home.

Of course, this sounds like a terrible way to learn and an exceptionally cruel way to teach, yet it is how we ask ML to work.

Actual people are taught in stages.

We begin with the basics that are needed for more complex problems, and once we have the hang of them we move on to harder problems and more complex information. We build upon our previous knowledge like a pyramid, adding to it layer by layer until we are able to solve the actual problems we care about.

We teach people this way because it's been shown to work; it turns out that just asking kids to solve quadratic equations isn't hugely effective, but teaching the basics of numbers, then numeracy, and then algebra and formulas means you can one day ask them to solve a quadratic equation and they can do it. It is done this way in various forms by all cultures, for all domains of knowledge.

Curriculum learning (CL) in ML asks the question, "If it works well for people, does it also work for ML?" In this chapter, we are going to take a look at how we can use curriculum learning to solve a problem by building it up in stages.

Curriculum Learning in ML

The main reason to use curriculum learning in your ML models is the same reason that we as humans use it: it's generally easier to master the basics of something before moving on to more advanced portions of a task.

When curriculum learning is successful, it is very successful. For example, in Unity, when teaching an agent to reach a goal (say, learning how to hop over a fence), the curriculum learning model learned both faster and better than a more traditional model. Other work in domains related to simulations (*https://oreil.ly/XwMcW*) have shown similar promising results (*https://oreil.ly/04bAa*). However, this isn't to say that the answer is always to "just use curriculum learning."

As with many things in ML, knowing when to use curriculum learning is not clear-cut. If the problem you're trying to solve has a clearly defined element of difficulty, or if the task itself has obvious stages, it may be an excellent candidate for CL. Unfortunately, you can't really tell whether CL is appropriate until you try it and see.

As an example, let's say you want to train an agent to chase after a goal that will be moving around; perhaps you are making a simulation of a dog chasing squirrels.

We, the authors, are from Australia, and we don't have squirrels in Australia, so we are assuming that dogs chase them for completely harmless reasons. Also, these squirrels can't climb trees; after all, we've never seen one do it!

We could start the dog off against a squirrel that moves itself about a space and let the agent just figure it out, or we could use curriculum learning.

To start our curriculum learning dog agent, we'll begin by having our dog move toward a squirrel that just happens to be over two meters wide, making it easier to reach.

Again, we don't have squirrels, so we are pretty sure they can get this big.

Additionally, the squirrel doesn't move, making things even easier for our dog. The squirrel could then start shrinking, forcing the dog to move more precisely to reach it.

Once the dog has the hang of reaching a stationary squirrel-sized squirrel, we could start moving the goal. We could even make it so that the squirrel slowly ramps up in speed from very slow to squirrel-speedy, eventually reaching all the way up to hypersquirrel.

So, our curriculum here is we first taught our agent to move, then to follow, and then to follow against faster and faster targets, essentially teaching it how to chase.[1]

Often, curriculum learning is shown being used in very complex scenarios that make it feel almost a bit like a magic bullet. Some problems it is used for feel like they'd be next to impossible to achieve if it weren't for the magic wand of curriculum learning being waved over it, but the thing to remember is that at its core, it is a means of improving training, not doing the impossible. In general, any problem you can solve with curriculum learning could be solved without it, but it will usually just take a lot longer.

It turns out that just throwing more compute power at a problem can solve it, although it is a bit inelegant. Curriculum learning is at its best, in our opinion, when it is used to speed up or improve your agent's training, and in that role it may well be the future of training models.

---

1 Editor's note: this is a joke, which the Australians have informed us is hilarious.

A Curriculum Learning Scenario

Let's create and then solve a problem using curriculum learning. The problem we want to solve will be teaching an agent how to throw a ball at a target.

While throwing a ball is something that we as humans are intrinsically good at, it's actually a really complex task. You have to take into account distance, throw force, angles, and ballistic arcs if you want to hit something.

The agent will always start in the center of the room, but the target will be scattered randomly around the space. The agent will have to figure out how strongly to throw the ball, on which vertical angle to aim, and in which direction to face before throwing.

This begs the question of what our curriculum will be and how we will ramp up the difficulty of the scenario.

Like all reinforcement learning approaches, we'll have a reward structure that encourages the agent to improve by giving it a small reward for near misses.

This reward structure will be the basis of our curriculum. We will start with a very large radius that counts as "near miss," and over time, that radius will shrink, thus encouraging the agent to become more accurate to keep gaining rewards. Much like our earlier example (where the squirrel started off at an extremely large size, then was repeatedly shrunk down as the agent got the hang of what it was meant to do), the same applies here.

Our curriculum, then, will be broken up into several lessons of increasing difficulty where the distance the agent has to successfully throw near the target will be shrunk.

We can make as many levels of difficulty here as we feel we want or will need, but the core approach of our curriculum will be the same each time.

Building in Unity

Let's begin by building the environment in Unity. The finished environment will look something like Figure 8-1.

Unlike every other example we have created so far in the book, we will be doing something a little bit different with the simulation side in this one.

We won't be throwing our object and then waiting for the Unity physics engine to move it. Instead, we'll calculate the landing point instantly and use that calculated point.

Figure 8-1. The environment in our scene, ready for curriculum learning

Once the model is trained, we will make it so that we fling objects around because it will look cool, but not for training. We don't need to throw the object in a way we can see, because we can calculate whether it would have hit our target. Simulating the visual component of actual flinging would unnecessarily slow things down during training, and we don't need that. Once we train the model, we can add an appropriate visual that maps to what's happening under the hood.

The reason for this is because otherwise we'd have to add memory into our agent so that it learns to associate the throw action it took with the reward it gets a little while later. So we can do some testing and hook up heuristics (for manual human control, for testing, like we've done before), we will be visualizing the arc and the end point of the throw.

> The ML-Agents framework does support adding memory to your agents, but because it *massively* increases complexity and training time, we are shying away from it where possible.
>
> The math of ballistics (*https://oreil.ly/DU3M0*) is well understood, so we don't have to actually go through the steps; instead, we can mathematically model it.
>
> When we later make it so that our agent is throwing actual game objects, they will land exactly where the math says they will land. In situations where this isn't possible, memory will be needed, but not here.

Create a new Unity project, add the Unity ML-Agents package, and get an empty scene ready before continuing. Our project is, quite imaginatively, named "CurriculumLearning."

Creating the Ground

First up we will need some ground; for this environment, we will be creating a single plane:

1. Create a new plane in the Hierarchy.

2. Use the Inspector to name it "ground," and set its position to (0, 0, 0) and its scale to (20, 1, 20).

With our ground created, we're going to apply a color to it (as usual), so it is easier to visually distinguish the different pieces of the simulation from each other (for us, the human):

1. Create a new material, and give it a name like "GroundGrass_Mat."

2. Use the Inspector to set the material's albedo color to a nice green color.

3. Drag the material from the Project pane onto the ground plane in either the Hierarchy or the scene itself.

Now our ground has a material to help us tell everything apart. With that done, we'll move on to make our target. Don't forget to save your scene.

Creating the Target

For this part of the scenario, our target will just be a simple cube. During training, it will be used to extract a position. However, during inference, it will be shot by our agent and flung around based on the laws of physics, so we need to set up the target to cover both scenarios.

 The "inference phase" is when you're using a trained model. Your agent infers actions from the model, hence inference phase.

1. Create a new cube in the Hierarchy.

2. Use the Inspector to name it "Target," and set its position to (0, 0.5, 0).

3. Add a Rigidbody component to it.

Our target needs to have a Rigidbody for later, when we run our simulation in inference mode, as we want it to react to having something thrown at it. This will have no impact on the training, but we need to set it up now.

With that done, we can start work on our agent. Save the scene before continuing.

The Agent

Now it's time to build our agent: the basis of our agent is very straightforward, as it's going to be based on a cube (much like our target). What a surprise!

1. Create a new cube in the Hierarchy.

2. Name the cube "Agent," and set its position to (0, 0, 0).

   It's simple, but it's useful to have something to visualize here. However, there is one problem: it has a collider, because cubes by default have one. This will only get in the way when it comes time to spawn projectiles later during inference.

3. In the Inspector, remove the Box Collider component from the agent.

   Now, the whole reason to have a mesh for our agent is to help us visualize what it is doing, but not all aspects of a ballistic trajectory are easily shown.

   Because the agent is a cube, we can kind of see in which direction it's facing, but we will want another element to show the pitch of its aim.

4. Add a new cylinder in the Hierarchy.

5. Drag the cylinder underneath the agent (in the Hierarchy), so it is a child of the agent.

6. Use the Inspector to set the position of the cylinder to (0, 1, 0) and the rotation to (0.2, 1, 0.2).

7. In the Inspector, remove the Collider component from the cylinder.

This gives us a small cylinder on top of the box that we can use to visually judge elevation.

While this will hinge in a strange way and clip through the box, it is fine for this as we only need it for the heuristic stage, and it has no impact on the simulation either in training or in inference.

That's most of the scene done. Save it before we continue.

Building the Simulation

With the basic structure of the scene ready to go, it's time to start building out the simulation side of things. Specifically, as you hopefully guessed by now, we will be creating the actions, observations, and rewards our agent will need.

Making the Agent an Agent

While we may have the agent physically ready in the scene, it has no code; if nothing else, it will need to be made an Agent subclass.

1. Create a new C# file, and name it *Launcher.cs*.

2. Open *Launcher.cs* and replace it with the following:

```csharp
using System.Collections;
using System.Collections.Generic;
using UnityEngine;
using Unity.MLAgents;
using Unity.MLAgents.Actuators;
using Unity.MLAgents.Sensors;

public class Launcher : Agent
{
    public float elevationChangeSpeed = 45f;

    [Range(0, 90)]
    public float elevation = 0f;

    public float powerChangeSpeed = 5f;
    public float powerMax = 20f;
    public float power = 10f;

    public float maxTurnSpeed = 90f;

    public float hitRadius = 1f;
    public float rewardRadius = 20f;

    public float firingThreshold = 0.9f;

    public Transform target;
    public Transform pitchCylinder;
}
```

In the preceding code, we are declaring a number of variables that control the minimum and maximum values, along with some additional values we'll use later on for adjusting rewards. Finally, there are two references: one for the target and one for the cylinder. We'll need these elements shortly, so we might as well handle them now.

Each of these numeric variables relate to different elements of a ballistic throw:

- *Elevation* is the vertical throw angle; it is capped between 0 and 90, and *Elevation Change Speed* is how quickly the elevation angle can be changed.

- *Power* is how much force the throw is to be delivered with, and *Power Max* and *Power Change Speed* put a limit on the maximum power and how quickly the agent can ramp its power up and down.

- *Max Turn Speed* is how quickly the agent can rotate its facing; we don't need to track the facing itself because unlike elevation, we are just going to be throwing forward.

- *Hit Radius* and *Reward Radius* are used to give rewards, so we will speak more about them shortly.

- *Firing Threshold* caps how often the agent is allowed to throw a projectile.

Now we need to hook up these various pieces:

1. Drag *Launcher.cs* onto the agent object in the scene.

2. Drag the target object from the Hierarchy into the `target` field on the Launcher component in the Inspector.

3. Drag the cylinder object from the Hierarchy into the `cylinder` field on the Launcher component in the Inspector.

Lastly, we need to add and configure the other necessary components for our agent:

1. Select the agent from the Hierarchy.

2. In the Inspector, click the Add Component button and choose ML Agents → Decision Requester.

3. In the Inspector, click the Add Component button and choose ML Agents → Behavior Parameters.

4. In the Behavior Parameters component section, rename the behavior to "Launcher."

5. Set the Vector Observations Space Size to 9.

6. Set the number of Continuous Actions to 4.

7. In the Agent component, set the Max Step to 2000.

Now that our agent has its basics done, we can start adding in the actions. Don't forget to save everything.

Actions

The actions by our agent are quite simple. It will be able to rotate its facing (or yaw), rotate its vertical aim direction (or pitch), increase or decrease its throwing strength, and finally, throw or fire its projectile.

This means the actions buffer will have four values: *yaw change, pitch change, force change,* and *decision to fire* (or not).

Here we'll gate the value of the firing action based on a threshold value (firingThreshold), which essentially forces a continuous action into a discrete one.

A *discrete action* is something the agent can do that is either happening or not, as compared to a *continuous action*, which is a spectrum of possible values the agent responds to.

Unity supports using both continuous and discrete actions in a single agent; however, we are not doing that here.

It's extremely useful to be able to adjust this value on the fly so that we can make the model more aggressive just by tweaking how often it releases a projectile. Just know that you can mix and match continuous and discrete actions if you want.

Before we create our action code, we need to create a few helper functions:

1. Add the following code to the Launcher class:

```
public Vector3 LocalImpactPoint
{
    get
    {
        var range = (power * power *
          Mathf.Sin(2.0f * elevation * Mathf.Deg2Rad)) /
              -Physics.gravity.y;
        return new Vector3(0, 0, range);
    }
}
public static Vector2 GetDisplacement
    (float gravity, float speed, float angle, float time)
{
    float xDisp = speed * time *
      Mathf.Cos(2f * Mathf.Deg2Rad * angle);
    float yDisp = speed * time *
      Mathf.Sin(2f * Mathf.Deg2Rad * angle) - .5f * gravity * time * time;
    return new Vector2(xDisp, yDisp);
}
```

The first of these methods, LocalImpactPoint, will give us a point on the ground plane where the projectile, once loosed, will land. GetDisplacement, the second method, returns the specific point in space where the projectile is based on its current point in time based on the ballistic arc.

Because the physics of ballistic projection is so well understood, these two functions will give us the exact same results as if we used the Unity physics simulation directly, just without having to wait for all that pesky time to pass.

The GetDisplacement method is a slightly modified version of Freya Holmer's Trajectory class (*https://oreil.ly/5GuvT*) available under the MIT License. It's part of a library of mathematical functions you might find useful; for more details and license information, see the repository (*https://oreil.ly/NilGU*). We only needed this one function, so we didn't include everything, but it's a really cool library of code; you should check it out.

Next up we want to be able to visualize the ballistic arc so that we can check if it's working and so that it can help us when we are testing the system heuristically:

2. Add the following method to the Launcher.cs class:

```
private void OnDrawGizmos()
{
    var resolution = 100;
    var time = 10f;

    var increment = time / resolution;

    Gizmos.color = Color.yellow;

    for (int i = 0; i < resolution - 1; i++)
    {
        var t1 = increment * i;
        var t2 = increment * (i + 1);
        var displacement1 = Launcher.GetDisplacement
            (-Physics.gravity.y, power, elevation * Mathf.Deg2Rad, t1);
        var displacement2 = Launcher.GetDisplacement
            (-Physics.gravity.y, power, elevation * Mathf.Deg2Rad, t2);

        var linePoint1 = new Vector3(0, displacement1.y, displacement1.x);
        var linePoint2 = new Vector3(0, displacement2.y, displacement2.x);

        linePoint1 = transform.TransformPoint(linePoint1);
        linePoint2 = transform.TransformPoint(linePoint2);

        Gizmos.DrawLine(linePoint1, linePoint2);
    }

    var impactPoint = transform.TransformPoint(LocalImpactPoint);
```

```
        Gizmos.DrawSphere(impactPoint, 1.5f);
    }
```

This method will draw out the arc of the trajectory as well as a small sphere at the point where it will intersect with the ground plane.

This works by iterating through the imagined throw, drawing a new segment of a line after each iteration, and finally just drawing a sphere at the end point.

The OnDrawGizmos method is built into Unity itself, and is called on every frame. It can draw a variety of useful debug and assistance information (most of the helper visuals, like the translation arrows in the Scene view, are drawn using gizmos). These gizmos only appear in the Scene view and are never shown in the game or in builds.

Now we are ready to build out our actions.

3. Add the following method to the Launcher.cs class:

```
public override void OnActionReceived(ActionBuffers actions)
{
    int i = 0;
    var turnChange = actions.ContinuousActions[i++];
    var elevationChange = actions.ContinuousActions[i++];
    var powerChange = actions.ContinuousActions[i++];
    var shouldFire = actions.ContinuousActions[i++] > firingThreshold;

    transform.Rotate(0f, turnChange * maxTurnSpeed *
        Time.fixedDeltaTime, 0, Space.Self);

    elevation += elevationChange * elevationChangeSpeed *
        Time.fixedDeltaTime;
    elevation = Mathf.Clamp(elevation, 0f, 90);
    pitchCylinder.rotation = Quaternion.Euler(elevation, 0, 0);

    power += powerChange * powerChangeSpeed * Time.fixedDeltaTime;
    power = Mathf.Clamp(power, 0, powerMax);

    if (shouldFire)
    {
        var impactPoint = transform.TransformPoint(LocalImpactPoint);
        var impactDistanceToTarget = Vector3.Distance
            (impactPoint, target.position);
        var launcherDistanceToTarget = Vector3.Distance
            (transform.position, target.position);

        var reward = Mathf.Pow(1 - Mathf.Pow
            (Mathf.Clamp(impactDistanceToTarget, 0, rewardRadius) /
                rewardRadius, 2), 2);

        if (impactDistanceToTarget < hitRadius)
```

```
        {
            AddReward(10f);
        }

        AddReward(reward);
        EndEpisode();
    }
}
```

There is quite a lot going on in this method. First we get the actions out of the buffer, and we check if the firing action is above its threshold.

Then we start working our way through the actions, adjusting the pitch, yaw, and throw force based on the action values.

The real magic happens inside the `if (shouldFire)` section. It's where we grant rewards.

First up we determine how far away from the target our projectile will land and then we give a scaling reward based on that distance. The distance factor conforms to a sigmoid shape.

We decided to scale the reward like this because, during our testing, we found that it worked better than a linear reward. Although linear does still work, it just takes longer. A lot of reinforcement learning involves this kind of trial and error.

Next, if we are within the `hitRadius`, as in we directly hit the box, we give the agent a very large reward. Finally, we end the episode.

Because the agent only ends the episode and gets rewards once it releases a throw, sometimes it might take a little while before it gets any points.

You can wait this out, try adjusting the throw threshold, or cancel the training and restart it, hoping its random start is a bit more release-eager the next time around.

All options work: just pick the one you find the most appealing.

Observations

The next step is to make our agent perceive the world through observations. We mentioned earlier that there would be nine observations, so let's make them now. In this activity, we'll be providing all the observations via code within an overriden `CollectObservations`, and we won't be adding any sensors inside the Unity Editor.

Add the following method to *Launcher.cs*:

```
public override void CollectObservations(VectorSensor sensor)
{
    sensor.AddObservation(transform.InverseTransformDirection
        (target.position - transform.position));
    sensor.AddObservation(elevation);
    sensor.AddObservation(power);
    sensor.AddObservation(LocalImpactPoint);
    sensor.AddObservation(Vector3.Distance
        (transform.InverseTransformPoint(target.position), LocalImpactPoint));
}
```

The first three observations we add represent the *facing relative to the target*, the *elevation of the throw*, and the *force of the throw*.

The next two are the *position where it will hit if thrown* and the *distance of the hit point relative to the goal*.

So, if we pretend the agent is an arm, we are essentially telling the agent the setup of its arm and how far off it would be if it were to throw based on this current setup.

Even though this seems like a lot of information, it's not that different from how we (as humans) think about throwing things. We are pretty good at estimating the landing point of a throw before we make it, and we use this information to adjust.

Our agent is just given a bit of extra help in that their "estimate" will be perfect. However, as humans, we can also estimate travel time and can even adjust our throws to hit a moving target that compensates for movement—our agent would have no idea how to handle that.

Heuristic Controls for Humans

This is a pretty complex scenario, so we want to test it first to make sure we haven't made some sort of huge mistake before we start our agent off on training.

Let's hook up some heuristic controls so that we can do a quick test of the basics of the scenario.

 Also, it's fun to play with.

As with all our previous activities, we're doing this so that we, as humans, can control things during testing, and not for anything that will be used in training (unlike recording demonstrations for BC):

---

1. Add the following method to the Launcher class:

```csharp
private bool heuristicFired = false;
public override void Heuristic(in ActionBuffers actionsOut)
{
    var continuousActions = actionsOut.ContinuousActions;

    var input = new Vector3();

    var keysToVectors = new (KeyCode, Vector3)[]
    {
        (KeyCode.A, new Vector3( 0, -1,  0)),
        (KeyCode.D, new Vector3( 0,  1,  0)),
        (KeyCode.W, new Vector3(-1,  0,  0)),
        (KeyCode.S, new Vector3( 1,  0,  0)),
        (KeyCode.Q, new Vector3( 0,  0, -1)),
        (KeyCode.E, new Vector3( 0,  0,  1)),
    };

    foreach (var e in keysToVectors)
    {
        if (Input.GetKey(e.Item1))
        {
            input += e.Item2;
        }
    }

    var turnChange = input.y;
    var elevationChange = input.x;
    var powerChange = input.z;

    int i = 0;
    continuousActions[i++] = turnChange;
    continuousActions[i++] = elevationChange;
    continuousActions[i++] = powerChange;

    if (Input.GetKey(KeyCode.Space))
    {
        if (heuristicFired == false)
        {
            continuousActions[i++] = 1;
            heuristicFired = true;
        }
        else
        {
            continuousActions[i++] = 1;
        }
        continuousActions[i++] = 1;
    }
    else
```

```
        {
            heuristicFired = false;
            continuousActions[i++] = 0;
        }
    }
```

This looks more complex than it is. While there is a fair chunk of code here, all it does is detect whether any of the specified QWEASD keys are held down, and if so, it increments the relevant action (W and S for pitch, A and D for rotation, Q and E for power) in the actions buffer.

This gives us full control over the facing, the pitch, and the power of the throw.

Then, if the space bar is pressed, we also set the firing threshold to 1 to ensure that the agent will release its throw.

Let's give it a go and see how it all works.

2. Select the agent in the Hierarchy.

3. In the Inspector, find the Behavior Parameters component.

4. Change the Behavior Type property from Default to Heuristic.

5. Play the scene and try your best to hit the target.

Because we clearly made no mistakes and didn't have to fix anything (right?), we are good to move on to the curriculum side of things.

Creating the Curriculum

We said earlier that the curriculum will ramp up the difficulty by reducing the size of the radius that gives rewards, thus forcing the agent to get closer and closer to the target in order to keep getting rewards. This means we need to do several things: define a curriculum, determine the values that map to the difficulty, and make the environment reset be based on the curriculum values. Let's start with resetting the values first.

Resetting the Environment

We haven't actually done any of the work to reset the environment yet. As mentioned earlier, we want to change the environment based on the curriculum, but this isn't all we need to change.

There are three pieces in play in our simulation: the agent, the target, and the reward signal.

We want all three to be modified for each reset, but only one of these is to be impacted by the curriculum. This means we can reset most of the environment without caring at all about the curriculum itself.

Add the following method to the Launcher class:

```
public override void OnEpisodeBegin()
{
    power = Random.Range(0, powerMax);
    elevation = Random.Range(0f, 90f);
    transform.eulerAngles = new Vector3(0, Random.Range(0, 360f), 0);

    var spawn = Random.insideUnitCircle * 100f;
    target.position = new Vector3(spawn.x, 0, spawn.y);

    rewardRadius =
        Academy.Instance.EnvironmentParameters.GetWithDefault
        ("rewardRadius", 25f);
}
```

This will be called by the training when a new training episode starts. Now, it doesn't have a lot of code, but it does include all our curriculum learning-relevant code.

Here we randomize the initial facing, elevation, and power of the throw. Then we also pick a random point on our ground plane and move the target there. Finally, we set our rewardRadius, which is the element that determines how close we have to be to the target to get any rewards at all.

This final step is the magic one as far as curriculum learning is concerned. The rewardRadius value is going to be set based on the value it gets from the Academy environment variables, specifically from the environment variable rewardRadius, which we haven't set yet but will shortly. The environment variable here has a default value set, which in our case is going to be 25, and this is used in case the environment variable can't be found.

With that done, if you were to run the simulation as is and check the value of rewardRadius on the agent, you will see it's always 25, because we haven't actually created a configuration yet, so it's using the default. Still, that is our resetting done, so we can now move on to creating the curriculum side of things.

Curriculum Config

Our environment is correctly configured now to use the values the curriculum provides to ramp up difficulty, but we haven't actually created a curriculum yet, so let's fix that.

To create our curriculum, we will be using a section of the YAML config file we've not hugely explored: the environment parameters. Here is where we can configure our curriculum to slowly build up the difficulty of the scenario.

All our curriculum essentially boils down to an extra set of values we add to our YAML file for training:

1. Create a new YAML file, and name it "launcher.yaml".

2. Add the following text to the YAML file:

```
behaviors:
  Launcher:
    trainer_type: ppo
    hyperparameters:
      batch_size: 2048
      buffer_size: 20480
      learning_rate: 3.0e-4
      beta: 1.0e-2
      epsilon: 0.2
      lambd: 0.95
      num_epoch: 3
      learning_rate_schedule: linear
    network_settings:
      normalize: false
      hidden_units: 256
      memory_size: 256
      num_layers: 2
      vis_encode_type: simple
    reward_signals:
      extrinsic:
        gamma: 0.995
        strength: 1.0
    keep_checkpoints: 5
    max_steps: 10000000
    time_horizon: 120
    summary_freq: 10000
```

This is a mostly straightforward setup of using PPO to train an agent, and if we weren't showing off curriculum learning, this would be where we would stop.

Now we are going to add in the parts relevant for our curriculum.

3. Add the following to the bottom of the YAML file:

```
environment_parameters:
  rewardRadius:
    curriculum:
      - name: Lesson0
        completion_criteria:
          measure: reward
          behavior: Launcher
          signal_smoothing: true
          min_lesson_length: 100
          threshold: 1.0
          require_reset: true
        value: 100
```

Here we are declaring a new environment parameter called `rewardRadius`, which is the same one we were using earlier in our code, and then setting it up to be modified by a curriculum.

We only have a single lesson in our curriculum currently: we named it `Lesson0`, but we could call it anything we want. We will be adding some more in a moment, but for now let's take a look at this one alone.

First up, we have the `name`. As we mentioned before, we aren't going to explicitly refer to this by name, but logs will make use of it, so it's worth setting one.

Next we have two different properties, the `completion_criteria` and the `value`.

The `completion_criteria` is responsible for handling when the current lesson is finished and the next one can begin.

In particular, the two most important elements are the `measure` and the `min_lesson_length`.

The `measure` can be either `reward` or `progress`. Instead of taking cues from the reward signal for when to change, `progress` uses the ratio of steps taken to maximum steps.

In our case, we want the reward itself to be the process by which we get better, hence why we are using it.

Next, the `min_lesson_length` is a control to prevent essentially a lucky start from putting the agent into a harder environment than it is ready for.

The value of `100` means the agent has to perform a minimum of 100 iterations at or above the `threshold` value before the next lesson will begin.

Finally, the `value` property is where we can control the actual values that our environment parameter will get.

In our case, we are setting it to a value of `100`, which gives it a nice large initial region in which to acquire rewards.

Instead of a single value, you can set the `value` to have a minimum and maximum value range and have the curriculum pick randomly from that range.

You can even configure if you want it to be a uniform or Gaussian sampling of the values across the range.

Now with our first lesson done, it's time to finish off our curriculum.

4. Add the following to the curriculum section of the YAML file:

```
- name: Lesson1
  completion_criteria:
      measure: reward
      behavior: Launcher
      signal_smoothing: true
      min_lesson_length: 100
      threshold: 3.0
      require_reset: true
  value: 75
- name: Lesson2
  completion_criteria:
      measure: reward
      behavior: Launcher
      signal_smoothing: true
      min_lesson_length: 100
      threshold: 6.0
      require_reset: true
  value: 50
- name: Lesson3
  value: 25
```

We've added three more lessons to the model here, and each is basically the same as the first—except that the values for how far away the box will be upon reset have increased.

Environment parameters set in the YAML file here don't have to be used just for curriculum learning. Unity ML-Agents also uses them for any environment randomization. They are simply variables ML-Agents can access and then inject into the simulation, and you can use them however you want.

The only difference is that in the final lesson, we are setting the reward radius to be quite small and don't have completion criteria because we want the agent to be fully challenged. It's important to mention the lessons in the curriculum are all part of a list, which is why the little dash (-) is next to the named lesson in the YAML file. Without this, the lessons won't work.

If you are planning or need a lot of lessons in your curriculum, you can declare them as arrays instead of fully constructing each one like we have. We only have a few lessons, so writing them all out like we have is fine.

With our curriculum now written, we are finally ready to move on to training our model.

 We only modified a single variable, `rewardRadius`, but you can have as many variables modified as you want, or you can use them to fundamentally alter the environment far more than we are doing. Another good candidate for this scenario would be to also reduce the radius of the `hitDistance` so that the perfect hits have to get more accurate as well. We are trying to keep things simple so that you can see how to use curriculum learning, but the principle is the same regardless of how many variables you modify in the lessons. As with all things in ML, working out the right touch to use a technique is often more "guess and check" than we might like.

Training

With everything set up, it's time to get going with our training:

1. In the Inspector, in the Behavior Parameters component of the agent, change the Behavior Type from Heuristic to Default.

2. Run the following command:

   ```
   mlagents-learn config/launcher.yaml --run-id=launcher
   ```

3. Sit back, relax, and wait for the training to finish.

 There are a bunch of different variables you can tweak on the agent to adjust how the ballistic arc feels. You should play around with the settings in heuristic mode and see if you can find some you like. If you just want the ones we used, however, here they are:

- Elevation Change Speed = 45
- Power Change Speed = 5
- Power Max = 50
- Max Turn Speed = 90
- Hit Radius = 3
- Reward Radius = 100
- Firing Threshold = 0.9

In our case, we found that training took approximately an entire day, so definitely don't wait up for this one. But once it is done, you will have a nice neat little agent that is able to very accurately throw projectiles toward a target.

Running It

Because we are training the agent without actually lobbing virtual rocks around the scene, it would be quite dull to watch the trained agent.

If you add your freshly trained model into Unity and hook it up to the agent, you'll see it rotate and adjust its angle, but the only part of the process you'll actually be able to see is it changing the yellow line arc that we added as a gizmo.

What we want to see, though, is the agent adjusting pitch and yaw before throwing a virtual rock off into the distance; a yellow parabola just doesn't cut it.

Additionally, because the episode ends as soon as it launches a projectile, you wouldn't get to see the target actually being hit, even if it did spawn projectiles, because it would suddenly be teleported to another part of the world, so we'd also have to change that.

This chapter is already quite long, however, and to add in all the steps necessary to show off the agent actually doing this would make it truly enormous.

As such, we are going to skip over that side of things and, in the time-honored tradition of cooking shows everywhere, say, "Here's one we prepared earlier," and direct you to our website (*https://oreil.ly/1efRA*) if you want to check out the scene we created.

This is a scene not hugely different from the one we created for training, but designing it to make watching the agent play out its actions is a bit more exciting.

The core of this scene is similar to the previous training discussed earlier in this chapter. We have a target that will be placed randomly on the ground plane when the episode is reset. Unlike the training environment, we won't end the episode when the agent fires. Instead, we will spawn a projectile with the physical properties determined by the agent. This projectile then flies out from the agent, and hopefully hits the target.

Because it will likely hit the target a great deal of the time, we don't immediately reset the environment. Instead, we fling the target up in the air by applying an explosive force to the target. After three hits on the target, or if it falls off the edge of the world, we then reset the episode.

We picked three hits arbitrarily, as giving too many rewards can often muddy the waters a bit. Experiment to figure out what's best for each scenario you build. Trial and error! Likewise, in this context, "edge of the world" means falling below the y-axis that the plane sits on (in other words, the projectile didn't hit anything, and kept falling).

Now, we aren't limiting how many projectiles it can fire, so sometimes it will just be blasting them out, but we are deleting the projectiles if they fall off the edge of the world or if they hit something.

If you want to increase or decrease the number of projectiles it lets loose, the easiest parameter to tweak is the `firingThreshold`. Increasing it will make it less likely to spawn a projectile, and decreasing it makes it more likely.

We found `0.6` was a good threshold for firing lots of projectiles; try some different values and see what works for you.

Modifying the code to only support a single projectile isn't too difficult and is left as an exercise for the reader.

If you are curious, the majority of the changes are in *InferenceLauncher.cs* and *Projectile.cs*, which contain all the code for managing the agent and projectiles themselves.

From an agent perspective, however, it is identical to the original launcher code we wrote earlier. The only real difference is we don't have any rewards here, since they are unnecessary, so we took them out.

All other changes are visual tweaks. You can find these files in the book's resources, which are available on the book's special website.

Curriculum Versus Other Approaches

The entire point of curriculum training is to improve training; that is, to either increase the speed of training or the overall score of training (i.e., the quality), or both. If you were starting to design a scenario like the one we used as the initial lesson, the reward radius of 100 might feel pretty large, as it covers a significant portion of the ground. It's much more likely that designing something with a reward radius of, say, 25 will suit your needs better. In fact, we also created a training with a smaller radius of 25, and you can see the difference in Figure 8-2.

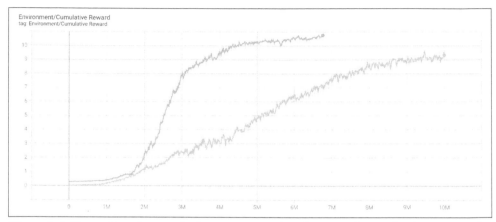

Figure 8-2. TensorBoard rewards showing curriculum learning (upper line) versus traditional training (lower line)

When you show the plots side by side, you can see that not only was the curriculum learning faster, it was also learning better; that is to say, it got a higher average reward and it got to that higher reward with fewer steps. We actually stopped training the curriculum learning at a bit under 7 million iterations because it was basically getting the maximum rewards possible, whereas even after 10 million iterations the traditional learning approach was only getting about 90% of the maximum rewards possible. It's worth pointing out that we also had some situations in which curriculum learning with the same setup was significantly slower (shown in Figure 8-3) than the traditional learning approach, although it did still get a higher overall score.

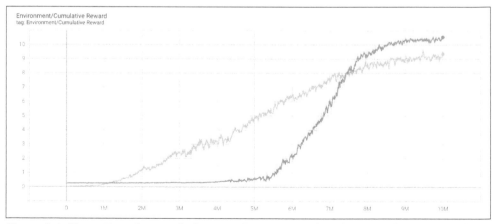

Figure 8-3. TensorBoard rewards showing slower curriculum learning (lower, curved line) versus traditional training (upper, straighter line)

Our guess on this is that when it was seeded with initial random weighting in the neural net, it coincidentally happened to result in a low firing threshold, making it hesitant to throw a projectile. We believe this to be the case because it wasn't struggling to learn once it worked out `Lesson0` in our curriculum; it just seemed to struggle to learn that first part. If you essentially shift the slower curriculum learning line over to the left, it's basically identical to the first, resulting in a nigh identical shape and the same total reward. So, it goes to show that curriculum learning isn't a magic bullet for every situation and those early stages of training do heavily influence the overall training, but even then it still has advantages in complex scenarios.

What's Next?

With that done, we've unpacked a simple curriculum learning example. You can use curriculum learning for almost any kind of problem in which it makes more sense to break it down into steps.

Unity's documentation comes with a couple of great curriculum learning examples, and if you want to explore this more, we've got some links to the best starting points in the book's online materials (*https://oreil.ly/9WmyP*).

CHAPTER 9

Cooperative Learning

In this chapter, we're going to take another step forward with our simulations and reinforcement learning, and create a simulation environment in which multiple agents must work together toward a common goal. These sorts of simulations involve *cooperative learning*, and agents will usually receive their rewards as a group, instead of individually—including agents that might not have contributed to the actions that resulted in the rewards.

In Unity ML-Agents, the preferred training algorithm and approach for cooperative learning is known as Multi-Agent POsthumous Credit Assignment (or MA-POCA, for short). MA-POCA involves the training of a centralized *critic* or *coach* for a group of agents. The MA-POCA approach means agents can still learn what they need to do, even though the group is the entity being rewarded.

 In cooperative learning environments, you can still give rewards to individual agents if you want. We'll briefly touch on this later. You can also use other algorithms, or just PPO like usual, but MA-POCA has specialized features to make cooperative learning better. You could *wire together* a collection of PPO-trained agents to get a similar result. We don't recommend it, though.

A Simulation for Cooperation

Let's build a simulation environment with a collection of agents that need to work together. This environment has a lot of pieces, so take your time, step through slowly, and take notes if you need to.

Our environment will involve three identical agents, and two of three different sizes of cube (totaling six cubes). The agents will need to work together to move the goals efficiently into a goal area, particularly the larger cubes, which will require the pushing force of more than one agent.

Building the Environment in Unity

Create a new Unity project, add the Unity ML-Agents package, and open a new scene in the editor. Our project is called "Coop."

With the project read, the first thing we need to do is make the physical elements of our cooperative learning simulation, so we need:

- A floor
- Some walls
- A goal area
- Some blocks, of differing sizes
- The agents

Let's do that now.

Assembling the floor and walls

Our walls and floor will be scaled cubes, as usual. In your scene, in the Unity Editor do the following:

1. Create a cube in the Hierarchy, name it "Floor," and scale it to (25, 0.35, 25), so it's a big square shape.
2. Create a new material in the Project pane, assign a color (ours is light brown), and assign this material to the floor.
3. Create four cubes in the Hierarchy, name them name them "Wall1," "Wall2," "Wall3," and "Wall4," and scale them to (25, 1, 0.25), so they're long enough to run the length of each side of the floor.
4. Rotate and position walls to be on either side of the floor, as shown in Figure 9-1.

Figure 9-1. The walls positioned on the floor

5. Create a new material in the Project pane, assign a color (ours is light blue), and assign this material to all four wall objects.

6. Create an empty GameObject in the Hierarchy, name it "Walls," or something similar, and drag the four wall objects under it, as children.

Your world should look like Figure 9-1 at this point. You're ready to continue after you save the scene.

Adding the goal

Next we need a goal area. The goal area, as we saw earlier, will be a section of the floor where the agents must push the blocks. It will be brightly colored so that we as humans can tell where it is when we're looking at it in Unity, and it will have a large Box Collider volume for the agents:

1. Create a new plane in the Hierarchy, name it "Goal," and scale it to (0.5, 1.16, 2.5).

2. Create a new material in the Project pane, and assign a bright, distracting color (ours is red). Assign this material to the goal.

Just a reminder that the agent in this case, doesn't have any sensors that might reveal the color of the goal to it. It learns where the goal is based on the information it gets from sensors, which will be covered shortly. It does not see the color. The color is for the humans watching.

3. Position the goal on the floor, against one edge of it, as shown in Figure 9-2.

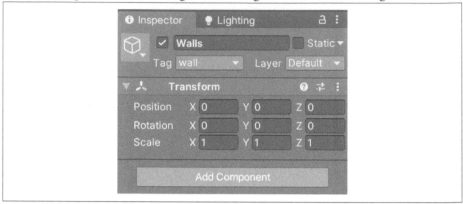

Figure 9-2. The goal area

4. In the goal's Inspector, click on the Edit Collider button and resize the goal's box collider so that it encompasses a large volume, as shown in Figure 9-3. This will be used to detect when the agent manages to push one of the blocks into the goal area.

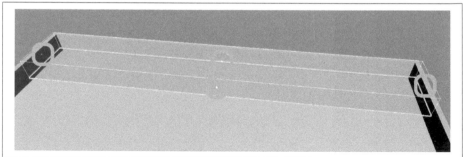

Figure 9-3. The goal's collider

5. Likewise, in the goal's Inspector, tick the Is Trigger button. We don't want the agent or the blocks to actually collide with the goal's volume, we just want to know they're in the goal's volume.

That's everything for the goal area. Yours should look like Figure 9-4 now. Save the scene before you continue.

Figure 9-4. The area with the goal in place

Blocks of differing sizes

Now we're going to create some blocks for the cooperative agents to push into the goal. We want to have three different types of blocks, as shown in Figure 9-5:

- Small blocks
- Medium blocks
- Large blocks

We'll create duplicates of each one we make so that there are two of each type. Each type will be worth a different reward amount, which the whole group of agents will receive when it pushes a block into the goal.

Additionally, via the physics system, some of the blocks will be heavier than others, which means the agents will need to work together to push them into the goals, and thus the group of agents will get a higher score.

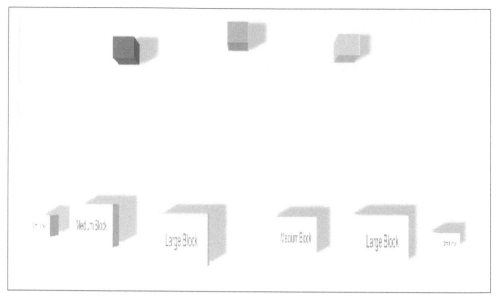

Figure 9-5. The three kinds of blocks

Follow these steps to create the blocks:

1. Add a new cube to the Hierarchy, and name it "Small Block 1" or something similar. We will leave it at the default scale.

2. Add a Rigidbody component to it, using the Add Component button in its Inspector.

3. Set up the Rigidbody component as per Figure 9-6.

Figure 9-6. The Rigidbody component on the small block

4. Duplicate Small Block 1, and create (and name) Small Block 2.

 You might notice that we've added a canvas, displaying some text, to our blocks. You could do this too, if you wanted. It's not connected to the ML components, and is just for human visibility.

5. Position them both in the scene, as shown in Figure 9-7.

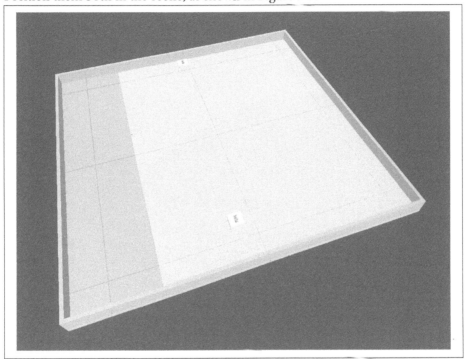

Figure 9-7. Both small blocks

6. Next, duplicate one of the small blocks, and name it "Medium Block 1."

7. Change the scale of Medium Block 1 to (2, 1, 2), so it's a bit bigger than Small Block 1.

8. Using the Inspector, set Medium Block 1's mass in the Rigidbody component to 100, making it quite heavy.

9. Duplicate Medium Block 1, and create (and name) Medium Block 2.

10. Position both of the medium blocks in the scene, as shown in Figure 9-8, alongside the small blocks.

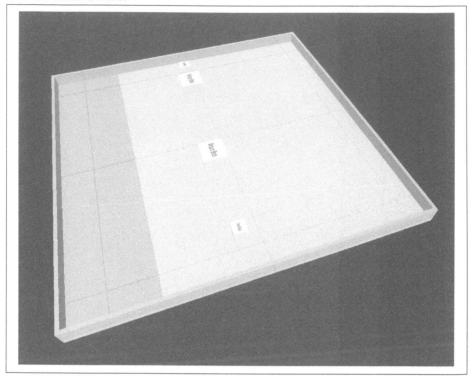

Figure 9-8. The medium blocks added

11. Finally, duplicate one of the medium blocks, and name it Large Block 1.

12. Change the scale of Large Block 1 to (2.5, 1, 2.5).

13. Using the Inspector, set Large Block 1's mass in the Rigidbody component to 150, so it's really heavy.

14. As with the small and medium blocks, duplicate Large Block 1, and create and name Large Block 2.

15. Position the two large blocks in the scene, as shown in Figure 9-9, alongside all the other blocks.

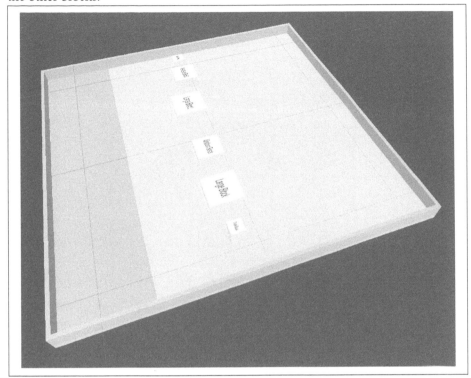

Figure 9-9. The large blocks added

That's it for the blocks for now—we'll come back to them in a bit to add some code. Save the scene.

The agents

The agents are quite simple, and all their cooperative behavior comes from the script we'll write shortly, rather than anything special in their editor setup:

1. Create a new cube in the Hierarchy, and rename it "Agent 1." Leave it at the default scale.

2. Add a Rigidbody component to it, with the settings as shown in Figure 9-10.

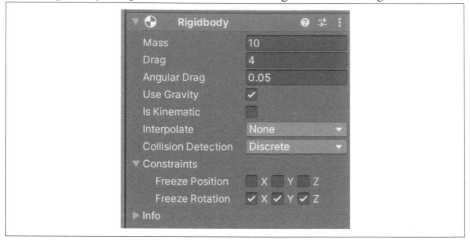

Figure 9-10. The agent's Rigidbody component

3. Duplicate it twice, and rename the two new copies Agent 2 and Agent 3.

4. Create three new materials—one for each agent—of differing colors, and assign them to the agents.

5. Position them similarly to ours, as shown in Figure 9-11.

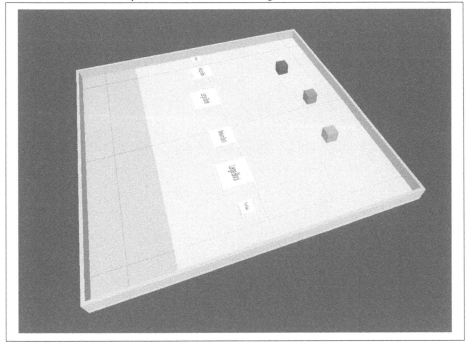

Figure 9-11. The three agents

That's it for now, for the agents. We'll be adding some code next, and after that we'll need to come back to the Unity scene to implement some more things. Don't forget to save the scene.

Coding the Agents

With the majority of the scene constructed, it's time to write the code for the agent. The code for this agent is actually quite simple, since a lot of the logic is moved elsewhere—we'll get to that soon.

For the agent, we'll only need to implement the following methods:

- `Initialize()`
- `MoveAgent()`
- `OnActionReceived()`

Let's get going:

1. Make a new C# script asset in the Project pane, and name it "Cooperative Block Pusher" or something similar.

2. Open the new script in your code editor, delete the entirety of the boilerplate, and add the following imports:

```
using UnityEngine;
using Unity.MLAgents;
using Unity.MLAgents.Actuators;
```

3. Next, implement the skeleton of the class, making sure it descends from `Agent`:

```
public class CoopBlockPusher : Agent
{

}
```

4. Add a member variable to hold a reference to the agent's `Rigidbody`:

```
private Rigidbody agentRigidbody;
```

5. Override the agent's `Initialize()` function to get a handle on that `Rigidbody`:

```
public override void Initialize() {
    agentRigidbody = GetComponent<Rigidbody>();
}
```

6. Next, create a `MoveAgent()` method:

```
public void MoveAgent(ActionSegment<int> act) {

}
```

This method takes an array as a parameter (`act`), using the ML-Agents `Action Segment` data structure. This will be called in the `OnActionReceived()` that we'll override shortly, passing in the array of discrete actions to move the agent.

 There will only be one specific discrete action that comes through each time, so we're only ever looking at the first entry of the array. This agent will have seven different possible actions (doing nothing, rotating one way, rotating the other way, going forward, going backward, going left, and going right).

7. Now, inside the new method, zero some temporary variables for a direction and a rotation:

```
var direction = Vector3.zero;
var rotation = Vector3.zero;
```

8. Get a handle on the first (and only) entry of the array we're working with, which represents the specific action of the moment:

```
var action = act[0];
```

9. Now, `switch` on that `action`:

```
switch(action) {
    case 1:
        direction = transform.forward * 1f;
        break;
    case 2:
        direction = transform.forward * -1f;
        break;
    case 3:
        rotation = transform.up * 1f;
        break;
    case 4:
        rotation = transform.up * -1f;
        break;
    case 5:
        direction = transform.right * -0.75f;
        break;
    case 6:
        direction = transform.right * 0.75f;
        break;
}
```

This `switch` statement sets one of the temporary variables for either rotation or direction, depending on which action is passed through.

It's entirely arbitrary which action maps to which actual action of the agent. We've just decided that in advance, and stuck to it. The machine learning system learns what's applied to what, and deals with it.

10. Next, actually implement whatever action has been set by rotating the agent's `transform`, and applying a force to the agent's `Rigidbody`, for the rotation and direction, respectively:

```
transform.Rotate(rotation, Time.fixedDeltaTime * 200f);
agentRigidbody.AddForce(direction * 3, ForceMode.VelocityChange);
```

11. That's all for the `MoveAgent()` method, so now we turn to `OnActionReceived()`, where we actually call it:

```
public override void OnActionReceived(ActionBuffers actionBuffers) {
    MoveAgent(actionBuffers.DiscreteActions);
}
```

All this does is take the discrete component of the `ActionBuffers` it receives and pass it to the separate `MoveAgent()` method we wrote a moment ago.

 We could have just put the code that we wrote in `MoveAgent()` in `OnActionReceived()` instead, but because `OnActionReceived()` is technically about handling actions and not specifically about movement, it's cleaner to call our `MoveAgent()` method even though the only possible actions are related to movement.

That's everything for our agent's code. Save the script, and return to the Unity Editor.

Coding the Environment Manager

Now we need to make a script that will be responsible for the environment itself. This script will do some of the heavy lifting to allow us to have cooperative agents:

1. Create a new C# script asset in the Project pane, and name it "CooperativeBlock-PusherEnvironment" or something similar.

2. Open the new script and delete the boilerplate.

3. Add the following imports:

   ```
   using System.Collections;
   using System.Collections.Generic;
   using Unity.MLAgents;
   using UnityEngine;
   ```

4. Create a class for everything else to go in:

   ```
   public class CoopBlockPusherEnvironment : MonoBehaviour {

   }
   ```

   This class does not need to be a child of `Agent`, and instead can just be a child of the default Unity `MonoBehaviour`.

5. Make a class to store all the agents that will be working together, as well as their starting positions:

   ```
   [System.Serializable]
   public class Agents {
       public CoopBlockPusher Agent;

       [HideInInspector]
       public Vector3 StartingPosition;

       [HideInInspector]
       public Quaternion StartingRotation;
   ```

```
    [HideInInspector]
    public Rigidbody RigidBody;
}
```

6. Now create a similar class for the blocks that they'll be pushing into the goal:

```
[System.Serializable]
public class Blocks {
    public Transform BlockTransform;

    [HideInInspector]
    public Vector3 StartingPosition;

    [HideInInspector]
    public Quaternion StartingRotation;

    [HideInInspector]
    public Rigidbody RigidBody;
}
```

7. We need to create a nice `int`, to store the max steps we want the environment to take, so we can easily configure it from the editor:

```
[Header("Max Environment Steps")] public int MaxEnvironmentSteps = 25000;
```

8. We also need to create a collection of member variables, to store handles to useful things like the ground, the overall area, the goal, something to check when we need to reset, and the count of blocks remaining undelivered to the goal:

```
[HideInInspector]
public Bounds areaBounds;

// The ground (we use this to spawn the things that need to be placed)
public GameObject ground;

public GameObject area;

public GameObject goal;

private int resetTimer;

// blocks left
private int blocksLeft;
```

9. And we need to create two lists, one of `Agents` and one of `Blocks`, using the classes we wrote a moment ago:

```
// List of all the agents
public List<Agents> ListOfAgents = new List<Agents>();

// List of all blocks
public List<Blocks> ListOfBlocks = new List<Blocks>();
```

10. Finally, we create a `SimpleMultiAgentGroup`, which we'll use to group the agents so that they can work together:

    ```
    private SimpleMultiAgentGroup agentGroup;
    ```

    More on the `SimpleMultiAgentGroup` shortly.

11. Next, we need to implement a `Start()` method, which we'll use to set everything up when a simulation is about to begin:

    ```
    void Start() {

    }
    ```

12. Inside `Start()`, we'll do all the necessary bits and pieces to make sure things are ready to go:

    - Get a handle on the ground's bounds.

    - Iterate through the list of `Blocks` (all the blocks in the scene) and store their starting position and rotation and their `Rigidbody`.

    - Initialize a new `SimpleMultiAgentGroup`.

    - Iterate through the `Agents` (all the agents in the scene) and store their starting position and rotation and their `Rigidbody`, and then call `RegisterAgent()` on the `SimpleMultiAgentGroup` we created, notifying it of the existence of each agent we want to cooperate together.

    - Call `ResetScene()`, which we'll be writing in a moment.

13. Inside `Start()`, add this code to do all the aforementioned things:

    ```
    areaBounds = ground.GetComponent<Collider>().bounds;

    foreach (var item in ListOfBlocks) {
        item.StartingPosition = item.BlockTransform.transform.position;
        item.StartingRotation = item.BlockTransform.rotation;
        item.RigidBody = item.BlockTransform.GetComponent<Rigidbody>();
    }

    agentGroup = new SimpleMultiAgentGroup();

    foreach (var item in ListOfAgents) {
        item.StartingPosition = item.Agent.transform.position;
        item.StartingRotation = item.Agent.transform.rotation;
        item.RigidBody = item.Agent.GetComponent<Rigidbody>();
        agentGroup.RegisterAgent(item.Agent);
    }

    ResetScene();
    ```

14. Next, we'll implement `FixedUpdate()`, which gets called regularly by Unity:

```
void FixedUpdate() {
    resetTimer += 1;
    if(resetTimer >= MaxEnvironmentSteps && MaxEnvironmentSteps > 0) {
        agentGroup.GroupEpisodeInterrupted();
        ResetScene();
    }

    agentGroup.AddGroupReward(-0.5f / MaxEnvironmentSteps);
}
```

Here, we increment the reset timer by 1 every time, and check if the reset timer is greater than or equal to the maximum environment steps (and that the maximum environment steps is above 0), and if so we interrupt the group of agents by calling `GroupEpisodeInterrupted()` on the agent group and call `ResetScene()`.

If the maximum environment steps had not been reached, all we would have to do is call `AddGroupReward()` on the agent group, assigning a group penalty of `-0.5` divided by the maximum environment steps to penalize it for existing. This will, hopefully, contribute to making sure the agents do their task as quickly as possible.

The `SimpleMultiAgentGroup` coordinates a collection of agents, and allows agents to work together to maximize a reward that is given to the whole group. The usual rewarding and ending of episodes takes place on the `SimpleMulti AgentGroup`, instead of on individual agents.

The `SimpleMultiAgentGroup` is a feature of Unity ML-Agent's implementation of MA-POCA, and thus it also only works when you're using MA-POCA to train the agents.

15. Now we're going to make a rather large `GetRandomSpawnPos()` method, which we'll use to randomly position the blocks and the agents in the environment, as needed:

```
public Vector3 GetRandomSpawnPos()
    {
        Bounds floorBounds = ground.GetComponent<Collider>().bounds;
        Bounds goalBounds = goal.GetComponent<Collider>().bounds;

        // Stores the point on the floor that we'll end up returning
        Vector3 pointOnFloor;

        // Start a timer so we have a way
        // to know if we're taking too long
        var watchdogTimer = System.Diagnostics.Stopwatch.StartNew();
```

```
    do
    {
        if (watchdogTimer.ElapsedMilliseconds > 30)
        {
            // This is taking too long; throw an exception to bail
            // out, avoiding an infinite loop that hangs Unity!
            throw new System.TimeoutException
                ("Took too long to find a point on the floor!");
        }

        // Pick a point that's somewhere on the top face of the floor
        pointOnFloor = new Vector3(
            Random.Range(floorBounds.min.x, floorBounds.max.x),
            floorBounds.max.y,
            Random.Range(floorBounds.min.z, floorBounds.max.z)
        );

        // Try again if this point is inside the goal bounds
    } while (goalBounds.Contains(pointOnFloor));

    // All done, return the value!
    return pointOnFloor;
}
```

16. Next, we'll make a `ResetBlock()` method, which takes a `Blocks` type (which we made earlier) and gives it a random spawn position (using that handy `GetRandomSpawnPos()` method we wrote a moment ago) and zeroes the velocity and angular velocity:

```
void ResetBlock(Blocks block) {
    block.BlockTransform.position = GetRandomSpawnPos();

    block.RigidBody.velocity = Vector3.zero;

    block.RigidBody.angularVelocity = Vector3.zero;
}
```

17. Now we need a method that can be used to log when an agent or group of agents has successfully delivered a block to the goal:

```
public void Scored(Collider collider, float score) {
    blocksLeft--;

    // check if it's done
    bool done = blocksLeft == 0;

    collider.gameObject.SetActive(false);

    agentGroup.AddGroupReward(score);
```

```
    if (done) {
        // reset everything
        agentGroup.EndGroupEpisode();
        ResetScene();
    }
}
```

This might look slightly mysterious, but all that's happening is that our `Scored()` method takes a `Collider`, and a `float` (representing a score), and because this method is only being called if a block has definitely been delivered to the goal, it:

- Decrements the count of remaining blocks by 1

- Checks if there are 0 blocks left, and if so, sets a bool named `done` to `true`

- Deactivates the game object belonging to the `Collider` that was passed in (in other words, it gets rid of the block that was pushed into the goal)

- Adds a reward to the `SimpleMultiAgentGroup`, based on the score being passed in

- Then checks if the `done` bool is `true`, and if it is, it calls `EndGroupEpisode()` on the `SimpleMultiAgentGroup`, and then calls `ResetScene()`

18. Next, we'll create a quick helper method to return a random rotation:

```
Quaternion GetRandomRot() {
    return Quaternion.Euler(0, Random.Range(0.0f, 360.0f), 0);
}
```

19. And, for the environment script, we'll write the oft-called `ResetScene()`:

```
public void ResetScene() {
    resetTimer = 0;

    var rotation = Random.Range(0,4);
    var rotationAngle = rotation * 90f;
    area.transform.Rotate(new Vector3(0f, rotationAngle, 0f));

    // first reset all the agents
    foreach (var item in ListOfAgents) {
        var pos = GetRandomSpawnPos();
        var rot = GetRandomRot();

        item.Agent.transform.SetPositionAndRotation(pos,rot);
        item.RigidBody.velocity = Vector3.zero;
        item.RigidBody.angularVelocity = Vector3.zero;
    }

    // next, reset all the blocks
    foreach (var item in ListOfBlocks) {
        var pos = GetRandomSpawnPos();
        var rot = GetRandomRot();
```

```
        item.BlockTransform.transform.SetPositionAndRotation(pos,rot);
        item.RigidBody.velocity = Vector3.zero;
        item.RigidBody.angularVelocity = Vector3.zero;
        item.BlockTransform.gameObject.SetActive(true);
    }

    blocksLeft = ListOfBlocks.Count;
}
```

This function:

- Sets the `resetTimer` back to 0.

- Then rotates the whole area, so the goal is not always in the same side.

- Iterates through all the `Agents` in the `ListOfAgents`, gives them a random location and a random rotation using our helper methods, and zeroes their velocity and angular velocity.

- Iterates through all the `Blocks` in the `ListOfBlocks`, gives them a random location and a random rotation using our helper methods, zeroes their velocity and angular velocity, and sets them to active.

 We set each of the blocks to active because they might be coming back from inactive after a reset, as the simulation may have been running, and some of the blocks may have been pushed into the goal (which, per the earlier code, means they get set to inactive).

That's it for the environment manager script. Save it and return to Unity.

Coding the Blocks

The last bit of coding we need to do is for the blocks themselves:

1. Make a new C# script asset in the Project pane, and name it "GoalScore" or something similar.

2. Open the script in your code editor and delete the boilerplate.

3. Add the following imports:

   ```
   using System.Collections;
   using System.Collections.Generic;
   using UnityEngine;
   using UnityEngine.Events;
   ```

4. Implement a class named `GoalScore`, a child of Unity's default `MonoBehaviour`:

```
public class GoalScore : MonoBehaviour
{

}
```

5. Inside, add some member variables to store the specific Unity tag we want to
   detect, the value of pushing the specific block this script will be attached to into
   the goal, and the block's `Collider`:

```
public string tagToDetect = "goal"; //collider tag to detect

public float GoalValue = 1;

private Collider blockCollider;
```

6. Next, implement the class `TriggerEvent`, as follows, inside the `GoalScore` class:

```
[System.Serializable]
public class TriggerEvent : UnityEvent<Collider, float>
{
}
```

This class is required to use Unity's event system the way we'll be using it. More
on this in a moment.

7. After the `TriggerEvent` class, but still inside the `GoalScore` class, add the following trigger callbacks:

```
[Header("Trigger Callbacks")]
public TriggerEvent onTriggerEnterEvent = new TriggerEvent();
public TriggerEvent onTriggerStayEvent = new TriggerEvent();
public TriggerEvent onTriggerExitEvent = new TriggerEvent();
```

These represent the events of something entering the collider of the object in
question, staying in it, and exiting it.

8. Now, create the functions that are called for each of these:

```
private void OnTriggerEnter(Collider col)
{
    if (col.CompareTag(tagToDetect))
    {
        onTriggerEnterEvent.Invoke(blockCollider, GoalValue);
    }
}

private void OnTriggerStay(Collider col)
{
    if (col.CompareTag(tagToDetect))
    {
        onTriggerStayEvent.Invoke(blockCollider, GoalValue);
    }
}
```

```
private void OnTriggerExit(Collider col)
{
    if (col.CompareTag(tagToDetect))
    {
        onTriggerExitEvent.Invoke(blockCollider, GoalValue);
    }
}
```

Each of these maps to one of the trigger callbacks we created, taking a Collider, and if that Collider has the tag we want to look for (which is defined in one of the member variables we made earlier), we trigger the callback event, passing the Collider and GoalValue (which is one of the member variables we made a moment ago).

Save the script, and jump back to Unity.

Finalizing the Environment and Agents

We've made three scripts, and now we need to hook them up.

Start by doing the following:

1. Drag the Agent script from the Project pane onto each agent in the Hierarchy (three agents total).

2. Drag the Environment script from the Project pane onto the environment (the parent object) in the Hierarchy.

3. And drag the GoalScore script from the Project pane onto each block in the Hierarchy (six blocks in total).

Next, we need to configure everything. We'll start with the agents. Do the following for each agent in the Hierarchy:

1. Select the agent, and use the Inspector to add a Behavior Parameters component.

2. Configure the Behavior Parameters component as shown in Figure 9-12.

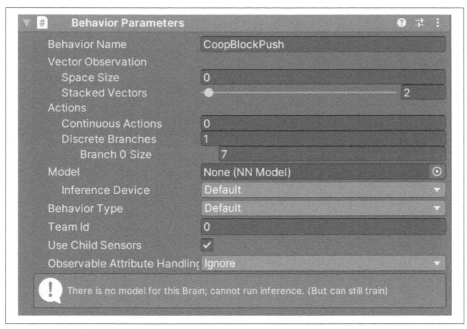

Figure 9-12. The configured Behavior Parameters component

3. Use the Inspector to add a Decision Requester component to the agent, leaving its settings at the defaults.

4. Use the Inspector to add a Rigidbody Sensor component to the Agent, taking care to assign the root body to be the agent's Rigidbody component, and the virtual root to be the agent itself, ticking the boxes as shown in Figure 9-13.

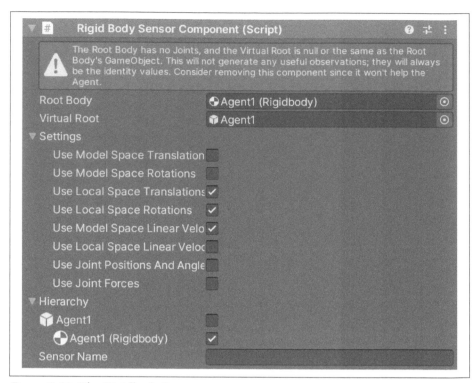

Figure 9-13. The Rigidbody Sensor component

5. Next, add an empty child object to the agent in the Hierarchy, and name it "Grid Sensor" or something similar.

6. Select the Grid Sensor child of the agent in the Hierarchy, and use the Add Component button in its Inspector to add a Grid Sensor component.

7. Use the Inspector to configure the Grid Sensor component as shown in Figure 9-14.

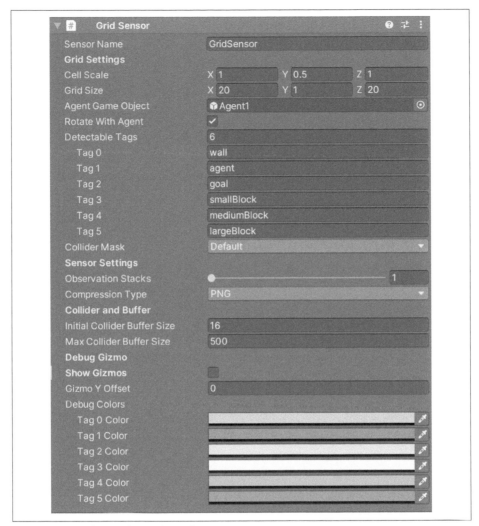

Figure 9-14. The configured Grid Sensor component

The Grid Sensor component creates a grid sensor. A grid sensor is an incredibly flexible sensor that creates a grid shape around an agent, and based on what kind of objects (defined by tags) that it's set up to look for, it can detect the presence of objects in specific cells in a top-down 2D view around the agent. An example of the grid sensor attached to the selected agent is shown in Figure 9-15.

Eidos, the video game development studio, contributed the Grid Sensor component to the Unity ML-Agents project (*https://oreil.ly/ryu3F*). The grid sensors combine the generality of data extraction from raycasts with the computational efficiency of convolutional neural networks (CNNs—neural networks that work with images). The grid sensor collects data from your simulations by querying the physics properties and then structures the data into a "height x width x channel" matrix. This matrix is analogous to an image in many ways, and can be fed into a CNN. Another benefit is that the grid can have a lower resolution than an actual image, which can improve training times.

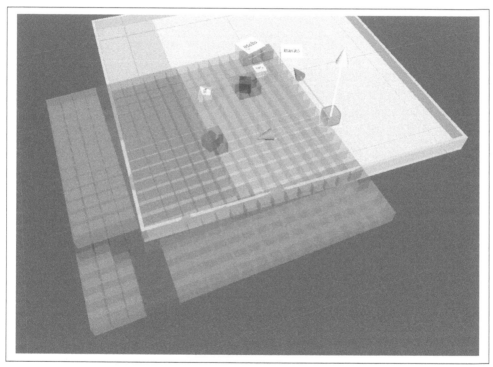

Figure 9-15. The Grid Sensor component in action

Next, do the following for each of the blocks in the Hierarchy:

1. Select the block, and use the Inspector to set the Goal Score component (the script we wrote and dragged onto it a moment ago) to detect things tagged with "goal."

2. Set the appropriate goal value: 1 for small blocks, 2 for medium blocks, and 3 for large blocks.

3. Next, click the + button below the Trigger Callbacks section, and set the drop-down to Runtime Only, as shown in Figure 9-16.

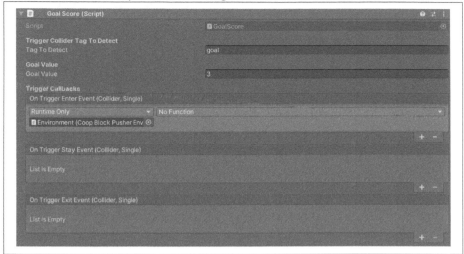

Figure 9-16. Setting to Runtime Only

4. Drag the Environment object from the Hierarchy into the field below the drop-down containing Runtime Only, and then set the drop-down to the right to point to the Scored() method in the environment script we created earlier, as shown in Figure 9-17.

Figure 9-17. Choosing the Scored() method

Next, do the following for the environment parent object:

1. Select the environment parent object in the Hierarchy.

2. In its Inspector, under the Environment component (which belongs to the script we wrote and dragged on), set Max Environment Steps to 5000.

3. Then drag the floor, environment parent object, and goal into the appropriate fields, as shown in Figure 9-18.

Figure 9-18. Configuring the environment

4. Update the List of Agents shown in the component to have 3, and drag in each of the three agents, as shown in Figure 9-19.

Figure 9-19. The list of agents

5. Update the List of Blocks shown in the component to have 6, and drag in each of the six blocks, as shown in Figure 9-20.

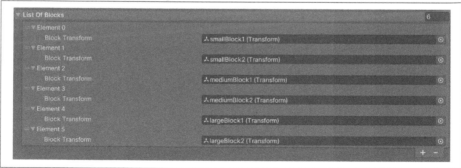

Figure 9-20. The list of blocks

That's it! Save the scene.

Training for Cooperation

It's almost time to train our cooperative environment. As usual, first we need to create a YAML file:

```
behaviors:
  CoopBlockPush:
```

```
trainer_type: poca
hyperparameters:
  batch_size: 1024
  buffer_size: 10240
  learning_rate: 0.0003
  beta: 0.01
  epsilon: 0.2
  lambd: 0.95
  num_epoch: 3
  learning_rate_schedule: constant
network_settings:
  normalize: false
  hidden_units: 256
  num_layers: 2
  vis_encode_type: simple
reward_signals:
  extrinsic:
    gamma: 0.99
    strength: 1.0
keep_checkpoints: 5
max_steps: 15000000
time_horizon: 64
summary_freq: 60000
```

Now, save it somewhere! To run the training, fire up your terminal and run the following:

```
mlagents-learn CoopBlockPush.yaml --run-id=BlockCoop1
```

And that's it. Your training might take a few hours—on our testing MacBook Pro, it took about 18 hours to get somewhere.

Grab the resulting *.onnx* file, drag it into the Project pane in Unity, then assign it to the appropriate field in all your agents, as shown in Figure 9-21, and run your simulation to watch your little agent friends work together to push blocks.

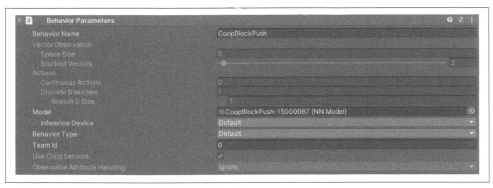

Figure 9-21. The model is attached to the agents

Cooperative Agents or One Big Agent

It's sometimes difficult to conceptualize when you might want to take a cooperative multi-agent approach in which each agent is genuinely separate, but they are rewarded and guided through the systems discussed in this chapter, versus making a single agent that manifests in the simulation as an assortment of entities.

In other words, you could replicate the behavior of the simulation you built here by making a single "giant" agent that has three cube entities in the world, each of which can move independently.

It's usually easier to make separate agents, because each agent will have a much simpler model which will result in more reliable training, and you'll converge on a solution much more quickly. The neural network stored in the model for each agent will be a lot smaller than the theoretical giant agent, and the behaviors will be more predictable and, likely, reliable. But yes, you could make a giant agent.

One agent "cooperating" with other agents is no different from a lone agent in that no communication can happen between the brains of different agents (they cannot share intent, and information about the state of other agents can only come from external observations of them). Other agents existing in the simulation simply act as another part of the environment that this agent must consider and observe—albeit a potentially chaotic one.

The problem space for a collection of legitimately individual but cooperatively learning agents, instead of limbs of a giant agent, is much smaller than one agent trying to deal with the exponential interactions that can happen between the entities under its control. Thus, it's usually better to make a cooperative collection of agents if you need to.

If you want to explore cooperative agents in more detail, check out Unity's fantastic Dodgeball environment (*https://oreil.ly/BETZi*).

CHAPTER 10

Using Cameras in Simulations

It's time to get some real vision. And we don't mean the shiny robot man, we mean cameras (and lights, and action). In this chapter, we're going to look at how you can use a camera that sees the world of your simulation as an observation for your agents.

No longer will your observations be bound by feeding your agent numbers from code, and from sensors! Instead, you'll be bound by what the camera you choose to set up can see. (Which, if we're getting technical, are also numbers, but we digress.)

Observations and Camera Sensors

So far, all the observations we've been using are basically numbers—usually `Vector3`s —that we've been providing to the agent via our `CollectObservations` method, or collecting by using sensors of some kind, looking into our environment to measure things, or using grid-based observations for a 2D spatial representation of things.

We've either implemented `CollectObservations()` in our `Agent`, and passed in vectors, and other forms of numbers, or we've added components to the agent in the Unity Editor, which have—under the hood—created raycasts (perfect lasers to measure distances and what they hit) and automatically passed the numbers arising from those into the ML-Agents system.

There's another way to provide observations to our agent: by using `CameraSensor` and `RenderTextureSensor`. These allow us to pass image information, in the form of a 3D Tensor, to the convolutional neural network (CNN) of the agent policy. So, basically, more numbers. But from our perspective, it's a *picture*.

Convolutional neural network (*https://oreil.ly/kPfSW*) is often used as a term to describe any form of neural network that deals with images.

Using images as observations allows an agent to learn from spatial regularities in the images it receives in order to form a policy.

You can combine visual observations with the vector observations you've already used. We'll get to that later.

Broadly speaking, adding a CameraSensor to your agents is quite straightforward, and as with many things in Unity, it involves adding a component in the Inspector.

We'll be working through a full example in this chapter momentarily, but the typical steps are as follows:

1. In the Unity Editor, locate your agent in the Hierarchy and select it.
2. In the Inspector for the agent, use the Add Component button to add a Camera Sensor component.
3. In the Camera Sensor component that gets added, assign the camera (from any camera in the Hierarchy) to the Camera field.
4. You can also name the camera sensor, and specify a width and height and whether you want the image the neural network is working with to be grayscale or not.

Every sensor component (whether it's a camera or otherwise) must have a unique sensor name, on a per-agent basis.

We'll come back to the camera sensor shortly, and discuss how to connect a camera to it.

Visual observations are useful when it's difficult to numerically represent the state you want your agent to work with using vectors, but they can make your agent slower to train.

Building a Camera-Only Agent

To demonstrate the use of a camera sensor, our activity for this chapter is the creation of a very simple simulation that solely relies on a camera for its observations.

The simulation we're going to build is a cube agent (surprising nobody, dear reader, it exists in a void) that must keep a sphere (also known as a ball, but not an agent ball) balanced on its top.

First, as you've done a few times, create a new empty Unity project and import the ML-Agents package. Then, in a new scene, do the following:

1. Create a new cube in the Hierarchy, and name it "Agent."

2. Create a new sphere in the Hierarchy, and name it "Ball."

3. Set the scale of the agent cube to (5, 5, 5).

4. Move the ball sphere above the agent, as shown in Figure 10-1. An approximate placement is fine; you just need the ball floating in the space above the cube somewhere.

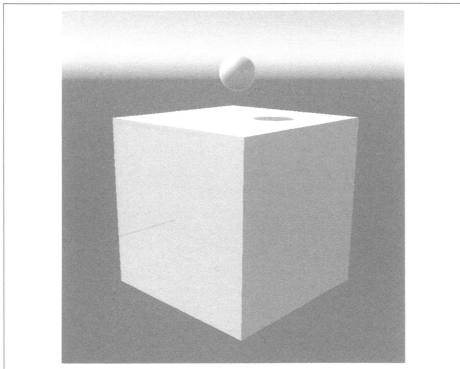

Figure 10-1. The ball above the cube

5. Next, create a new empty object in the Hierarchy, name it something like "Balancing Ball," and drag the agent and the ball under it, as children. This represents the entire simulation environment.

That's it for now. We promise we're going somewhere with this.

Coding the Camera-Only Agent

Now we're going to write the code that drives our simple agent. To get coding, as usual create a new script asset as a component on the agent. We named ours "BalancingBallAgent." Double-click the new asset file for your code in the Project view to open it in your code editor.

Once you've got the file open in your code editor, follow these steps:

1. Add the following imports so that you get all the bits of Unity you need:

```
using UnityEngine;
using Unity.MLAgents;
using Unity.MLAgents.Actuators;
using Unity.MLAgents.Sensors;
using Random = UnityEngine.Random;
```

We obviously need a bunch of stuff from ML-Agents, but we also want Unity's random number system so that we can generate random numbers.

2. Next, delete the entire class that's been provided for you, and replace it with:

```
public class BalancingBallAgent : Agent
{

}
```

Note that you'll need to make sure the class name is the same as the asset file you created. Naturally, it will descend from Agent.

3. Add some member variables, one to store a reference to the GameObject that is the ball, and another to that ball's Rigidbody:

```
public GameObject ball;
Rigidbody ball_rigidbody;
```

4. Next, override the Initialize() method, which comes from Agent and is called once when the agent is first enabled:

```
public override void Initialize()
{
    ball_rigidbody = ball.GetComponent<Rigidbody>();
}
```

Inside Initialize(), we get a handle on the ball's Rigidbody, and could do other setup if we needed to (but we don't right now).

5. Override the `Heuristic()` method, which also comes from `Agent` and allows us to manually control the agent:

```
public override void Heuristic(in ActionBuffers actionsOut)
{
    var continuousActionsOut = actionsOut.ContinuousActions;
    continuousActionsOut[0] = -Input.GetAxis("Horizontal");
    continuousActionsOut[1] = Input.GetAxis("Vertical");
}
```

As usual, `Heuristic()` allows the agent to choose an action using a custom heuristic. This means you can provide some sort of custom decision-making logic that's separate from any machine learning. Most commonly this is used to provide manual control of an agent, by a human, and that's what we're doing here. We'll use it to test the agent, and not train it, though (we're not doing IL or GAIL this time).

Our code should be pretty familiar to you by now, if you've been working through the book sequentially, but essentially it:

- Gets the continuous component of the `ActionBuffers` being passed to the method.

- Gets the first entry in the array of continuous actions, and assigns the negative value of the horizontal input to it.

- Gets the second entry in the array of continuous actions, and assigns the value of the vertical input to it.

> For information on Unity's Input Manager, check the Unity documentation (*https://oreil.ly/WOjxC*).

6. Next, we'll implement the `OnEpisodeBegin()` function, also from `Agent`:

```
public override void OnEpisodeBegin()
{
    gameObject.transform.rotation = new Quaternion(0f, 0f, 0f, 0f);
    gameObject.transform.Rotate
        (new Vector3(1, 0, 0), Random.Range(-10f, 10f));
    gameObject.transform.Rotate
        (new Vector3(0, 0, 1), Random.Range(-10f, 10f));
    ball_rigidbody.velocity = new Vector3(0f, 0f, 0f);
    ball.transform.position = new Vector3
        (Random.Range(-1.5f, 1.5f), 4f, Random.Range(-1.5f, 1.5f))
        + gameObject.transform.position;
}
```

In this function, we do what we need to do to set the agent and environment up at the beginning of a training episode. For our ball-balancing agent, we need to:

- Set the agent's rotation to the default position.

- Randomly rotate the agent on the x-axis, somewehere between -10 and 10.

- Randomly rotate the agent on the z-axis, somewhere between -10 and 10.

- Set the ball's `Rigidbody` velocity to nothing.

- Randomly position the ball itself to somewhere between -1.5 and 1.5 on the x- and z-axes, and at 4 on the y-axis (which should roughly be the height you placed it earlier), so it's always at the same height above the agent, but in a different place above it.

7. Finally, for the code, we implement `OnActionReceived()`. We'll do this in pieces, because it's quite a bit of code. First, we'll implement the skeleton:

```
public override void OnActionReceived(ActionBuffers actionBuffers)
{
    var action_z = 2f *
        Mathf.Clamp(actionBuffers.ContinuousActions[0], -1f, 1f);
    var action_x = 2f *
        Mathf.Clamp(actionBuffers.ContinuousActions[1], -1f, 1f);
}
```

This method is called to allow the agent to execute some actions. What it executes is based on the contents of the `ActionBuffers` passed in.

The `ActionBuffers` bits of the `Agent` system come specifically from the `Unity.MLAgents.Actuators` component that we imported earlier.

The code we've implemented so far creates some temporary variables holding z-axis and x-axis actions for our agent. Specifically, we use `Clamp`, and pass in the contents of each of the components of the continuous actions component of the `ActionBuffers`, clamping between -1 and 1, then we multiply the result by 2 to magnify the effect a bit.

The `Clamp` function we use here, which we've done a few times in the past, takes a value (in this case something from the `ActionBuffers` array), and returns that value if it is between the subsequent two values (in this case, -1 and 1). Otherwise, it returns the smaller value if the initial value is less than it, or the larger value if the initial value is greater than it.

8. Next, below this initial code but still within `OnActionReceived()`, add:

```
if ((gameObject.transform.rotation.z < 0.25f && action_z > 0f) ||
    (gameObject.transform.rotation.z > -0.25f && action_z < 0f))
{
    gameObject.transform.Rotate(new Vector3(0, 0, 1), action_z);
}

if ((gameObject.transform.rotation.x < 0.25f && action_x > 0f) ||
    (gameObject.transform.rotation.x > -0.25f && action_x < 0f))
{
    gameObject.transform.Rotate(new Vector3(1, 0, 0), action_x);
}
```

This code checks whether the z-axis of our agent's rotation is less than `0.25` and the passed-in z-axis action is greater than `0`, or whether the z-axis of our agent's rotation is greater than `-0.25` and the passed-in z-axis action is less than `0`. If either of those is true, it calls `Rotate` (*https://oreil.ly/VpVXb*), asking for a rotation on the z-axis of the amount specified in the `action_z` variable we created earlier (which contains the passed-in z-axis action).

Then we do the same thing again, but for the x-axis.

9. Next, still within the method, and below the code you just wrote, add the following:

```
if ((ball.transform.position.y - gameObject.transform.position.y) < -2f ||
    Mathf.Abs
    (ball.transform.position.x - gameObject.transform.position.x) > 3f ||
    Mathf.Abs
    (ball.transform.position.z - gameObject.transform.position.z) > 3f)
{
    SetReward(-1f);
    EndEpisode();
}
else
{
    SetReward(0.1f);
}
```

This code checks if the difference between the position of the ball on the y-axis and the position of the agent on the y-axis is less than `-2`, or similarly on the x- and z-axes, checks if the difference is greater than 3. Why? Any of these things might indicate the ball has left the top of the agent and fallen off or done something else strange. And that means the simulation should end the episode, and the agent should receive a penalty (in this case, of `-1`).

Otherwise, a small reward of `0.1` is provided, as the ball is probably still on the top surface of the agent, and all is well in the world.

That's all the code! Don't forget to save before you switch back to the Unity Editor.

Adding a New Camera for the Agent

Next we need to add an additional camera for the agent to use as its observations. We'll do this by adding objects to the world in our scene, in the Unity Editor. Cameras are, by default, not coded by you, and are physical but invisible things that we add to the Unity world.

Cameras do have coordinates (i.e., they have a `transform`), and we can see them in the Unity Editor (which helps us position them, and where they point), but if you had two cameras looking at each other in a scene, they wouldn't "see" each other. There's nothing physical present.

To add a camera, follow these steps:

1. Use the Hierarchy, and create a new camera as a child of the Balancing Ball object (the parent of Agent and Ball), as shown in Figure 10-2.

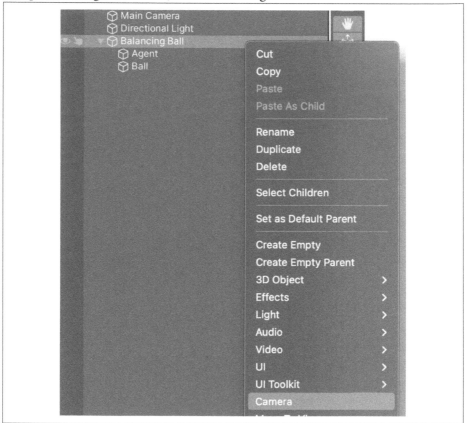

Figure 10-2. Adding a new camera

2. Rename the new camera something sensible, like "Agent Camera."

3. Position the new agent camera so that it's pointing down toward the agent and the ball, as shown in Figure 10-3.

 There will already be a camera in the scene, because every scene comes with one. Don't remove that one. It's the one you, a human, will use to view the simulation as it runs.

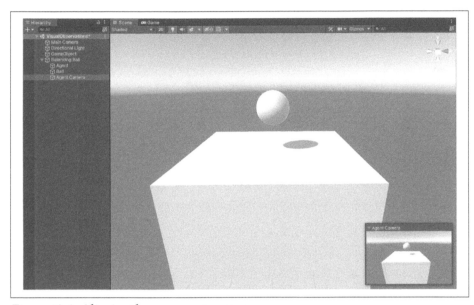

Figure 10-3. Aligning the new agent camera

4. Select the agent in the Hierarchy, and use the Add Component button to add a Camera Sensor component.

5. Now, use the Inspector to assign the new agent camera to the Camera field in the Camera Sensor component, as shown in Figure 10-4.

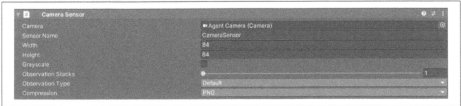

Figure 10-4. Assigning the camera

6. Assign the ball object, from the Hierarchy, to the Ball field in the agent's Inspector, as shown in Figure 10-5.

Figure 10-5. Assigning the ball in the script

7. Use the Add Component button to make sure you have Decision Requester and Behavior Parameters components attached to the agent.

8. Make sure your Behavior Parameters component has a space size of 0 for Vector Observations (in that there are none), and 2 Continuous Actions.

9. You'll also want to give the behavior a name. We suggest "BalancingBall" or something similar.

That's all we need to do to add a camera. Save your scene before continuing.

Seeing What the Agent's Camera Sees

There are a few ways you can see what the agent's camera sees. The first is quite obvious, and you probably already did it in order to position the camera suitably:

1. Select the agent's camera in the Hierarchy.

2. The Scene view will show a preview of what the camera sees in the bottom righthand corner, as shown in Figure 10-6.

Figure 10-6. Showing what the agent's camera sees

You can also create a view, showing the special agent camera's view, and display that on top of the Game view, as shown in Figure 10-7.

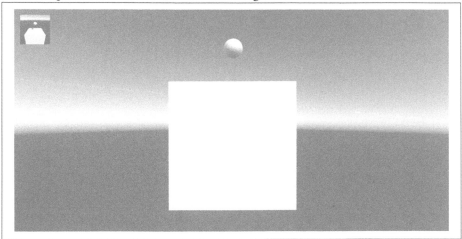

Figure 10-7. A special view to show the new camera's view

3. To create this view in your scene in the Unity Editor, create a new Custom Render Texture asset in the Project view, as shown in Figure 10-8.

Figure 10-8. Creating a Custom Render Texture asset

4. Set it up as shown in Figure 10-9. The defaults should be correct.

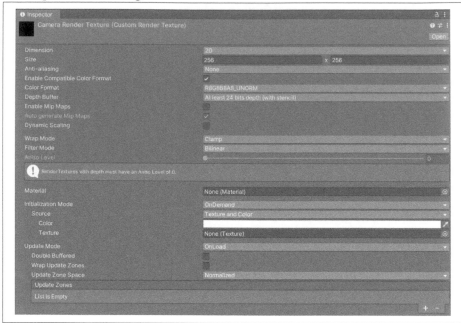

Figure 10-9. The new render texture asset

5. Name it something sensible, like "cameraRenderTexture."

6. Select the agent's camera in the Hierarchy, and in the Target Texture field of its Inspector, assign the render texture asset that you just created to it, as shown in Figure 10-10.

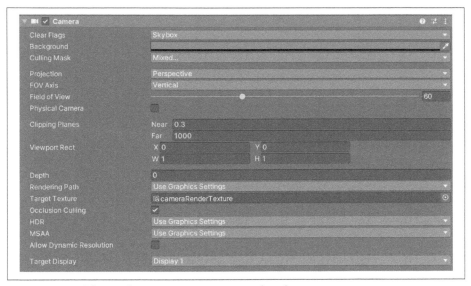

Figure 10-10. The render texture asset assigned to the agent camera

Render texture is a game development term, common across all game engines, that is created by the engine and updated at runtime. Accordingly, a render texture is useful when you want to put the view of a camera in the scene onto something that's shown in the scene or on top of the scene. Render textures are commonly used in video games, for example, to display the contents of in-game screens: the screen's view is a render texture, showing what a camera somewhere else (out of the player's view) sees. Learn more about render textures in the Unity documentation (*https://oreil.ly/HkqTA*).

7. Next, create a canvas in the Hierarchy, as shown in Figure 10-11, leaving everything at the defaults.

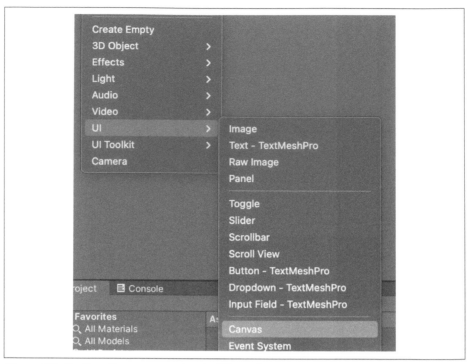

Figure 10-11. Creating a canvas in the Hierarchy

A canvas (*https://oreil.ly/OtlT6*) is an object provided by Unity for screen rendering; this means it's typically used for displaying things that go on top of the scene (screen versus scene), like the user interface. We're going to use it for a rudimentary noninteractive interface: showing what a camera sees.

1. As a child of the canvas, in the Hierarchy, add an empty object and name it "Camera View" or something similar, as shown in Figure 10-12

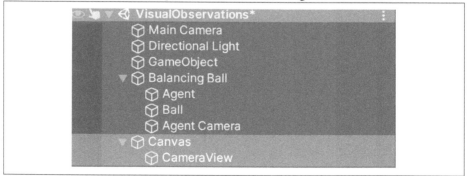

Figure 10-12. The Hierarchy, showing the new canvas and camera view

2. In this new object's Inspector, use the Add Component button and add a Raw Image component.

3. Then, assign the Render Texture asset (from the Project view) that you created earlier to the Texture field of the Raw Image component, as shown in Figure 10-13.

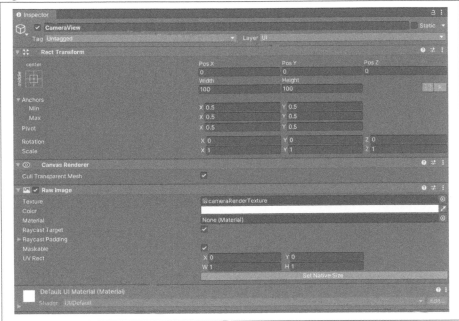

Figure 10-13. Assigning the texture to the Raw Image component

4. Now, using the Rectangle tool (shown in Figure 10-14), resize the Raw Image component in the Scene view and put it in a corner, as shown in Figure 10-15.

Figure 10-14. The rectangle tool

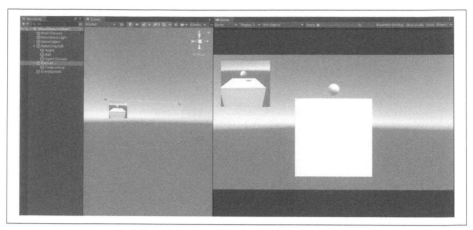

Figure 10-15. Putting the Raw Image component into the corner

Now when you run the simulation, you'll see the main camera's view as normal, as well as a small view of the agent's camera. You can use this technique to add views for your own consumption to any of the simulations you make. Even if the agent doesn't use a camera, there's nothing stopping you from adding cameras to capture different perspectives.

Training the Camera-Based Agent

To train the agent, you'll need a YAML file for your hyperparameters, as usual (what a huge surprise, you say!). Here's the one we recommend using, but feel free to experiment:

```
behaviors:
  BalancingBall:
    trainer_type: ppo
    hyperparameters:
      batch_size: 64
      buffer_size: 12000
      learning_rate: 0.0003
      beta: 0.001
      epsilon: 0.2
      lambd: 0.99
      num_epoch: 3
      learning_rate_schedule: linear
    network_settings:
      normalize: true
      hidden_units: 128
      num_layers: 2
      vis_encode_type: simple
    reward_signals:
      extrinsic:
```

```
        gamma: 0.99
        strength: 1.0
  keep_checkpoints: 5
  max_steps: 500000
  time_horizon: 1000
  summary_freq: 12000
```

With the YAML file ready to go, run the training by executing `mlagents-learn` on the command line:

```
mlagents-learn BalancingBall.yaml --run-id=Ball1
```

 Your behavior name on the Behavior Parameters component of the agent will need to match the behavior name in the YAML file, as usual.

Training using only visual observations will take a lot longer than training using vector observations. Our training process, using the preceding YAML file, took about two hours on a recent MacBook Pro.

When the training is complete, run your agent with the *.onnx* file that's been output, and see how it goes.

 Explore combining visual observations with vector and other observation types. See if you can combine them to produce an agent that can be trained more quickly.

Cameras and You

It's very tempting to use cameras constantly and for everything. We get it! They're exciting, and it's kind of magical to give your agent virtual eyes and just let them loose to solve whatever problem you might need them to address. But it's rarely the best approach.

Cameras are at their most obviously useful when you're building a simulation that represents *something* you might then build in the real world, and when that *something* will actually have cameras. If you're building a simulation of a complex self-driving car, or a drone, or a pick-and-place robot, and plan to use part or all of the model that you generate in a real-world version of the same, and it has cameras, then of course it makes sense to use cameras in your simulation.

Giving an agent *just* a camera is about the same as a human that only has sight—only receiving visual information about our environment is a very complex proposition. It's much better paired with or complementary to other sensory inputs. Agents often have objectives that are performing some action, but not necessarily physically changing an environment. There are quite often actions an agent can take that won't change camera input, which means they might not get any feedback about it because there wasn't a *visible* state change to the environment. An agent needs its actions to have a measurable impact on the environment (beyond its rewards) if it's only got visual observations coming in, as it needs to know *something* has happened in the environment as a result of its actions.

If you're building something that's purely destined to live in a simulation, you should be judicious in your use of cameras. It's relatively unusual to use cameras and vector observations together to observe the same elements of the simulation, but there are scenarios in which it makes sense: vectors might add context to the camera, or give additional environmental information about what's going on that can't be gleaned from the camera alone.

For example, if you were building a pick-and-place robot, and it could see, for example, a bag of pasta sitting in front of it via its camera, it might be strange to also use a raycast observation that detects a tagged bag of pasta, and identifies it as such. The image recognition system alone could deal with identifying a bag of pasta and the additional information from the raycast is, at best superfluous, and at its worst, an impediment to the training process.

Basically, if you're using your agent out of engine (in the real world), you should try and mimic the inputs it really will have as best as possible, and if you're doing something that's solely virtual, you can give it a camera if you want a computer vision model as a result.

You could give any agent a camera. But that doesn't mean it would be useful. Any observations that don't give an agent more information about how to fulfill its objectives is just muddying the waters, making the resulting neural network more complex and making training slower and more difficult. You should always have as few observations as possible.

Cameras are great fun, and you should definitely play with them as you explore making your own simulations. But when it gets down to business, you want to be careful not to use too many, or not to only use cameras if there is a better option.

CHAPTER 11

Working with Python

In this chapter, we're going to explore the possibilities for using Unity's ML-Agents together with Python, in a more active way. Everything we've done so far has focused on the combination of Unity and (by way of ML-Agents) Python, but we've taken a Unity-centric approach.

This chapter is going to present a few ways you can do things from a Python-centric approach. Specifically, we'll look at how you can use Python to interact with Unity and ML-Agents.

Python All the Way Down

We've been using Python throughout the book, but we're also using a script that runs the training and connects it to Unity. PyTorch is also being used deep under the hood to do the training. Beyond that, though, it's not really relevant that we're using Python. It just happens to be Python that powers the scripts we're running. It could be anything.

In this chapter, we'll experiment more with Python and get a handle on the capabilities generated by combining Python with ML-Agents, beyond the provided scripts. We'll prove that it's actually Python you're using when you run `mlagents-learn` to train an agent, and look beyond the provided scripts a little bit.

The environment we'll spend most of our time poking at in this chapter, via Python, is called the GridWorld environment. It's a simple 3x3 grid, where the agent is a blue square that needs to touch a green +, and not touch a red x. It uses an exclusively visual observation system: a camera pointed down at the grid.

Its actions are one of five discrete options:

- Do nothing
- Move up
- Move down
- Move right
- Move left

The agent is rewarded with `1.0` if it touches the goal (green plus sign), and penalized with `-1.0` if it touches the red x. There's an existential penalty of `-0.01` for every step.

You can see what the GridWorld looks like in Figure 11-1.

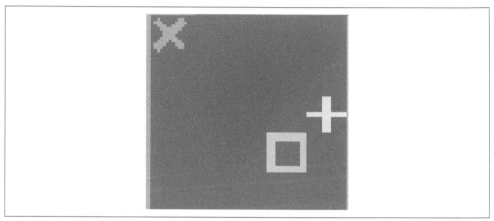

Figure 11-1. The GridWorld, a digital frontier

Experimenting with an Environment

To work with Python, naturally you'll need to set up a new Python environment. This is almost exactly the same as the Python environment we worked on all the way back in "Setting Up" on page 19, with a few small differences.

To get ready, you'll need to do the following:

1. Set up a new Python environment, per "Setting Up" on page 19.
2. Once it's configured to those specifications, install a few extra things. First, install matplotlib:

   ```
   pip install matplotlib
   ```

We'll use matplotlib to show some images on the screen as we explore Python and ML-Agents. It's beyond the scope of this book to discuss matplotlib in detail, but if you search O'Reilly's Learning Platform, or DuckDuckGo, you'll find *plenty* of material. There's also a website (*https://matplotlib.org*).

3. Next, install Jupyter Lab:

   ```
   pip install jupyterlab
   ```

4. And fire up Jupyter Lab:

   ```
   jupyterlab
   ```

   Jupyter Lab is a tool for creating "notebooks," which allow you to execute Python in a form that's easy to run and write. It's commonly used for scientific computing, and you might have been exposed to it as Jupyter Notebooks, IPython, or Google's branded version, Google Colab.

5. Once it's running, create an empty notebook, as shown in Figure 11-2.

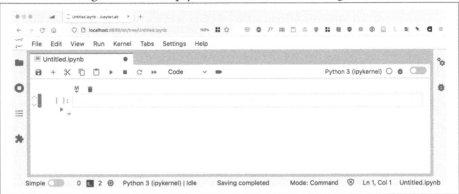

Figure 11-2. The empty Jupyter notebook

That's it.

Next, we're going to start coding, and we'll explain what's up as we go:

1. Right away, we need to import ML-Agents:

   ```
   import mlagents
   ```

   This brings the Python-based ML-Agents package into our notebook.

2. Next, we're going to import `matplotlib.pyplot`, so we can display plots:

   ```
   import matplotlib.pyplot as plot
   ```

3. And we'll tell `matplotlib` that we want it to be displayed `inline`:

   ```
   %matplotlib inline
   ```

   This makes sure `matplotlib` will display images inline, within the notebook.

4. Now we ask ML-Agents for its default registry:

```
from mlagents_envs.registry import default_registry
```

This provides a database of prebuilt Unity environments (called the "Unity Environment Registry" (*https://oreil.ly/pDNML*)), based on the ML-Agents examples. These environments can be used to experiment with the Python API without having to build out an environment to a binary, or run Unity at the same time.

5. With the default registry imported, we can take a quick look to see what we've got:

```
environment_names = list(default_registry.keys())
for name in environment_names:
    print(name)
```

If you run your notebook at this point (using the Run menu → Run all cells), you'll see a list of environments, as shown in Figure 11-3.

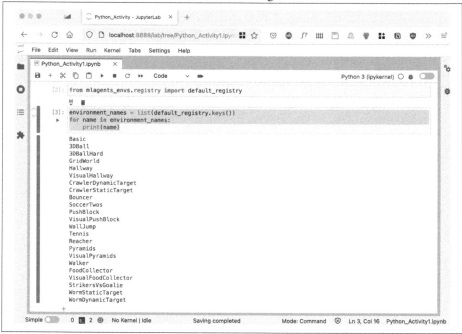

Figure 11-3. The list of environments

6. Next, we're going to load one of the provided environments:

```
env = default_registry["GridWorld"].make()
```

This will load the GridWorld environment from the default environments.

7. With the GridWorld environment loaded, the first thing we want to do is ask for the behavior:

```
behavior = list(env.behavior_specs)[0] # get the first behavior
print(f"The behavior is named: {behavior}")
spec = env.behavior_specs[behavior]
```

This gets a handle on the behavior of the environment (corresponding to the Behavior Parameters component attached to the agent in the environment), and prints its name and team ID (which will be 0, because the environment doesn't use teams).

8. Next, we'll find out how many observations it has:

```
print("The number of observations is: ", len(spec.observation_specs))
```

9. And we'll take a look to see if it has any visual observations:

```
vis_obs = any(len(spec.shape) == 3 for spec in spec.observation_specs)
print("Visual observations: ", vis_obs)
```

10. We'll also check how many continuous and discrete actions there are:

```
if spec.action_spec.continuous_size > 0:
 print(f"There are {spec.action_spec.continuous_size} continuous actions")
if spec.action_spec.is_discrete():
 print(f"There are {spec.action_spec.discrete_size} discrete actions")
```

11. And we'll check the options on the discrete branches:

```
if spec.action_spec.discrete_size > 0:
 for action, branch_size in enumerate(spec.action_spec.discrete_branches):
  print(f"Action number {action} has {branch_size} different options")
```

We can run the notebook again to get a bit of information about it. You should see something like Figure 11-4.

```
                    Behaviours

[6]:  behavior = list(env.behavior_specs)[0] # get the first behaviour
      print(f"The behaviour is named: {behavior}")
      spec = env.behavior_specs[behavior]

      The behaviour is named: GridWorld?team=0


[7]:  print("The number of observations is: ", len(spec.observation_specs))

      The number of observations is:  1


[8]:  vis_obs = any(len(spec.shape) == 3 for spec in spec.observation_specs)
      print("Visual observations: ", vis_obs)

      Visual observations:  True


[9]:  if spec.action_spec.continuous_size > 0:
          print(f"There are {spec.action_spec.continuous_size} continuous actions")
      if spec.action_spec.is_discrete():
          print(f"There are {spec.action_spec.discrete_size} discrete actions")


      # How many actions are possible ?
      #print(f"There are {spec.action_size} action(s)")

      # For discrete actions only : How many different options does each action has ?
      if spec.action_spec.discrete_size > 0:
        for action, branch_size in enumerate(spec.action_spec.discrete_branches):
          print(f"Action number {action} has {branch_size} different options")

      There are 1 discrete actions
      Action number 0 has 5 different options
```

Figure 11-4. Exploring the environment

Next, we'll step through the environment:

1. First, we'll store the number of steps from the environment:

    ```
    decision_steps, terminal_steps = env.get_steps(behavior)
    ```

2. We'll set the actions for the agent's behavior, passing in the behavior we want to use, and a tensor of dimension 2:

    ```
    env.set_actions
        (behavior, spec.action_spec.empty_action(len(decision_steps)))
    ```

3. Then, we'll move the simulation forward by one step:

    ```
    env.step()
    ```

4. With the simulation stepped once, it's time to take a look at what it can see. First, we'll check for any visual observations:

    ```
    for index, obs_spec in enumerate(spec.observation_specs):
      if len(obs_spec.shape) == 3:
        print("Here is the first visual observation")
    ```

```
plot.imshow(decision_steps.obs[index][0,:,:,:])
plot.show()
```

This will grab the first visual observation from one of the agents in the environment and display it using `matplotlib`.

5. Next, we'll check for any vector observations:

```
for index, obs_spec in enumerate(spec.observation_specs):
    if len(obs_spec.shape) == 1:
        print("First vector observations : ", decision_steps.obs[index][0,:])
```

6. Running the notebook at this point should result in an image of the agent's first visual observation, as shown in Figure 11-5.

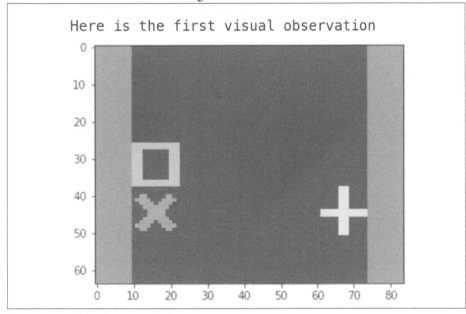

Figure 11-5. The first visual observation

7. Now we'll step the environment through three episodes:

```
for episode in range(3):
    env.reset()
    decision_steps, terminal_steps = env.get_steps(behavior)
    tracked_agent = -1 # -1 indicates not yet tracking
    done = False # For the tracked_agent
    episode_rewards = 0 # For the tracked_agent
    while not done:
        # Track the first agent we see if not tracking
        # len(decision_steps) = [number of agents that requested a decision]
        if tracked_agent == -1 and len(decision_steps) >= 1:
            tracked_agent = decision_steps.agent_id[0]
```

```
# Generate an action for all agents
action = spec.action_spec.random_action(len(decision_steps))

# Set the actions
env.set_actions(behavior, action)

# Move the simulation forward
env.step()

# Get the new simulation results
decision_steps, terminal_steps = env.get_steps(behavior)
if tracked_agent in decision_steps: # The agent requested a decision
    episode_rewards += decision_steps[tracked_agent].reward
if tracked_agent in terminal_steps: # Agent terminated its episode
    episode_rewards += terminal_steps[tracked_agent].reward
    done = True
print(f"Total rewards for episode {episode} is {episode_rewards}")
```

8. Run the entire notebook again, and you should see some familiar-looking training information, as shown in Figure 11-6.

```
Total rewards for episode 0 is −1.4899999890476465
Total rewards for episode 1 is 0.9400000013411045
Total rewards for episode 2 is 0.570000009611249
```

Figure 11-6. Training in a notebook

9. Finally, close the environment:

```
env.close()
```

What Can Be Done with Python?

The mlagents Python package we're using is the same package that's used to drive the mlagents-learn script we've been using to train agents in simulations.

 It's out of scope, and thoroughly unnecessary, for this book to explore the entirety of the mlagents Python API. There's a lot in there, and we're just here to give you the highlights in a tutorial form. But if you're curious, you can find all the mlagents Python API documentation online (*https://oreil.ly/7O0h3*).

You can use the Python API to control, interact with, and get information from a Unity simulation environment. This means you could use it to develop entirely custom training and learning algorithms, instead of relying on the provided algorithms (which you use via the mlagents-learn script).

Later, in Chapter 12, we'll look at connecting Unity-built simulation environments to the OpenAI Gym.

Using Your Own Environment

You can, of course, use your own environment instead of one of the Unity-provided examples from the registry.

Before you can use your own environment, you'll need to build it. We'll build one of Unity's example projects, the GridWorld we used earlier, as an example:

1. Open the ML-Agents Unity project that comes as part of the ML-Agents GitHub Repository, as shown in Figure 11-7.

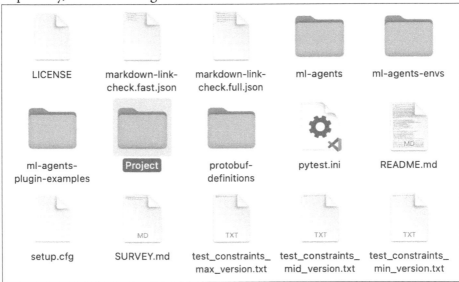

Figure 11-7. The project in the ML-Agents repository

2. Once you're in the project, open the GridWorld scene from the Project pane, as shown in Figure 11-8.

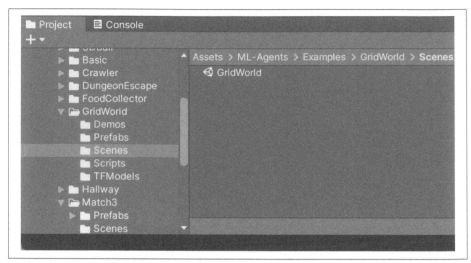

Figure 11-8. The GridWorld scene

3. To simplify things, select and delete all the numbered areas from the Hierarchy view, as shown in Figure 11-9.

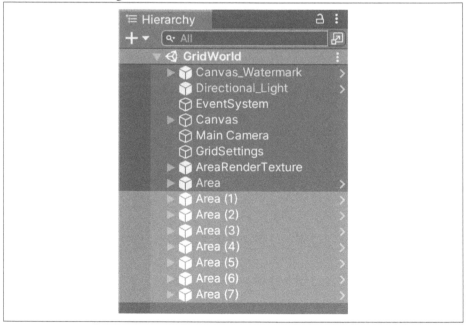

Figure 11-9. The areas you'll need to delete

These are duplicates of the main area used to speed up training by training multiple agents at once. Because we'll be experimenting with this environment in Python, we only want the one area.

4. Next, open the Player settings via the Edit menu → Project Settings → Player. Find the Resolution and Presentation section, as shown in Figure 11-10, and check Run in Background. Close the Player settings.

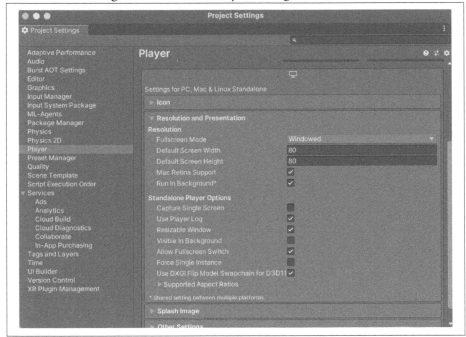

Figure 11-10. The Player settings

5. Open the Build settings from File → Build Settings, as shown in Figure 11-11. Choose the platform you want to run this on (we're using a MacBook Pro for our screenshots), and make sure the GridWorld scene is the only scene checked in the list.

If the list of scenes is empty, only the currently open scene will be built. That's also fine.

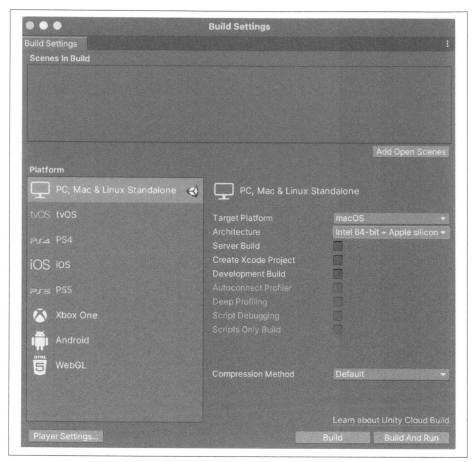

Figure 11-11. The Build settings

6. Click the Build button, and save the resulting output to a path you're familiar with, as shown in Figure 11-12.

 On macOS, the saved output will be a standard *.app* file. On Windows, the output will be a folder that contains an executable.

Figure 11-12. Choosing where the build goes

7. Unity will build the environment, as shown in Figure 11-13.

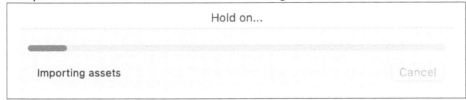

Figure 11-13. The build occurring

Completely Custom Training

Because the Python package is, effectively, just an API to control the processes occurring within the Unity simulation environment, we can actually use it to replace the training processes supplied by the `mlagents-learn` script. In this section, we're going to take a quick look at an example largely based on one of Unity's examples.

Before we get started, you'll need a Python environment set up, as per "Setting Up" on page 19. Once you've done that, make sure Jupyter Lab is running, and you're ready to continue.

In this example, we're going to once again use Unity's GridWorld example environment, and instead of training it using one of the training algorithms supplied in Unity, we'll train it using Q-learning. Q-learning is a model-free reinforcement learning algorithm that is designed to learn the value of actions for particular states.

The "model-free" aspect of Q-learning refers to the way Q-learning does not require a model of the environment. Everything relates to states and actions, rather than a specific understanding of the environment. PPO, the standard algorithm employed by Unity ML-Agents, is also model-free. Exploring the specifics of Q-learning (*https://oreil.ly/4UjqA*) is beyond the scope of this book, however.

We're going to jump-start the process here by supplying some code, since there's a fair bit of it. Locate the `PracticalSims_CustomTraining.ipynb` notebook in the resources you downloaded for the book, and load it into Jupyter Lab.

Let's take a look at what the code in this notebook does:

- The `import` statements bring in `mlagents`, as usual, as well as `torch` (PyTorch), and some Python `math` and `typing` (Python's type hinting library), as well as `numpy`.

- After that, a class to represent the neural network that'll be trained is created: `VisualQNetwork`. This class defines a neural network that takes some images as input, and spits out a collection of numbers as output.

- Next, we create an `Experience` class, which stores an action, observation, reward combination. The experiences that will be stored as an `Experience` will be used to train the neural network that will be made.

- Now, the bulk of the notebook, the `Trainer` class, will take data from our Unity environment and generate a buffer of `Experience` objects, using the policy from the `VisualQNetwork`.

With the setup provided, we'll write the training loop together. We're going to do this step by step as usual, since it's good to get a picture of what's going on:

1. First we'll make sure any existing environments are closed:

   ```
   try:
     env.close()
   except:
     pass
   ```

2. Then we'll get a GridWorld from the Unity default registry:

   ```
   env = default_registry["GridWorld"].make()
   ```

3. Now we'll create an instance of the `VisualQNetwork` that we discussed a moment ago (using the class defined earlier in the notebook):

   ```
   qnet = VisualQNetwork((64, 84, 3), 126, 5)
   ```

4. And we'll create a `Buffer` (which is defined earlier, with `Experience`) to store experiences in:

   ```
   experiences: Buffer = []
   ```

5. We'll also create an optimizer, which is just a standard Adam optimizer, direct from PyTorch:

   ```
   optim = torch.optim.Adam(qnet.parameters(), lr= 0.001)
   ```

6. And we'll create a list of floats to store the cumulative rewards:

```
cumulative_rewards: List[float] = []
```

7. Next, we'll define a few environment variables, like the number of training steps we want, the number of new experiences we want to collect per training step, and the maximum size of the buffer:

```
NUM_TRAINING_STEPS = int(os.getenv('QLEARNING_NUM_TRAINING_STEPS', 70))
NUM_NEW_EXP = int(os.getenv('QLEARNING_NUM_NEW_EXP', 1000))
BUFFER_SIZE = int(os.getenv('QLEARNING_BUFFER_SIZE', 10000))
```

8. And, almost last (and definitely not least), we're going to write the training loop:

```
for n in range(NUM_TRAINING_STEPS):
  new_exp,_ =
    Trainer.generate_trajectories(env, qnet, NUM_NEW_EXP, epsilon=0.1)
  random.shuffle(experiences)
  if len(experiences) > BUFFER_SIZE:
    experiences = experiences[:BUFFER_SIZE]
  experiences.extend(new_exp)
  Trainer.update_q_net(qnet, optim, experiences, 5)
  _, rewards = Trainer.generate_trajectories(env, qnet, 100, epsilon=0)
  cumulative_rewards.append(rewards)
  print("Training step ", n+1, "\treward ", rewards)
```

Our training loop iterates through to the maximum number of training steps that we defined, creates a new experience for each step, stores it in the buffer, updates the model, updates the rewards, and continues. It's a pretty standard training loop.

9. Finally, we close the environment, and we use `matplotlib` to plot a nice training graph:

```
env.close()
plt.plot(range(NUM_TRAINING_STEPS), cumulative_rewards)
```

With that, we can run the notebook, and wait a while as it trains.

What's the Point of Python?

The ML-Agents Toolkit is actually a really powerful way to control a simulation entirely from Python. You don't need to use it for machine learning at all if you don't want to.

But of course, you *can* use it for machine learning. The Python API components of ML-Agents are useful if you want to go beyond what the `mlagents-learn` command allows you to do automatically (in concert with the YAML files, defining the hyperparameters). You can create a completely custom training pipeline, using all the glorious features of PyTorch (or TensorFlow, or anything you can get your hands on) to train the entities that live inside your Unity simulation beyond the limitations of the algorithms and scenarios provided by `mlagents-learn` (PPO, GAIL, and so on).

You could also use the Python API to add extra steps to the training and learning process, injecting calls to specialist domain libraries before or after in-engine observations take place, as needed.

CHAPTER 12

Under the Hood and Beyond

In this chapter, we're going to touch on some of the approaches we have used throughout the previous chapters on simulation.

We've covered the gist: in simulation-based agent learning, an agent undergoes a *training* process to develop a *policy* for its behavior. The policy acts as a mapping from previous *observations* to the *actions* it took in response and the corresponding *rewards* it earned for doing so. Training takes place across a large number of *episodes* during which the cumulative reward should increase as the agent improves at the given task, partially dictated by *hyperparameters* that control aspects of agent behavior during training—including the *algorithm* used to produce the behavior model.

Once trained, *inference* is used to query the trained agent model for the appropriate behavior (actions) in response to given stimuli (observations), but learning has ceased and thus the agent will no longer *improve* at the given task.

We've talked about most of these concepts already:

- We know about observations, actions, and rewards, and how the mapping between them is used to build up a policy.

- We know that a training phase occurs over a large number of episodes, and how once this is completed, the agent transitions to inference (only querying the model, not updating it any longer).

- We know we pass a file of hyperparameters to the `mlagents -learn` process, but we kind of glossed over that part.

- We know there are different algorithms to choose from during training, but maybe not why you would choose a specific one from among the options.

So, this section will take a further look at the *hyperparameters* and *algorithms* available in ML-Agents, where and why you should choose to use each of them, and how they impact other choices you will make in training, such as your choice of rewards scheme.

Hyperparameters (and Just Parameters)

When training begins with ML-Agents, a YAML file needs to be passed with the necessary *hyperparameters*. This is commonly referred to in the machine learning world as a *hyperparameters file*, but that's not all it contains, so ML-Agents documentation prefers to instead call this a *configuration file*. This contains variables used in the learning process whose values will do one of the following:

- Specify aspects of the training process ("parameters")
- Change the behavior of the agent or model itself as it learns ("hyperparameters")

Parameters

Commonly configured training *parameters* include the following:

`trainer_type`
> The algorithm to use in training, selected from `ppo`, `sac`, or `poca`

`max_steps`
> The maximum number of observations an agent can receive or actions it can take before an episode ends, whether or not it has achieved the objective

`checkpoint_interval` *and* `keep_checkpoints`
> How often to output duplicate/backup models during training and how many of the most recent ones to keep around at a time

`summary_freq`
> How often to print out (or send to TensorBoard) details of how training is going

`network_settings` *and its corresponding subparameters*
> Allow you to specify some of the size, shape, or behaviors of the neural network that represents the agent policy

Your selection of `trainer_type` will depend on aspects of your agent and environment. We'll talk about that in depth in the next sections, where we take a look under the hood of each of these algorithms.

The definition of `max_steps` is important, because if a simulation is run thousands or millions of times—as occurs in the model training process—it is highly likely that at some point the agent will get stuck in an unrecoverable state. Without an enforced limit, the agent would remain in this state and continually pollute its own behavior model with irrelevant or unrepresentative data until Unity ran out of available memory or a user terminated the process. Not ideal. Instead, experience or estimation should be used to derive a number that allows for a slow-moving agent on the right track to achieve the objective without being cut off, but disallows excessive floundering.

For example, imagine you are training a self-driving car that needs to traverse a circuit and reach a goal location, and a previously trained model or test run tells you an ideal run will reach the goal location in around 5,000 steps. If `max_steps` were set to `500,000`, a *junk* episode in which the agent achieved nothing would result in 10 times the information as an episode with optimal performance—likely muddying the model in the process. But if `max_steps` were set to `5,000` or lower, the model would never be afforded the chance to achieve middling results, instead having its attempts cut short each time before eventually (maybe) it happened to achieve a perfect episode with no prior knowledge. Highly unlikely. In between these numbers is best; say, around `10,000` for this example. For your own agents, the ideal will depend on the complexity of the task it is to perform.

The checkpoint functionality allows intermediate models to be saved as every `check point_interval` changes, keeping the last `keep_checkpoints` models around at all times. This means if you see the agent is performing well long before training is set to end, you can terminate the training process and just use the latest checkpoint. Training can also be resumed from a checkpoint, allowing training to begin with one algorithm and then continue with another—such as the BC to GAIL example given in Chapter 1.

The `network_settings` accessor can be used to set subparameters that dictate the shape of the neural network used as the behavior model. This can be helpful for reducing the size of the resulting model if it is to be used in an environment where storage or compute resources are limited (e.g., edge devices), such as with `network_settings→num_layers` or `network_settings->hidden_units`. Other settings can give finer control over specific aspects such as the method used to interpret visual input, or whether to normalize continuous observations.

Reward Parameters

Further parameters then need to be defined to specify how rewards are treated during training. These fall under `reward_signals`.

Where explicit rewards are used, the `reward_signals->extrinsic->strength` and `extrinsic->gamma` must be set. Here, `strength` is simply a scale applied to the rewards sent by `AddReward` or `SetReward` calls, which you might want to reduce if you were experimenting with a hybrid learning approach or some other combination of extrinsic and intrinsic rewards.

Meanwhile, gamma is a scale applied to *estimations* of the reward, based on how long it would take to achieve. This is used when the agent is considering what it should do next, based on the reward it thinks it will receive for each of the options. gamma can be viewed as a measure of how much an agent should prioritize long-term gain over short-term gain. Should the agent forego rewards in the next few steps to hopefully achieve a larger objective and receive a larger reward at the end? Or should it do whatever will give it rewards most immediately in the moment? The choice will depend on your rewards scheme and the complexity of the task the agent is to achieve, but generally higher values (suggesting more long-term thinking) tend to produce smarter agents.

Other types of rewards may be enabled that will come directly from the training process, and they are called *intrinsic* rewards—similar to those used by imitation learning methods. But where IL rewards the agent for similarity to demonstrated behaviors, these rewards encourage general attributes—almost like a certain agent *personality*.

The most generally applicable intrinsic reward is curiosity, defined by reward_signals->curiosity. Curiosity in an agent means level of tendency to prioritize mapping the unknown (i.e., try new things and see how many points they get) over known good actions (i.e., things that have gotten them points in the past). Curiosity is encouraged through rewards that scale based on how new an action is or how unforeseen its result is, and this helps avoid the local maxima problem that commonly occurs in sparse reward environments.

For example, an agent may be designed to seek out and stand on a platform to open a door and then move through the open door to reach a goal. To incentivize each step and speed up training, you would give the agent a reward for standing on the platform and an exponentially larger reward for then reaching the goal. But a noncurious agent may recognize that it got a reward for the first step, and decide the best course of action is to continually step on and off the platform until each episode—and eventually training—ends. This is because it *knows* that standing on the platform is good, and the results of any other action (of which there could be infinite as far as it knows) are unknown. So, it will just stick with what it is good at. This is why multistage objectives will often require the introduction of artificial curiosity to make the agent more willing to try new things.

To enable curiosity, simply pass the same hyperparameters as are required for extrinsic rewards:

`reward_signals->curiosity->strength`
> A number to scale curiosity rewards by when trying to balance them against other rewards such as extrinsic rewards (must be between `0.0` and `1.0`)

`reward_signals->curiosity->gamma`
> A second scale to apply to temper the perceived value of rewards based on how long they would take to achieve, the same as in `extrinsic->gamma` (also between `0.0` and `1.0`)

Other, less commonly used intrinsic reward signals can be used to introduce other agent tendencies, such as random network distillation, or to enable particular learning types, such as GAIL.

Hyperparameters

Commonly configured model *hyperparameters* include:

`batch_size`
> Controls how many iterations the simulation does per update of the model. The `batch_size` should be large (in the thousands) if you're using continuous actions at all, and small (in the tens) if you're only using discrete actions.

`buffer_size`
> Controls different things depending on the algorithm. For PPO and MA-POCA, it controls the number of experiences to collect before we do any updating of the model (it should be multiple times larger than `batch_size`). For SAC, `buffer_size` corresponds to the maximum size of the experience buffer, so SAC can learn from both old and new experiences.

`learning_rate`
> Corresponds to how much of an impact each update makes on the model. It will typically be between `1e-5` and `1e-3`.

> If training is unstable (in other words, the reward does not consistently increase), try decreasing the `learning_rate`. A larger `buffer_size` will also correspond to more stable training.

Some hyperparameters are specific to the trainer being used. Let's start with the important ones for the trainer you'll probably use most often (PPO):

- `beta` incentivizes exploration. Here, high `beta` values will have a result similar to the curiosity intrinsic reward, in that it will encourage the agent to try new things even once early rewards have been discovered. Lower `beta` values are preferred in simple environments, so agents will tend to limit their behaviors to those that have been beneficial in the past—which may decrease training time.

- `epsilon` dictates how receptive the behavior model is to change. Here, high `epsilon` values will allow the agent to adopt new behaviors quickly once rewards are discovered, but this also allows the agent behavior to change easily and often even into late training. Lower `epsilon` values mean an agent will need more attempts to learn from an experience, and may result in longer training but will ensure consistent behavior in late training.

- Schedule hyperparameters such as `beta_schedule` and `epsilon_schedule` can be used to make the values of other hyperparameters change during training, such as to prioritize `beta` (curiosity) more during early training, or to reduce `epsilon` (fickleness) during late training.

 POCA/MA-POCA uses the same hyperparameters as PPO, but SAC has a few dedicated hyperparameters of its own (*https://oreil.ly/SuApG*).

For a full list of the parameters and hyperparameters currently supported by ML-Agents, see the ML-Agents documentation (*https://oreil.ly/4M3An*).

 If you don't really know (or want to know) what the required hyperparameters mean for your chosen model, you can look at the ML-Agents example files for each trainer type (*https://oreil.ly/0048b*) on GitHub. Once you see how training goes, if you encounter some hyperparameter-specific issues as described here, you may choose to tweak those specific values.

Algorithms

The Unity ML-Agents framework allows agents to learn behaviors through optimization of rewards defined in one of the following ways:

Explicitly (extrinsic rewards) by you
RL approaches in which we've used the `AddReward` or `SetReward` method: we give an agent a reward when we know it did something right (or a penalty when it's wrong).

Implicitly (intrinsic rewards) by selected algorithm
IL approaches in which rewards are given based on similarity to the provided behavior demonstration: we demonstrate behavior to an agent, and it attempts to clone it and gets rewarded automatically based on how well it clones it.

Implicitly by training process
The hyperparameter settings we discussed, in which the agent can be rewarded for exhibiting certain attributes such as curiosity. We haven't touch on this one in this book as much, as it's a bit out of scope.

But that's not all that differs between the different algorithms available in ML-Agents.

Proximal policy optimization (PPO) is probably the most sensible default choice for your ML efforts with Unity. PPO (*https://oreil.ly/6rCeP*) attempts to approximate an ideal function that maps an agent's observations to the best possible action available for a given state. It's designed to be a general-purpose algorithm. It's unlikely to be the most effective, but it will usually get the job done. That's why Unity ML-Agents ships it as the default.

Soft actor-critic (SAC) is an *off-policy* RL algorithm. This basically means that optimal training behavior and optimal resulting agent behavior can be defined separately. This can reduce the training time required for an agent to arrive at optimal behavior, because you can encourage certain attributes that may be desirable during training but not in the final agent behavior model.

The best example of such an attribute is *curiosity*. Curious exploration is great during training, when you don't want your agent to discover one thing that gives it points and then never try anything else. But it's not so great once the model is trained, because if training has gone as intended, it will already have discovered all the desirable behaviors.

So, SAC (*https://oreil.ly/jPlxp*) can be faster for training but requires more memory to hold and update separate behavior models when compared to an *on-policy* approach like PPO.

There is debate as to whether PPO is *on-policy* or *off-policy*. We tend to think of it as on-policy, since it makes updates based on following the current policy.

Multi-Agent POsthumous Credit Assignment (POCA or MA-POCA) is a multiagent algorithm that uses a centralized *critic* to reward and penalize a group of agents. The rewards are similar to basic PPO, but are given to the critic. The agents should learn how best to contribute to receiving the reward, but can also be individually rewarded. It's considered *posthumous* because an agent can be removed from the group of agents during the learning process, but will still learn which of its actions contributed to the reward achieved by the group, even after being removed. This means agents can take actions that are beneficial to the group, even if they result in their own death.

We used MA-POCA (*https://oreil.ly/aDvvz*) in Chapter 9.

Unity Inference Engine and Integrations

During agent training, the neural network that represents agent behavior is constantly updated as the agent performs actions and receives feedback in the form of rewards. This is often a lengthy process, as a neural network graph can be very large, and the calculations required to adjust it between steps or episodes scales with its size. Likewise, the number of episodes required for an agent to consistently succeed at the desired task is commonly in the hundreds of thousands or even millions.

Thus, training an agent of moderate complexity in ML-Agents will easily occupy a personal computer for hours or even days. And yet a *trained* agent can easily be included in a Unity game or exported for use in simple applications. So, how is it that their use becomes more feasible following training?

 If you want to train models for use in ML-Agents outside of ML-Agents, start by understanding the Tensor names (*https://oreil.ly/J59hl*) and Barracuda model parameters (*https://oreil.ly/pu3YM*). It's outside the scope of this book, but it's very interesting!.

The answer is the difference between the performance required during training versus during *inference*. Following the training phase, the neural network of agent behavior is locked in place; it will no longer be updated as the agent performs actions, and rewards will no longer be sent as feedback. Instead, the same observations will be served to the agent as they were during training, but the rules that define which observations will be responded to with which actions are already defined.

Figuring out the corresponding reaction is as simple as tracing a graph. For this reason, inference is a performant process that can be included even in applications where compute resources are limited. All that is needed is an *inference engine* that knows how to take input, trace the network graph, and output the appropriate action to be performed.

The Unity ML-Agents inference engine is implemented using *compute shaders*, which are tiny specialized programs that run on a GPU (also known as a graphics card), but are not used for graphics. This means they may not work on all platforms (*https://oreil.ly/Iaj5s*).

Luckily, Unity ML-Agents comes with one, called the *Unity inference engine* (sometimes called Barracuda). So, you don't need to make your own—or ship around the underlying framework you used for training, such as PyTorch or TensorFlow.

You can learn more about Barracuda in the Unity documentation (*https://oreil.ly/0jyye*).

If you've trained a model outside of ML-Agents, you will not be able to use it with Unity's inference engine. You could, in theory, make a model outside of ML-Agents that complies with the names of constants and tensors that ML-Agents expects, but it's not officially supported.

It might be counterintuitive (or really intuitive, depending on your background), but for models generated using ML-Agents, running inference using the CPU will be faster than using the GPU unless you have a significant number of visual observations on your agent.

Using the ML-Agents Gym Wrapper

The OpenAI Gym is an (almost de facto standard at this point) open source library used for developing and exploring reinforcement learning algorithms. In this section, we're going to take a quick look at using the ML-Agents Gym Wrapper to explore reinforcement learning algorithms.

Before we get started with the ML-Agents Gym Wrapper, you'll need to have your Python and Unity environments set up. So, if you haven't done so already, create a new environment via the steps from "Setting Up" on page 19. Once you've done this, continue here:

1. Activate your new environment, and then install the `gym_unity` Python package:

   ```
   pip install gym_unity
   ```

2. You can then, from any Python script, launch a Unity simulation environment *as a gym*:

```
from gym_unity.envs import UnityToGymWrapper
env = UnityToGymWrapper
    (unity_env, uint8_visual, flatten_branched, allow_multiple_obs)
```

In this case, unity_env is a Unity environment to be wrapped and presented as a gym. That's it!

Unity environments and OpenAI Baselines

One of the most interesting components of the OpenAI project is OpenAI Baselines, a set of high-quality implementations of reinforcement algorithms. It's in maintenance mode now, but it still provides an incredibly useful collection of algorithms with which you can explore reinforcement learning.

Conveniently, you can use OpenAI Baselines together with a Unity simulation environment, via the Unity ML-Agents Gym Wrapper.

As a quick example, we'll train the GridWorld that we were using in Chapter 11 with the DQN algorithm from OpenAI.

First, you'll need to build a copy of the GridWorld environment:

1. Open the Project folder in the copy of the ML-Agents GitHub repository that you cloned or downloaded (see "Setting Up" on page 19) as a Unity project using the Unity Hub, and then use the Project view to open the GridWorld scene.

2. Then open File menu → Build settings, and choose your current platform.

3. Make sure the only scene selected in the Scenes in Build list is the GridWorld scene.

4. Click Build and choose to save the build somewhere you're familiar with on your system.

 You might be wondering why we cannot use the default registry to grab a copy of GridWorld, since we're exclusively working in Python here. The reason is that the ML-Agents Gym Wrapper only supports environments in which there is a single agent. All the prebuilt default registry environments have multiple areas in them, for speedier training.

Next, we'll move to Python:

5. In your Python environment, you'll need to install the Baselines package:

```
pip install git+git://github.com/openai/baselines
```

You might need to install TensorFlow, via `pip install tensorflow==1.15`, before you can do this. You'll need this specific version of TensorFlow in order to maintain compatibility with OpenAI Baselines: specifically, it uses the TensorFlow `contrib` module, which is not part of TensorFlow 2.0. Such is the joy of Python.

6. Next, fire up Jupyter Lab, following the process we used in "Experimenting with an Environment" on page 244 and create a new notebook.

7. Add the following `import` lines:

```
import gym

from baselines import deepq
from baselines import logger

from mlagents_envs.environment import UnityEnvironment
from gym_unity.envs import UnityToGymWrapper
```

8. Next, get a handle on the Unity environment we built out a moment ago, and convert it to a gym:

```
unity_env =
    UnityEnvironment("/Users/parisba/Downloads/GridWorld.app", 10000, 1)
env = UnityToGymWrapper(unity_env, uint8_visual=True)
logger.configure('./logs') # Change to log in a different directory
```

Note that the equivalent of /Users/parisba/Downloads/GridWorld.app should point to a *.app* or *.exe* or other executable (depending on your platform), which is the built copy of GridWorld we made a moment ago.

9. Finally, run the training:

```
act = deepq.learn(
    env,
    "cnn", # For visual inputs
    lr=2.5e-4,
    total_timesteps=1000000,
    buffer_size=50000,
    exploration_fraction=0.05,
    exploration_final_eps=0.1,
    print_freq=20,
    train_freq=5,
    learning_starts=20000,
    target_network_update_freq=50,
    gamma=0.99,
    prioritized_replay=False,
    checkpoint_freq=1000,
    checkpoint_path='./logs', # Save directory
    dueling=True
```

```
)
print("Saving model to unity_model.pkl")
act.save("unity_model.pkl")
```

Your environment will launch, and it will be trained using the OpenAI Baselines DQN algorithm.

Side Channels

Unity's Python ML-Agents components provide a feature called side channels, which allow you to share arbitrary information back and forth between C# code running in Unity and Python code. Specifically, ML-Agents supplies two side channels for you to use: `EngineConfigurationChannel` and `EnvironmentParametersChannel`.

Engine configuration channel

The engine configuration channel allows you to vary parameters related to the engine: timescale, graphics quality, resolution, and such. It's intended to be used to increase performance during training by varying the quality, or to make things prettier and more interesting or useful for human review during inference.

Follow these steps to create an `EngineConfigurationChannel`:

1. Make sure the following are part of your `import` statements:

   ```
   from mlagents_envs.environment import UnityEnvironment
   from mlagents_envs.side_channel.engine_configuration_channel
        import EngineConfigurationChannel
   ```

2. Create an `EngineConfigurationChannel`:

   ```
   channel = EngineConfigurationChannel()
   ```

3. Pass the channel into the `UnityEnvironment` that you're using:

   ```
   env = UnityEnvironment(side_channels=[channel])
   ```

4. Configure the channel as needed:

   ```
   channel.set_configuration_parameters(time_scale = 2.0)
   ```

In this case, the configuration for this `EngineConfigurationChannel` sets the `time_scale` to 2.0.

And that's it! There is a range of possible arguments that can be used with `set_configuration_parameters`, such as `width` and `height`, for resolution control, `quality_level`, and `target_frame_rate`.

Environment parameters channel

The environment parameters channel is more general than the engine configuration channel; it allows you to work with any numerical values you need to pass back and forth between Python and the simulation environment.

Follow these steps to create an EnvironmentParametersChannel:

1. Ensure that you have the following import statements:

   ```
   from mlagents_envs.environment import UnityEnvironment
   from mlagents_envs.side_channel.environment_parameters_channel import
       EnvironmentParametersChannel
   ```

2. Create an EnvironmentParametersChannel and pass it to the UnityEnvironment, as we did for the engine configuration channel:

   ```
   channel = EnvironmentParametersChannel()
   env = UnityEnvironment(side_channels=[channel])
   ```

3. Next, use the channel to set_float_parameter on the Python side, naming a parameter:

   ```
   channel.set_float_parameter("myParam", 11.0)
   ```

   In this case, the parameter is named myParam.

4. This allows you to get access to the same parameter from C# in Unity:

   ```
   var environment_parameters = Academy.Instance.EnvironmentParameters;
   float myParameterValue = envParameters.GetWithDefault("myParam", 0.0f);
   ```

The 0.0f in the call here is a default value.

And with that, we're done with this chapter, and more or less done with simulations for the book. We've provided some next steps in the code download; if you're curious about reinforcement learning and want to explore more, open the Next_Steps folder in the resources bundle you can find on the book's website (*http://secretlab.com.au/books/practical-sims*).

PART III

Synthetic Data, Real Results

CHAPTER 13

Creating More Advanced Synthesized Data

In this chapter, we'll return to synthesis and build upon the introduction to synthesizing data using Unity's Perception that we worked through back in Chapter 3.

Specifically, we'll use randomizers to add a random element to the images generated from our dice, and learn how to explore the data we're synthesizing, making use of the labels we added earlier.

Adding Random Elements to the Scene

To generate useful synthetic data, we need to add random elements to the scene. The random elements we're going to add are:

- A random *floor color*
- A random *camera position*

By randomly changing the color of the floor and the position of the camera, we'll be able to generate a variety of random images of dice, which can then be used to train an image recognition system outside of Unity to recognize dice in a huge range of situations.

We're going to be working with the same project we ended up with way back at the end of Chapter 3, so either duplicate it or re-create it from scratch before continuing. We duplicated it and renamed it "SimpleDiceWithRandomizers."

 Don't forget that it needs to be a 3D URP project, which is different from the projects you've been making throughout Part II for simulations. Refer back to "Creating the Unity Project" on page 56 if you need a reminder.

Randomizing the Floor Color

To randomize the floor color, we first need a randomizer. To add a randomizer, open the Unity scene and do the following:

1. Find the Scenario component attached to the Scenario object, and click the Add Randomizer button shown in Figure 13-1.

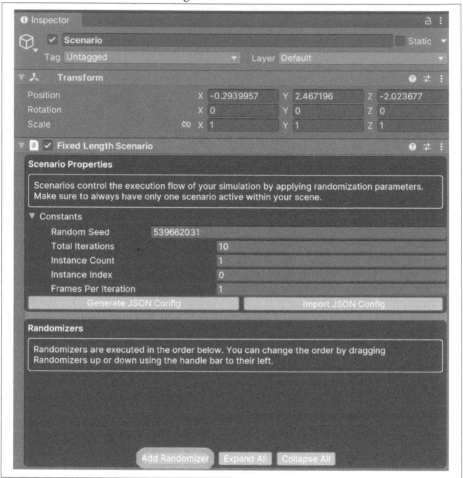

Figure 13-1. Adding a randomizer

2. Choose the perception category, as shown in Figure 13-2, and choose Color Randomizer, as shown in Figure 13-3.

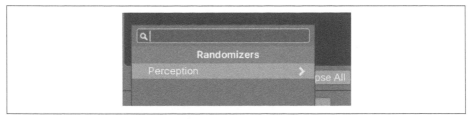

Figure 13-2. Choose the perception category

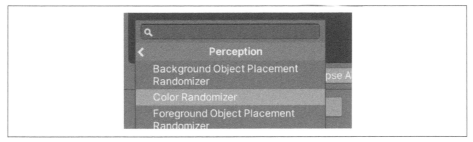

Figure 13-3. Picking the color randomizer

A color randomizer needs to know which objects it should change the color of. To do this, we need to add a Color Randomizer Tag component to the floor plane (which is the object we want the color to change on):

3. Select the floor in the Hierarchy panel, and add a Color Randomizer Tag component to it using its Inspector.

4. Verify that it's added to the object, as shown in Figure 13-4.

Figure 13-4. A color randomizer tag

That's all. To test that the randomizer is working, run the project, and check the filesystem locations noted in "Testing the Scenario" on page 72.

If it's all working, you'll find the dice pictures with a variety of colored backgrounds, as shown in Figure 13-5.

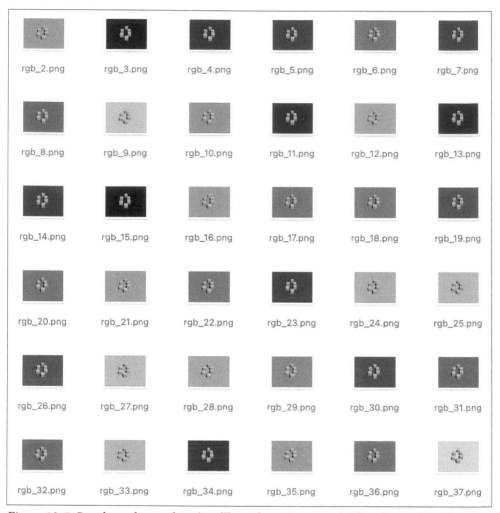

Figure 13-5. Random plane colors (you'll see these in grayscale if you're reading the print version)

Randomizing the Camera Position

Next we'll add a random element to the position of the camera that captures the images we save.

To randomize the camera's position, we'll need a randomizer that doesn't come with Unity's Perception package. To do that, we'll code our own randomizer.

A randomizer is a script that's attached to a scenario. A randomizer encapsulates specific randomization activities that are performed during execution of the environment. Each randomizer exposes certain parameters to the Inspector.

A new randomizer can be created by making a new script that derives from the Randomizer class, and the implementing methods from that class, as needed.

Some of the methods you can override are:

- OnCreate(), which is called when a randomizer is loaded by a scenario
- OnIterationStart(), which is called when a scenario starts an iteration
- OnIterationEnd(), which is called when a scenario completes an iteration
- OnScenarioComplete(), which is called when a scenario has completed
- OnStartRunning(), which is called on the first frame on which a randomizer is enabled
- OnUpdate(), which is called on every frame

For example, here's the code for the ColorRandomizer we used a moment ago, which was created and supplied as part of the Unity Perception package:

```
[AddRandomizerMenu("Perception/Color Randomizer")]
public class ColorRandomizer : Randomizer
{
    static readonly int k_BaseColor = Shader.PropertyToID("_BaseColor");
    public ColorHsvaParameter colorParameter;
    protected override void OnIterationStart()
    {
        var taggedObjects = tagManager.Query<ColorRandomizerTag>();
        foreach (var taggedObject in taggedObjects)
        {
            var renderer = taggedObject.GetComponent<Renderer>();
            renderer.material.SetColor(k_BaseColor, colorParameter.Sample());
        }
    }
}
```

 It's crucial that each randomizer has the [Serializable] tag so that the Unity Editor can customize and save the randomizer as part of its UI. You can learn more about this tag in Unity's documentation (*https://oreil.ly/fOeu4*).

It's important to include the [AddRandomizerMenu] attribute and specify a path for the randomizer to appear in the submenu of the Add Randomizer button. In this case, [AddRandomizerMenu("Perception/Color Randomizer")] makes it display as shown in Figure 13-6.

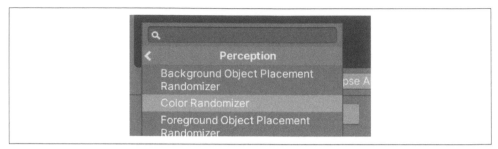

Figure 13-6. Pick color randomizer again

Follow these steps to make your own randomizer:

1. Create a new script by right-clicking in the Project pane and choosing Create → C# Script.

2. Name the new script *CamRandomizer.cs*, and open it, removing everything except the provided import lines.

3. Add the following imports:

```
using UnityEngine.Experimental.Perception.Randomization.Parameters;
using UnityEngine.Experimental.Perception.Randomization.Randomizers;
```

4. Add the aforementioned attribute (outside and above the class, not inside any methods) to make it appear in the submenu:

```
[AddRandomizerMenu("Perception/Cam Randomizer")]
```

5. Add the class, derived from Randomizer:

```
public class CamRandomizer : Randomizer
{

}
```

6. Create a place to store a reference to the scene's camera so that you can move it using the randomizer:

```
public Camera cam;
```

7. Create a FloatParameter so that the range for the camera's x position can be defined in the Unity Editor:

```
public FloatParameter camX;
```

8. Next, override the `OnIterationStart()` method mentioned earlier, use it to `Sample()` the camX parameter we just created, and position the camera:

```
protected override void OnIterationStart()
{
    cam.transform.position = new Vector3(camX.Sample(),18.62f,0.72f);
}
```

With the script written, you'll need to add it to the scenario:

1. Select the scenario from the Hierarchy and use the Add Randomizer button again, but this time find your newly created camera randomizer, as shown in Figure 13-7.

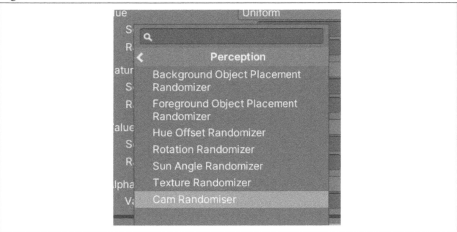

Figure 13-7. The newly created camera randomizer

2. Find the settings for the camera randomizer, and set the range between -7 and 7, as shown in Figure 13-8.

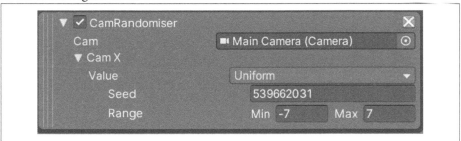

Figure 13-8. The camera randomizer settings

3. Drag the Main Camera into the camera randomizer's camera field.

Test the randomizer by running the scenario. This time, the position of the camera as well as the floor color will be random, as shown in Figure 13-9.

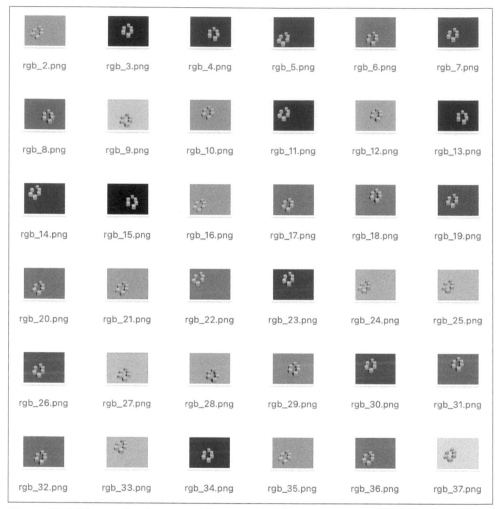

Figure 13-9. The randomly generated images with both random color and camera position

What's Next?

We've covered all the basic principles of synthesis with Unity over our two simulation-related chapters. Next, we're going to combine all our new knowledge and build a dataset for training an image recognition system (again, this training would occur outside of Unity, and stepping through the process is beyond the scope of this book).

CHAPTER 14

Synthetic Shopping

You've had some initial exposure to using Unity to generate a custom synthetic dataset, but you've only scratched the surface.

In this chapter, we'll combine what we've learned so far to further explore the possibilities and features of Unity Perception, and talk about how you can apply them to your own projects.

Specifically, we're going to create a full-featured set of synthetic data using Unity and Perception: a set of items that one might find at a supermarket, nicely annotated and tagged.

Imagine an AI-powered shopping trolley that knows what items you're touching as you take them from the shelves (you don't have to stretch far to imagine it, since it's real!). In order to train such a thing, you'd need a large corpus of data, showing packages of products you'd find in a supermarket. You'd need the images of packages at a huge variety of angles, with a variety of things behind them, and you'd need them tagged so that when you train the model using them, you'd be able to accurately train it.

We're going to make that dataset in this chapter.

Creating the Unity Environment

First, we need to build the world inside Unity that will create our randomized shop images. The world in this case will be a scene that we add randomizers to, in order to create the range of images we need.

To get the Unity environment up and running, follow these steps:

1. Create a brand-new Unity project, selecting the Universal Render Pipeline (URP) template again, as shown in Figure 14-1. Our project is called "SyntheticShopping," but feel free to get creative.

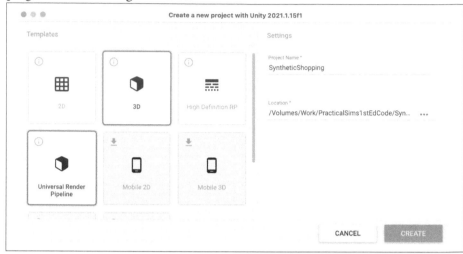

Figure 14-1. A new URP project

2. When the project opens, install the Unity Perception package using the Unity Package Manager, as shown in Figure 14-2.

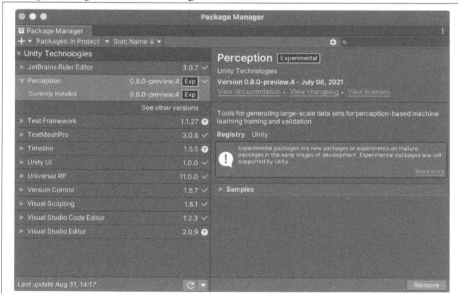

Figure 14-2. Adding the Perception package

You can add the package by name, `com.unity.perception`, browse the package repository, or download and install the it manually.

3. Click the Import button next to the tutorial files in the Package Manager pane, while the Unity Perception package is selected. This will import a collection of useful images and models into the project. We'll be using these for this chapter. This is shown in Figure 14-3.

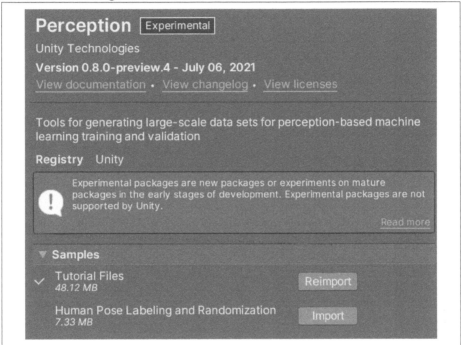

Figure 14-3. Importing the tutorial files

4. In the Project pane, create a new scene, as shown in Figure 14-4. Name it "SyntheticShop" or something similar.

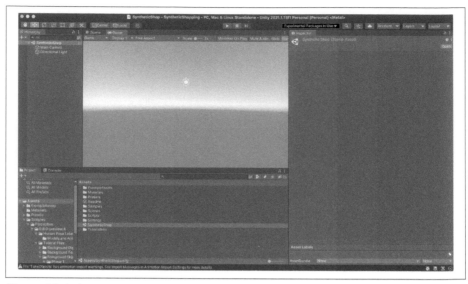

Figure 14-4. A new scene

5. Open the new, empty scene. Your Unity screen should look like Figure 14-4.

6. Next, locate the ForwardRenderer asset in the Project pane, as shown in Figure 14-5.

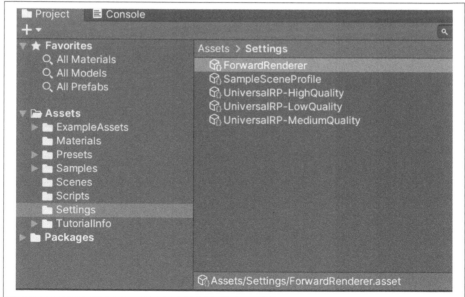

Figure 14-5. The ForwardRenderer asset

7. With the ForwardRenderer asset selected, using the Inspector click the Add Renderer Feature button and select Ground Truth Renderer Feature, as shown in Figure 14-6.

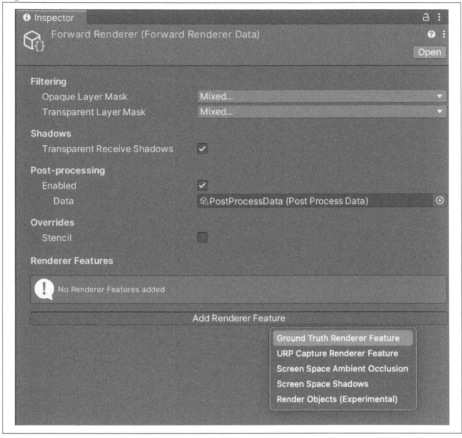

Figure 14-6. Configuring the forward renderer

That's everything we need for now; next we need to add a Perception Camera.

A Perception Camera

To allow ground truth to be labeled, we need to add a Perception Camera to the Main Camera in the SyntheticShop scene.

A Perception Camera is the camera, or the view, used to generate the images. What the Perception Camera sees is ultimately what will be rendered out for each image that's created for you when you generate synthesized images.

To add a Perception Camera, in Unity, follow these steps:

1. Select the Main Camera in the Hierarchy of your SyntheticShop scene, and use the Add Component button in its Inspector to add a Perception Camera component, as shown in Figure 14-7.

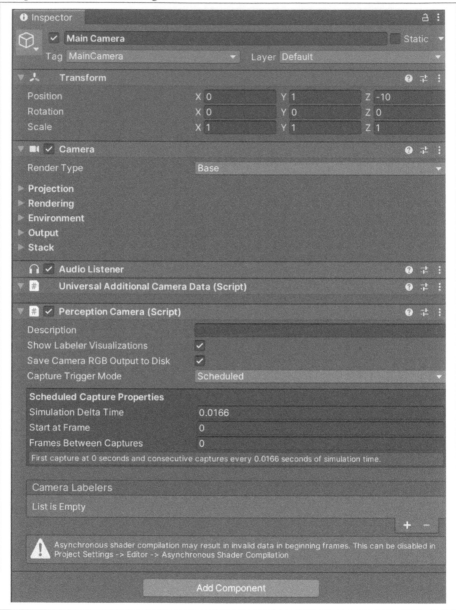

Figure 14-7. Adding the Perception Camera to the Main Camera

2. Next, in the Inspector for the Perception Camera component, choose the +
   button below the Camera Labelers section, and add a BoundingBox2DLabeler, as
   shown in Figures 14-8 and 14-9.

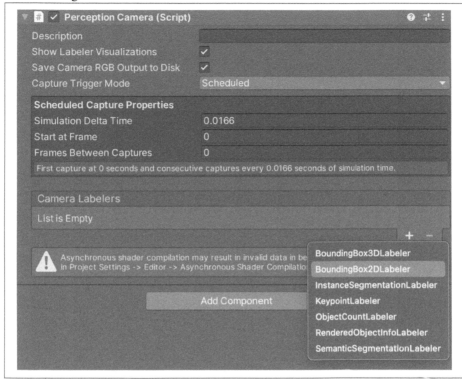

Figure 14-8. Adding a BoundingBox2DLabeler

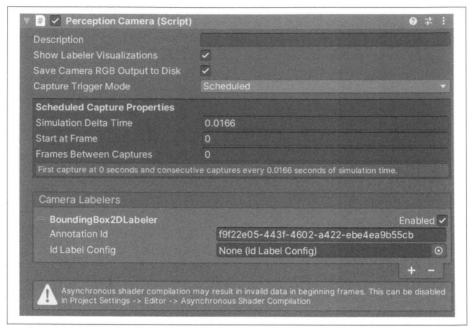

Figure 14-9. The labeler

3. Now we need to create a new asset to name the labels. In the Project panel, create a new ID Label Config asset, as shown in Figure 14-10. We named ours "SyntheticShoppingLabels."

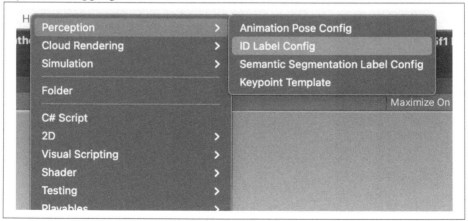

Figure 14-10. Creating the ID Label Config asset

4. Select the new asset in the Project pane, and find the Add All Labels to Config button (shown in Figure 14-11) in the Inspector to add the labels from the sample data you imported earlier.

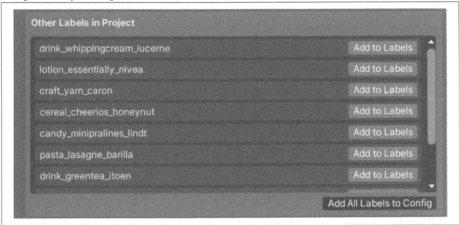

Figure 14-11. The labels and the Add All Labels to Config button

 The labels we just added come from the Label components that were on the assets we imported. Because the assets had labels, but we did not have an ID Label Config asset acknowledging and containing those labels, we needed to make one and add them.

5. Verify that the labels have moved into the Added Labels section, as shown in Figure 14-12.

Figure 14-12. The labels are added

6. Select the Main Camera in the Hierarchy again, and go back to the Perception Camera component. Drag the SyntheticShoppingLabels asset into the Id Label Config field (or use the button, shown in Figure 14-13).

 Be sure the Enabled checkbox is ticked in the Bound-Box2DLabeler section.

Figure 14-13. Assigning the ID Label Config asset

That's everything. Next, we need to test the labels.

Testing the labeler

To test that the labeler is working before we continue:

1. Locate the foreground object prefabs that were imported as part of the sample assets, as shown in Figure 14-14.

```
Assets > Samples > Perception > 0.8.0-preview.4 > Tutorial Files > Foreground Objects > Phase 1 > Prefabs
   candy_minipralines_lindt
   cereal_cheerios_honeynut
   cleaning_snuggle_henkel
   craft_yarn_caron_01
   drink_greentea_itoen
   drink_whippingcream_lucerne
   lotion_essentially_nivea
   pasta_lasagne_barilla
   snack_biscotti_ghiott_01
   snack_granolabar_naturevalley
```

Figure 14-14. The prefabs for the foreground

2. Drag one of the prefabs (it does not matter which one) from the Project pane into the Hierarchy.

3. Select the newly added prefab, and with the Scene view active, press the F key on your keyboard to focus the view on it, as shown in Figure 14-15.

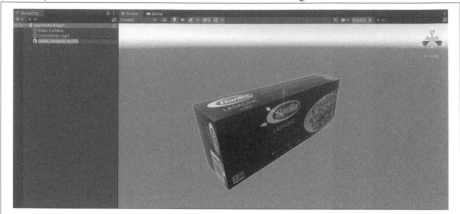

Figure 14-15. Focusing on some pasta

4. Move the Main Camera, in the Scene view, until it's showing the newly added prefab nicely in the Game view.

 Instead of manually aligning the camera, you can select the prefab, focus it in the Scene view, then ask the Main Camera to duplicate the Scene view's perspective by right-clicking on it in the Hierarchy and choosing Align with View.

5. Run the scene, using the Play button. You should see a bounding box displayed appropriately around the item represented by the prefab, as shown in Figure 14-16. If you do, this means everything is working so far!

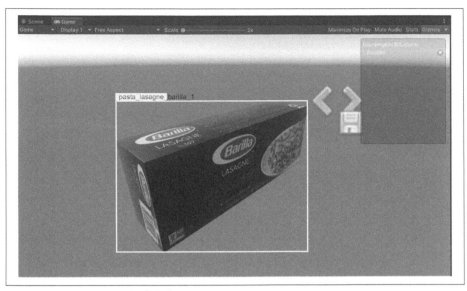

Figure 14-16. Testing the labeler

If everything works as expected, delete the prefab object from the scene.

Adding randomizers

Next, we need to add some randomizers to the environment. The randomizers will randomly position the foreground (and eventually the background) objects to generate a range of different images.

 By creating images that randomly position (and randomly do other things, too) the objects we want to train it to detect in images, we're helping the machine learning model that we might ultimately train using data like this to be more effective at finding the objects in images that we want it to find.

As we've discussed before, Unity Perception supplies a bunch of different randomizers, as well as allowing you to create your own as needed. For our synthetic shop, we want to randomize a lot of different things:

- The texture of things
- The objects behind the things we're interested in (background objects)
- The colors of the background objects
- The placement of the objects (foreground and background)

- The rotation of the objects (foreground and background)

Follow these steps to add the randomizers:

1. Create an empty Game object in the Hierarchy, and name it "Scenario" or something similar.

2. With the Scenario object selected, use its Inspector to add a Fixed Length Scenario component via the Add Component button, as shown in Figure 14-17.

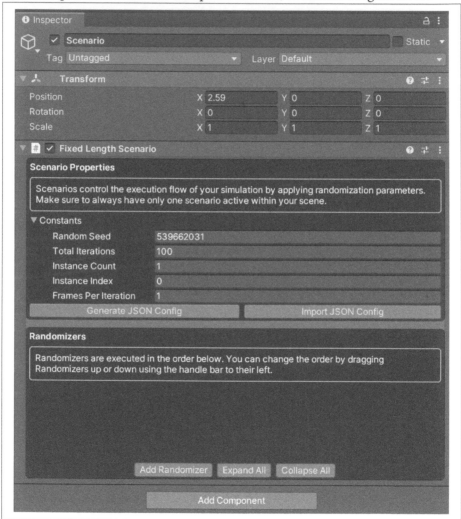

Figure 14-17. Adding a Fixed Length Scenario component

3. Add a BackgroundObjectPlacementRandomizer using the Add Randomizer button.

4. In the new BackgroundObjectPlacementRandomizer, click the Add Folder button, then navigate to the Prefabs folder in the Background Objects folder of the Tutorial Assets, as shown in Figure 14-18.

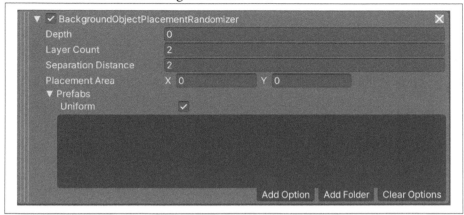

Figure 14-18. Adding a BackgroundObjectPlacementRandomizer

5. With the folder of background objects added, you may want to tweak the Depth, Layer Count, Separation Distance, and Placement Area settings: ours are shown in Figure 14-19.

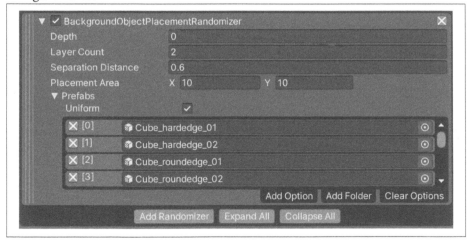

Figure 14-19. Settings for the BackgroundObjectPlacementRandomizer

 You could run the simulation again now, and you'd find a bunch of random shapes (of the same color) in front of the camera. There'd be no foreground objects yet, though.

6. Next, add a TextureRandomizer (using the same Add Randomizer button in the Fixed Length Scenario component in the Scenario object).

7. With the TextureRadomizer added, choose the Add Folder button, and find the Background Textures folder from the Tutorial Assets, as shown in Figure 14-20.

Figure 14-20. TextureRandomizer settings

8. Next we'll add a HueOffsetRandomizer, as shown in Figure 14-21. We'll use its default settings.

Figure 14-21. Adding a HueOffsetRandomizer

9. Now we need to add a ForegroundObjectPlacementRandomizer, and use the Add Folder button to point to the folder of foreground object prefabs (the groceries). Our settings are shown in Figure 14-22.

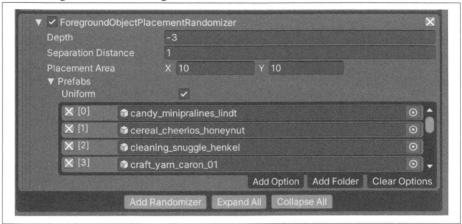

Figure 14-22. The ForegroundObjectPlacementRandomizer

10. For the final randomizer, we need a RotationRandomizer, as shown in Figure 14-23.

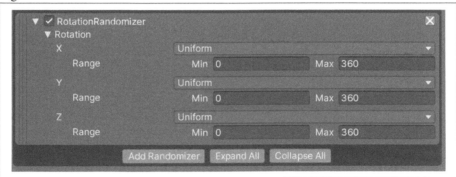

Figure 14-23. The RotationRandomizer

That's all the randomizers. To set which objects the randomizers affect, we need to give those objects some additional components:

1. Open the Background Objects Prefabs folder in the Project pane, and select all the prefabs (still in the Project pane), as shown in Figure 14-24.

Figure 14-24. Selecting the background prefab assets

2. Using the Inspector (while all the background object prefabs are selected), click the Add Component button and add a TextureRandomizerTag component, a HueOffsetRandomizerTag component, and a RotationRandomizerTag component, as shown in Figure 14-25.

Figure 14-25. Adding components to the assets

3. Navigate to the Foreground Objects Prefabs folder in the Project pane, select all of those prefabs, and use the Inspector to add a RotationRandomizerTag to all the Foreground Objects.

That's it!

Faking It Until You Make It

We're ready to generate some fake supermarket data.

You might need to position your camera so that it generates nicely framed images.

Run the environment, and Unity will repeatedly run the randomizers that we've set up, and save an image each time. The Unity console will show you where they've been saved to, as shown in Figure 14-26.

```
Project        Console
Clear  ▾  Collapse  Error Pause  Editor ▾

⊘  [15:33:20] Frame step forced all sensors to synchronize, changing frame timings.
   UnityEngine.GUIUtility:ProcessEvent (int,intptr,bool&) (at /Users/bokken/buildslave/unity/build/Modules/IMGUI/GUIUtility.cs:189)

⊘  [15:33:21] DC[I][1630388001]: USim Time (secs) : Wall(90.369) Simulation(0.060) Unscaled(0.080) FPS(0.098)
   UnityEngine.Debug:Log (object)

⊘  [15:33:21] Frame step forced all sensors to synchronize, changing frame timings.
   UnityEngine.GUIUtility:ProcessEvent (int,intptr,bool&) (at /Users/bokken/buildslave/unity/build/Modules/IMGUI/GUIUtility.cs:189)

⊘  [15:33:22] Frame step forced all sensors to synchronize, changing frame timings.
   UnityEngine.GUIUtility:ProcessEvent (int,intptr,bool&) (at /Users/bokken/buildslave/unity/build/Modules/IMGUI/GUIUtility.cs:189)

⊘  [15:33:23] Frame step forced all sensors to synchronize, changing frame timings.
   UnityEngine.GUIUtility:ProcessEvent (int,intptr,bool&) (at /Users/bokken/buildslave/unity/build/Modules/IMGUI/GUIUtility.cs:189)

⊘  [15:34:08] DC[I][1630388048]: USim Time (secs) : Wall(136.718) Simulation(0.100) Unscaled(0.140) FPS(0.064)
   UnityEngine.Debug:Log (object)

⊘  [15:34:08] Dataset written to /Users/parisba/Library/Application Support/DefaultCompany/SyntheticShopping/96b11f70-f266-4c48-bdc1-3787d77047b1
   UnityEngine.Perception.GroundTruth.DatasetCapture:ResetSimulation ()
```

Figure 14-26. The path to the image output

If you navigate to this folder on your system, you'll find a whole bunch of images, as well as some Unity Perception JSON files that describe the labels for the objects, as shown in Figure 14-27.

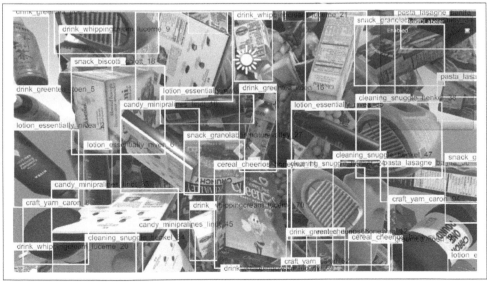

Figure 14-27. An example of one of the randomized images

You can use this collection of data to train a machine learning system outside of Unity. To train a machine learning system with that data, you could use any one of many approaches.

If you're curious, we'd recommend starting with the Faster R-CNN model, using a ResNet50 backbone pretrained on ImageNet. You can find implementations of all of these things in the PyTorch package, torchvision.

 We recommend finding a good book on PyTorch or TensorFlow if you want to learn more about this. In the meantime, a good starting point is Unity's datasetinsights repository on GitHub (*https:// oreil.ly/4FT3j*).

Using Synthesized Data

The synthesis chapters in this book focused on the use of a simulated *environment* to produce synthetic *data*, which is a growing trend in the broader machine learning space. This is because creating the kind of detection or classification model that is popular in hot ML areas like computer vision—where a computer can detect, recognize, and ideally make intelligent decisions about an object's presence in a photograph or video feed—requires an enormous amount of data representing the kinds of objects you want the model to be able to recognize or distinguish between.

Usually this means a dataset made up of millions of photographs, each individually labeled with the objects present within them. Sometimes it even requires labeling the *regions* in each image where a specific object occurs. And this is an unfeasible amount of work to do if such a dataset doesn't exist already for the problem you are trying to solve.

This has led to the popularization of *sharing* datasets, which is a nice thing to do, but given how opaque machine learning models can be about how they arrive at critical decisions, knowing little about the data it was based on only contributes to the existing problem of lack of accountability and understanding in the ML space. So, if you're training a model for something important, or as a learning exercise, it can still be desirable to create your own training datasets.

Data synthesis can reduce the amount of work needed to create a dataset by allowing someone to define rules for what should be present in the data and how aspects of it may vary. A simulated environment can then be used to generate any number of random variations within the given specifications, and output each in a specified form—such as labeled images. This can be used to create a dataset for:

- Recognition of a particular object—by generating pictures of the object in a virtual scene from different angles, among different objects, partially occluded, and shown in different lighting conditions

- Predicting distances or depth in a 2D image—by producing visual images and a corresponding depth map populated by the simulation (which knows the distances between objects and the camera)

- Partitioning regions in a scene—produced similarly to predicting depth in 2D images but where the output could allow something like a self-driving car to recognize objects relevant to its driving, such as signs or pedestrians (as shown in Figure 14-28)

- Anything else you can generate with random variations within a virtual scene

Figure 14-28. Example of visual images (left) and a corresponding map that signifies the category of objects recognized in the scene (right)

What you do with data once it's synthesized is up to you, as the kind of general-purpose machine learning required to ingest and learn from an image dataset is beyond the scope of this book. Here we focus on the simulation parts and how a simulation engine can enable unique kinds of machine learning.

For machine learning beyond simulation, you may wish to check out another of O'Reilly Media's books on the topic, such as *Practical Artificial Intelligence with Swift* by the same authors as this book or *Hands-On Machine Learning with Scikit-Learn, Keras, and TensorFlow* by Aurélien Géron.

Index

About the Authors

Dr. Paris Buttfield-Addison is cofounder of Secret Lab (*https://www.secret lab.com.au*) (@TheSecretLab on Twitter), a game development studio based in beautiful Hobart, Australia. Secret Lab builds games and game development tools, including the multiaward-winning ABC Play School iPad games, Night in the Woods, the Qantas airlines Joey Playbox games, and the Yarn Spinner narrative game framework. Paris formerly worked as mobile product manager for Meebo (acquired by Google), has a degree in medieval history, and a PhD in computing, and writes technical books on mobile and game development (more than 20 so far) for O'Reilly Media. Paris particularly enjoys game design, statistics, law, machine learning, and human-centered technology research. He can be found on Twitter at @parisba and online at *http://paris.id.au*.

Mars Buttfield-Addison is a computer science and machine learning researcher, as well as freelance creator of STEM educational materials. She is currently working toward her PhD in computer engineering at the University of Tasmania, collaborating with CSIRO's Data61 to investigate how large radio telescope arrays can be adapted to identify and track space debris and satellites in the near field while simultaneously performing deep space observations for astronomy. Mars can be found on Twitter @TheMartianLife and online at *https://themartianlife.com*.

Dr. Tim Nugent pretends to be a mobile app developer, game designer, tools builder, researcher, and tech author. When he isn't busy avoiding being found out as a fraud, he spends most of his time designing and creating little apps and games that he won't let anyone see. Tim spent a disproportionately long time writing this tiny little bio, most of which was spent trying to stick a witty sci-fi reference in, before he simply gave up. Tim can be found on Twitter at @The_McJones, and online at *http://lonely.coffee*.

Dr. Jon Manning is the cofounder of Secret Lab, an independent game development studio. He's written a whole bunch of books for O'Reilly Media about Swift, iOS development, and game development, and has a doctorate in jerks on the internet. He's currently working on Button Squid, a top-down puzzler, and on the critically acclaimed award-gwinning adventure game Night in the Woods, which includes his interactive dialogue system Yarn Spinner. Jon can be found on Twitter at @desplesda, and online at *http://desplesda.net*.

Colophon

The animal on the cover of *Practical Simulations for Machine Learning* is a panther grouper (*Cromileptes altivelis*), a ray-finned marine fish also known as a humpback grouper or, in Australia, a barramundi cod. The panther grouper can be found in the tropical waters of the Indo-Pacific, from southeast Asia to the north coast of Australia. Young panther grouper tend to live in shallow reefs or seagrass beds while adults can be found at depths of up to 120 feet.

This easily identifiable fish has characteristic black spots on a background of cream or green-gray, with blotches on its head, body, and fins. When alarmed, these brownish patches become darker as a form a camouflage. The grouper's small head and vertically compressed body give it the humpbacked appearance for which it is named.

Humpback grouper are carnivorous hunters that use powerful suction by extending their jaws to swallow prey whole. This fish will typically hunt on the ocean floor, waiting in ambush at dawn and dusk for small crustaceans and fish. When on the move, the panther grouper swims solo or in pairs, meandering slowly and with odd turns, almost as if it is attempting to swim upside down.

Panther grouper young are more strikingly patterned and are desired aquarium fish, while adults are a popular white fish for human consumption. Thus, the fishing industry poses as a potential threat to this species, but this species is currently designated as "data deficient" by the IUCN. It is a protected species of cod in Queensland, Australia, however. Many of the animals on O'Reilly covers are endangered; all of them are important to the world.

The cover illustration is by Karen Montgomery, based on an antique line engraving from *Fishes of India*. The cover fonts are Gilroy Semibold and Guardian Sans. The text font is Adobe Minion Pro; the heading font is Adobe Myriad Condensed; and the code font is Dalton Maag's Ubuntu Mono.

O'REILLY®

Learn from experts.
Become one yourself.

Books | Live online courses
Instant Answers | Virtual events
Videos | Interactive learning

Get started at oreilly.com.

9 781492 089926